LIKE WATER ON STONE

Jonathan Power was a foreign-affairs columnist for the *International Herald Tribune* for seventeen years; today his column is syndicated to over twenty papers around the world. He has written for *The New York Times*, the *Washington Post*, the *Los Angeles Times*, *The Times*, *Encounter* and *Prospect*. In 1972 he won the Silver Medal at the Venice Film Festival for the documentary *It's Ours Whatever They Say*. He has published five previous books and most recently edited the official history of the UN. Published on the occasion of the UN's fiftieth anniversary in 1995, it caused a media storm.

JONATHAN POWER

Like Water on Stone

THE STORY OF
AMNESTY INTERNATIONAL

ALLEN LANE
THE PENGUIN PRESS

ALLEN LANE
THE PENGUIN PRESS

Published by the Penguin Group
Penguin Books Ltd, 27 Wrights Lane, London w8 5TZ, England
Penguin Putnam Inc., 375 Hudson Street, New York, New York 10014, USA
Penguin Books Australia Ltd, Ringwood, Victoria, Australia
Penguin Books Canada Ltd, 10 Alcorn Avenue, Toronto, Ontario, Canada M4V 3B2
Penguin Books India (P) Ltd, 11 Community Centre, Panchsheel Park, New Delhi – 110 017, India
Penguin Books (NZ) Ltd, Private Bag 102902, NSMC, Auckland, New Zealand
Penguin Books (South Africa) (Pty) Ltd, 5 Watkins Street, Denver Ext 4, Johannesburg 2094, South Africa

Penguin Books Ltd, Registered Offices: Harmondsworth, Middlesex, England

First published 2001
1

Copyright © Jonathan Power, 2001

Set in 10.75/14.25 pt Linotype Sabon
Typeset by Rowland Phototypesetting Ltd, Bury St Edmunds, Suffolk
Printed and bound in Great Britain by Clays Ltd, St Ives plc
Cover repro and printing by Concise Cover Printers

A CIP catalogue record for this book is available from the British Library

ISBN 0-713-99319-7

For my children:
Jenny, Lucy, Miriam and Carmen

'I thought about the terrible uselessness of suffering. Love leaves behind its creation – the next generation coming into the world, the continuation of humanity. But suffering? Such a great part of human experience, the most difficult and painful, passes leaving no trace. If one were to collect the energy of suffering emitted by the millions of people here and transform it into the power of creation, one could turn our planet into a flowering garden.'

– from *Imperium* by Ryszard Kapuściński (Granta, 1998)

Contents

Acknowledgements

Begin at the beginning: the first person to thank is the one who gave me the idea: Derek Cross. After him comes Mark Lattimer of the British section of Amnesty International, who, finding me confronting what appeared to be an unmoveable road block – the resistance of some influential Amnesty International staff members who appeared to profoundly mistrust me – succeeded in moving enough boulders for me to find a way through the institutional labyrinth.

In the publishing world I have to thank Alastair Rolfe, then of Penguin, who rescued the book from HarperCollins after I'd crossed swords with its owner, Rupert Murdoch, over his peremptory decision to drop publication of Chris Patten's book *East and West*. Also my cerebral but charming editor at Penguin, Margaret Bluman, who has brought her perceptive and experienced eye to sharpen and improve the book's initial draft. And a thank you to my agent Jonathan Lloyd of Curtis Brown for looking after my interests with professional competence and good humour.

Then, a very special thank you to Richard Reoch, a former head of information at Amnesty International, who not only gave me an immense amount of help with my first study of the organization twenty years ago, but has once again given me sterling advice. I particularly want to thank him for helping me draft the introduction.

Without a lot of support over my journalistic career I would never have built up the mental resources, not to mention the contacts, to write this book. I think in particular of the late James Grant of the Overseas Development Council, who awakened my interest in human rights by inviting me to Washington DC to study the human rights policies of the new president, Jimmy Carter, and of the late Buddy Weiss, editor in chief of the *International Herald Tribune*, who gave me a column and encouraged me to follow that interest through. Later editors and editorial-page editors including the late Tom Kennedy, Robert Donahue and the late Philip Foisie also deserve my appreciation.

In the political world I have been encouraged and inspired to think through the issues of human rights by Andy Young, the former chief of staff of Martin Luther King and later ambassador of the US to the United Nations, and Olusegun Obasanjo, ex political prisoner and currently President of Nigeria.

A word of thanks to Betty Loxton, who typed innumerable drafts, and to Any Evason and Alex Grace, who dug deep into the Amnesty archives on my behalf. And to Mary White for help in researching the early years of Amnesty. Also to Elizabeth Stratford and Linda Ribera for copy-editing.

A kiss to Jeany, my wife, for giving me not just emotional and intellectual support but musical uplift, and to Carmen, my eldest daughter, for talking over the art of writing.

Finally, salud a mis amigos Javier Belmonte and Chris Van Hove of the Biblioteca in the unspoilt village of San Juan de la Rambla in Tenerife – as close to Africa as I could get my family! – who gave me writing space in the quiet corner of their shady courtyard.

Jonathan Power,
San Juan de la Rambla,
February, 2001

Introduction

Amnesty, founded forty years ago, was almost immediately dubbed 'one of the larger lunacies of our time'. The then bizarre idea was to collect information on people incarcerated in prison solely for their political views and then, by means of an army of volunteer activists, bombard the offending governments with massive numbers of letters, postcards and telegrams calling for the victims' immediate and unconditional release. For its early efforts, it was denounced as 'subversive' and 'an agent of Satan'. Its detractors have included Iran's Ayatollah Khomeini, Uganda's Idi Amin, Iraq's Saddam Hussein, Chile's Augusto Pinochet and former British Prime Minister Margaret Thatcher. In the 1990s the criticism has been more subtle.

The attacks have come not only from government leaders, but from sceptics in the media as well. Some have argued that Amnesty has become respectable, a part of the international establishment. Others have claimed that it has lost its unique profile and been submerged in a plethora of other human rights groups. Perhaps the unkindest cut of all has been the allegation that Amnesty's publicity campaigns have resulted in the development of even more insidious methods of torture and repression, designed to avoid the calumny of global exposure. 'Have the triumphs of the human rights lobby, in agitating so vociferously on behalf of individual prisoners, actually made political murder a more effective solution for repressive governments?' asked Caroline Moorehead, writing in *Index on Censorship* in 1994.

But the prisoners, often enough, have been released. The postcards, telegrams and parcels do get through. Letters come back, many of them smuggled out of prison or past airport censors. The same week that a young law student was sentenced to three years' imprisonment in an eastern European country – he had been arrested after collecting signatures calling for the release of political prisoners – his father wrote to Amnesty: 'I have experienced the blessing of your appeal, for you have raised your voice in defence of my son . . . Amnesty International is a light in our time, particularly for those on whose eyes darkness has fallen, when the prison doors close behind them. By your selfless work this light shines on the ever-widening circle of those who need it.' Among the many other victims was a teacher in Latin America. While he was being tortured by the police they opened a telephone line between the torture chamber and the prisoner's home, forcing his wife to listen to her husband's screams. During the ordeal she died of a heart attack. The prisoner himself survived and was eventually allowed to go into exile with his children. He told Amnesty: 'They killed my wife. They would have killed me too, but you intervened and saved my life.'

The most unexpected challenge came from the United States. Successive post-Vietnam War governments, starting with the administration of President Jimmy Carter, took up human rights as a geo-political crusade. Suddenly, US officials around the world were brandishing Amnesty International reports as they waged highly selective campaigns against their enemies, while often enough remaining tight-lipped or, at least reserved, about torture and 'disappearances' in the regimes they supported for 'reasons of state' in the Cold War age.

Famously, during his campaign to build up the coalition against Saddam Hussein prior to the Gulf War in 1990, George Bush took to quoting Amnesty reports on Iraq, even letting it be known he was sharing them with his wife, who said they made her very upset and angry. Yet at the same time, the US authorities were steadfastly ignoring Amnesty's critique of the role of the Central Intelligence Agency (CIA) in torture in Guatemala or the use of capital punishment. Amnesty was being used in a one-sided, high profile diplomatic war that threatened to poison international human rights efforts. In what must surely be one of the most extraordinary dialogues for a human rights organization, Amnesty sent one of its top people to Washington to plead with US officials to stop quoting from the organization's reports. She succeeded, and successive US State Department annual rights reports now depend on their own sources more and on Amnesty less.

By the beginning of the 1990s the question was not whether Amnesty would survive, but whether it could adapt to a changing world. The Cold War was over. Throughout Latin America, Africa, Asia and Eastern Europe, dictators and their regimes had crumbled. 'The world was becoming a different place,' recalls Franca Sciuto, the Italian lawyer who headed Amnesty's International Executive Committee in those days. 'We could already see the impact of globalization. People were speaking of a New World Order and the UN was given the power to send on-the-spot human rights monitoring teams into areas of conflict. The media, too, was starting to dispatch its own human rights reporters into the field. For the first time, human rights activists in many countries of the South and East were free to form their own organizations.' Governments, in some cases, have hijacked the traditional human rights vocabulary and the rhetoric of human rights, while permitting ferocious atrocities to continue. This has made it harder for campaigners to pin the blame squarely on the highest levels of government, and made the underworld of abduction, torture and extermination all the more shadowy and intractable. Moreover, offenders are not just governments, but opposition groups, rightist or nationalistic warlords, drug traffickers and leftist guerrilla organizations.

The need for change was felt not only at the top, but by Amnesty members. These are the people from all walks of life who pen the letters, send the faxes and stand on the street corners collecting signatures and donations. They are also Amnesty's antennae. In 1991 the organization's International Council, the democratic governing body that represents the membership and sets policy, voted to change the time-honoured mandate. The council decided to take on abuses such as hostage-taking, torture and the killing of captives by armed opposition groups – as well as by governments. Soon after it recognized, more controversially, that people imprisoned solely for their sexual orientation were prisoners of conscience. It also decided to argue that rape carried out in the course of military conflict should be regarded as a war crime.

At the time it was feared that these changes might spread Amnesty's resources too thinly or dilute its clear-cut public profile. Neither fear has materialized. Instead, the organization had answered two of the most common criticisms it faced. First, that it was indifferent to the victims of terrorism, unless it was state terrorism. Second, that it was blind to the oppression of homosexuals, or uncaring of the special needs of women prisoners or female war victims. With the appointment of Senegalese-born Pierre Sané as secretary-general in 1993, Amnesty embarked on one of its most searching self-examinations. It resulted in a major assessment of global trends. Increasing chaos and complexity were seen to characterize the international political system with a decline in the role of the all-powerful nation state. The newly emerging democracies were judged to be vulnerable to the ravages of political corruption, economic hardship and extremist movements. From South Africa and Mali in Africa to Guatemala and Haiti in Latin America to Pakistan and South Korea in Asia there was at one level a groundswell of pride and approval as they threw off their recent dictatorial past, but at another trepidation and nervousness as it became very apparent that many of the critical institutions of civic society were inexperienced, ill-formed and vulnerable.

On the economic front, growing disparities of income, the severe impoverishment of a number of countries and the danger of economic collapse in some of the new states of central and eastern Europe held the explosive potential for widespread political instability. Armed conflicts in Europe and Africa were seen to be spinning out of control, increasing tensions in the surrounding countries and creating vast refugee populations, while international peace-keeping efforts were on occasion proving impotent. Many observers both inside and outside Amnesty were worried that Amnesty might be becoming overstretched, perhaps even developing a tendency in the face of large-scale atrocities to shoot from the hip.

Some claimed Amnesty was moving too quickly and merely republishing rumours. Picking up the rumblings, the *New York Times* charged that there was a new culture in Amnesty which was 'a response to CNN – members who see atrocities on television demand to know what Amnesty has to say about them – and to a growth in the number of rights groups putting out reports in the middle of conflicts'. The mass killings in Rwanda brought the debate to the boil. Pierre Sané, determined that the genocide in Rwanda should not engulf the entire region, was passionate. 'We are moving forward,' he said. 'The objective of our report is to force governments to conduct their own investigations quickly.' He sensed that time was running out in Central Africa. And even without all the research completed, as was the norm in a more slow-moving situation, Amnesty had to fire all its cannons. He was right.

This book attempts to capture Amnesty International on the move. Forty years is a long time in anyone's life and for an organization that constantly works at a high tempo to tell the full story of what it has achieved would require many volumes. I have had to pick and choose and, inevitably, my own light has fallen on the areas I know best from my journalistic work, first as a foreign correspondent and later as a foreign affairs columnist.

The book begins with a personal story, built around my long-time friendship with one of Amnesty's best-known adopted political prisoners, Olusegun Obasanjo, now the democratically elected president of Nigeria. Next it looks at Guatemala, believed to be Amnesty's most difficult and demanding case, a country where Amnesty personnel have risked life and limb and yet have not always had much to show for it. Then the book travels back to Africa and back in time to the Central African Republic, where Amnesty's masterful detective work brought to the attention of the world the massacre (by the Emperor Bokassa) of defenceless children.

The Pinochet case follows next. It is one of the most important watersheds in the history of the human rights movement. Now war criminals, whether they be Saddam Hussein, Slobodan Milosevic, or people whose names we have yet to become familiar with, have been served warning that if they commit such evil acts they are prisoners in their own country, and even there they may be snatched and brought to international justice. Chapter 4 is about the history and the leaders of Amnesty International. Of all the chapters this is the most inadequate, as it gives insufficient attention to the rank and file researchers and support staff of Amnesty International who toil in some of the world's most difficult situations, working long hours for very modest financial reward, and are now finding, if they have been with the organization since its early days, that they look to a future pension that will cover only the bare necessities of life.

Northern Ireland may today be mainly at peace. But the thirty-two-year civil war has long taken its toll not just on the people of Ireland but on the standing of Britain itself. It has undoubtedly sullied the reputation of the United Kingdom as a bastion of liberty and good sense and, as it often likes to see itself, as a country that is at the forefront of the human rights crusade, not to mention being the home base of Amnesty International. For the enthusiasts who believe Amnesty can do no wrong the chapter on Germany and the Baader-Meinhof gang is, I hope, a sobering contribution. Excessive zeal led Amnesty to interpret the facts of the case in a manner that suggested it used a harsher set of guidelines when dealing with the Western democracies than with the outside world. The gang, with their fasts to death demanding political status and the right to associate in large groups, should not have been a cause to win so much of Amnesty's sympathy. It was a nihilistic group, their ideals long buried, seeking only the violent destruction of a democratically elected state. By contrast, Chapter 7 looks at a range of success stories. Success for Amnesty is, as Obasanjo says, often no more than the reward that comes from the constant dripping of water on a stone. Amnesty may not yet have changed the world, but it has not left it as it found it either.

The China story is, perhaps, the most interesting one. Amnesty's own work in China is interlinked and interwoven with the high-wire *realpolitik* of US and European foreign policy and the fast-changing policies of the Chinese leadership. Sometimes Amnesty has had an influence, sometimes not. If human rights could come to be taken seriously on a sustained basis in China it would do more to change the nature of world society than any other single event. Finally, the book homes in on the USA, the loudest contradiction of them all.

The land of Abraham Lincoln, Eleanor Roosevelt, Martin Luther King and Jimmy Carter, the first country in the world to attempt consciously to make human rights an integral part of its foreign policy, has a domestic record that cruelly undermines its political stance abroad. Only slowly is the penny beginning to drop among American opinion leaders that the USA is in danger of being seen as not only a political hypocrite but as a nation blinded to the finer and more important points of civilization.

The last chapter, says my editor, is my personal credo. Yes, I suppose it is. I do believe – have long believed – that those who since the Second World War have fought against barbarism, violence, human selfishness and blindness have made a great degree of progress. I have argued this on and off over thirty years in my eight-hundred-word weekly column[1] and value the chance to argue it further in this quite lengthy chapter. I wouldn't mind arguing it in a whole book, but that must wait for another day!

---

[1] Formerly in the *International Herald Tribune*, now syndicated world-wide; it can be read on the web at www.transnational.org.

PROLOGUE

The Wheel Turns in Nigeria

The day Nigeria came back into my life: 12 June. After a three-decade-long love affair with Africa, for the past few years I had tried most of the time to put the continent out of my mind. If I wrote anything it was a reflection of my mechanical optimism that tends to see, at least for publication, a spark of life where most would see mayhem, economic failure and the downhill road. All that was once present in African society – steadily improving health and schooling, sound and representative government, free opinions and individual human rights – had been whittled, often trampled, away. Nigeria, Africa's most populous country, was for me the worst case – the country that started with most had ended up with almost the least.

But that day in June I woke up in my hideaway in the Canary Isles, switched on my computer and read the BBC headlines, as is my routine, quicker and easier than the snap, crackle and pop of the World Service. Olusegun Obasanjo, an Amnesty International adopted prisoner of conscience, was out of jail. I couldn't believe it. I rushed into the kitchen to tell my wife, Jeany. She broke into an enormous smile. She knew how frustrated I'd felt that I'd been able to do so little for him as his health deteriorated and his formidable spirits struggled to maintain their vitality in a dank Nigerian jail. However, Obasanjo hadn't been short of friends. When I went to visit former German Chancellor Helmut Schmidt a few summers before, to win his support for my 'great' idea for a Euro-rival (more human-rights orientated) to my old newspaper, the *International Herald Tribune*, we'd ended up discussing Obasanjo. 'We've tried everything,' Schmidt said. 'Callaghan even got Thatcher to intervene.

Abacha is immovable.' 'Frankly,' he said, taking a pinch of his eternal snuff, 'he needs to be bumped off.'

I'd worked with Obasanjo on a Disarmament Commission chaired by the Swedish prime minister, Olof Palme, later assassinated returning from the cinema, walking alone with his wife. I'd learnt to rather dislike politicians and the only one I got on with in a commission stuffed with ex-prime ministers and foreign ministers was Obasanjo, a former military president, it is true, but the man responsible for engineering Nigeria's transition to democracy in the late 1970s. He'd spent the last three years in jail for struggling against the self-perpetuating clique of military officers who'd brought his efforts to dust.

In Moscow, we climbed over the protective fence of a government guest-house while the guards were distracted, and went off fishing together – or rather he borrowed a rod from some boys we met on the walk and showed them how to do it. In Hiroshima we bunked off from a boring reception and walked the streets, looking at people, now so ordinary, and wondering how mankind could be so evil. Inevitably, on our many expeditions, we talked a lot about the growing struggle for human rights and how it had passed much of Africa by. He was a great fan of Amnesty International and, once he knew my interest in the organization, became very eloquent on the subject. Later, he sent me an air ticket and I stayed with him on his farm, and a couple of years later, whilst filming, I stayed again. We ambled down to his old school, a mud-built structure on the edge of Abeokuta, and he inserted his big frame in his battered desk and smiled, the smile of a man who knew what he was doing and what he believed.

He is one of the world's tough guys, which is why in prison, instead of feeling sorry for himself, he wrote three books on Christianity and spiritual meditation, organized a productive farm on prison wasteland, sufficient to give all the prisoners a decent meal every day, jogged every morning and became the unofficial counsellor and religious adviser to all who needed his help – from murderers awaiting execution to men broken by torture. It had been the same toughness, the same single-minded application to difficult issues that led him, when president, at the time when the prime minister, Margaret Thatcher, refused to move to restore British authority in Rhodesia after it was usurped by the country's whites, to order the nationalizing of British Petroleum's interests in Nigeria and to threaten to boycott British exports. Thatcher not long after changed tack, and pushed for free elections and majority rule in what was now renamed Zimbabwe. Without a free Zimbabwe there would never have been a free South Africa.

At the age of 42 Obasanjo had walked away from the presidential palace in the continent's most populous and potentially richest country – where he had taken not a penny more than his salary – put on a pair of blue jeans and started a chicken and vegetable farm. He was so obsessed by his countrymen's refusal to come to terms with Nigeria's economic chaos, not least the running down of the country's precious agricultural base, that he decided to show what could be done with the land himself. Often, he would sleep rough in the farm's makeshift buildings still under construction, watching over every detail with the same tenacity that had made him a successful officer during the civil war, brought him to the top of the army and the country when he was only in his late thirties and led him to modernize the constitution.

Democracy, human rights, farming and disarmament are Obasanjo's passions and he has relentlessly promulgated them. As president, he once accused his countrymen of 'callousness and sadism'. To me he spoke often of the disequilibrium in a society that has been propelled so suddenly from ancient to modern. 'We got caught up in the conflict of culture, of trying to graft the so-called sophistication of Europe on to our African society.'

The first time I went to stay with him he apologized for being five hours late. Driving home from his farm he had come upon a long line of traffic halted by an accident. He went to investigate and found six bodies on the ground. There was a small crowd of onlookers and two policemen standing idly by. No one was helping. The policemen claimed that it was not their responsibility; they were *en route* to 'other business'. Obasanjo ordered the crowd to help move the bodies to the roadside and commandeered a car to rush one of the dead women, who was obviously pregnant, to the hospital, in the hope of saving the baby. He then directed traffic for three hours until the police arrived. The next day he learnt that the hospital had refused admission to the woman because there was no police certificate recording the accident. 'I should have done a Caesarean myself, by the roadside,' was his only comment.

We talked many evenings over dinner about this conflict between the old and the new. He sees a three- or four-generation timetable. 'The improvement of living standards and the wealth of nations are more of a journey and less of a destination,' he told me. 'Within our traditional society there are lots of things that we can pick, improve and develop into our own political concept. What, for example, is wrong with our traditional society, which respects age, experience and authority? Or the norm that everybody is his brother's keeper? Or the stigmatizing and ostracizing of evil-doers and the indolent?'

It is an immense and almost overwhelming struggle to achieve transition. When asked to predict which way the scales would tip, Obasanjo was always cautious. He has hopes for the future, but at the same time he is awed by the demand put upon the average Nigerian. He certainly doesn't believe that oil wealth has helped. Much of it has been wasted and 'the people put in a pressure cooker'.

On Monday June 8, 1988, General Abacha, Nigeria's strongman, had died in bed at the age of 54 of a supposed heart attack. (But the *New York Times* later reported that he was poisoned by four prostitutes who were specially recruited from India for the task, and were quickly flown in and out by plotting fellow officers.) His successor, General Abubakar, on Thursday had let Obasanjo and eight others walk free. I wanted to be there to celebrate, maybe to take a moment and do that short walk, past the flame trees that framed his house, down the dusty path to that old school-house with him again and say, 'Thank you, general, for being so brave, so strong. You give me courage and, I know, many, many other people too.'

2 MARCH 1999

'Obasanjo tops poll in Nigeria' is the headline in the freshly arrived *Financial Times*, always here by 9.30 a.m. on the day of publication. So my old friend is going to be president again.

Now I *do* want to jump on a plane to Africa. I phone the travel agent. 'Iberia non-stop, only an hour and a half to Senegal,' he says. 'Then Air Afrique to Ivory Coast, an hour there and on to Lagos.' It sounds so easy, until I realize I have no visa and the Nigerians, the world's worst bureaucrats, say they need five working days to issue one and I must present my passport myself in London.

I decide the better option is to contact Obasanjo. That, in a country that hasn't repaired its phone lines for thirty years, is easier said than done. I've been trying for weeks. Once in fifty times I caught a polite young man who answered the phone in the general's home in Abeokuta. 'He's never here,' he said. 'He's campaigning twenty-four hours a day. But try his e-mail.' 'E-mail?' 'Do you have e-mail in darkest Africa?' I feel like saying, but bite my tongue, reminding myself of the old adage, 'the darkest thing about Africa is our ignorance of it'. I try the e-mail, many times. Now I try it again with renewed intensity. Nothing happens. I try the phone again. A miracle. I get through. 'I wouldn't just come,' the young man says. 'In two days' time, he's off on a world trip.'

7 MARCH

All weekend I mull over what to do. I don't particularly want to sit in London for five days waiting for the Nigerian bureaucracy to tick over. Last time, they refused me a visa because I had a South African stamp in my passport. It needed a Cabinet decision to give me approval, which Obasanjo, then out of office, somehow engineered.

8 MARCH

With new energy I dial half a dozen times and then to my surprise the young man answers again. 'We received your e-mail,' he says, immediately recognizing my voice. 'The general is on his farm – phone this number.' 'So he hasn't dashed off on his world trip?' 'No, not yet.'

I dial again a few times and this time my luck holds and a voice, rather submerged in crackle, answers. 'Hold on, I'll get the general.' I wait for a few minutes. I hear many voices in the background. Jeany comes into my office. 'I think I can hear him. He's there!' The man comes back. 'Can you hold on another few minutes?' 'Of course I can,' I say, now starting, at the moment when success looms, to worry about my mounting phone bill. 'Jonathan, are you there?' Obasanjo it is. 'I can't believe it. I didn't know if I'd ever talk to you again. How did you survive?' 'Only by the grace of God,' he says. I love that voice, as I always have – slow, rich and kind – but I also know well enough his other side. A man, although bereft of arrogance, who doesn't suffer fools gladly, who, when he chooses, can intimidate, not just with his brain, which is shrewd, but with his massive bulk. I once saw him react to one of his farm workers who had started to argue with him. Obasanjo quickly stooped to pick up a piece of thick steel wire that had dropped on the floor to make as if to whip him. The man immediately begged for mercy and changed his tune. It was all over in a second, but I realized this is probably how Obasanjo kept his troops in order, battling the Ibo insurgency in Nigeria's fratricidal war, back when he was a young officer.

Jeany said she could see the tears in my eyes as we talked. I'm not embarrassed to admit it. I feel deeply for a man who always makes me think of Tom Paine's remark: 'My country is the world, and my religion is to do good.'

'I want to see you soon. In fact, I want to do one of my long, full-page interviews with you.' 'Well, come,' he says. 'I'll get someone to meet you at the airport.' I explain the visa problem and boldly suggest I should just come anyway. He doesn't sound keen on that idea – even the president-elect knows better than to waste energy with an unnecessary tangle with Nigerian bureaucracy. 'We'll do you a letter to the London High Commission,' he says. 'Talk to Ad-Obe, my assistant. He'll sort it out.'

I'm left in the hands of Ad-Obe, who comes on the phone to tell me how difficult it is to come to Nigeria and that I should wait until Obasanjo comes to London in ten days' time. But my journalistic instincts are in full swing and I want to get that *first* interview, just as I once caught Mrs Indira Gandhi two days before she swept back into power and persuaded her to give me two hours alone. I explain all this to Ad-Obe, who replies, 'Nigeria is not India, it's chaotic here.' What a silly remark. I remember waiting at Mrs Gandhi's house and then, when she appeared on the veranda, pushing through the crowd who'd been there, many waiting for promised appointments for days, to accost her nose with my request. The interview made the front page of the *Herald Tribune* and the *Washington Post* and she gave me the cleverest, wittiest Question and Answer I have ever done. But this time I was skewered by the visa problem. Precious days were slipping by, and I had to admit if I was still in Oxford I'd have nipped down to London and got my visa by now. For the first time, all was not so simple from the Canary Isles.

14 MARCH

Yesterday afternoon, Funmi, Obasanjo's helpful secretary, told me to call at 11 o'clock that evening, after he returned from a meeting. With some trepidation at the late hour, I dial again. This time the call goes straight through and Funmi's voice is as clear as a bell. Obviously, Obasanjo's phone lines are getting priority treatment – no doubt taps included – now he's president-elect. 'Hallo, Jonathan,' she says brightly, recognizing my voice. 'I'll put you through to his room. If he doesn't answer it means he's sleeping.' A mellow, sleepy voice answers. 'Where are you? Why aren't you here?' My nervousness at calling so late subsides. I'm obviously not the pain in the neck I feared.

I explain to him again more fully than I did before why I want to see him, how I think I know him well enough to bring out his deepest thoughts and can give him a platform to the world. 'I want to talk to you, too. Why don't you come on the 19th when I'm back from my African trip before I go to London? Phone Olokum, my friend the ambassador in Madrid, and say I told him to give you a visa.'

16 MARCH

At 8 a.m. I'm on the phone and, under the businesslike but always amusing prodding of Funmi, my plans for departure are put forward a day. She will meet me at Lagos airport tomorrow evening. Already imbued with the Nigerian wit that transcends all difficulties, I am transported to Africa. 'I'm your woman,' she says, when I call her to tell her I've squared the Nigerian ambassador to Spain yet again – yesterday he gave his approval for a visa on mention of Obasanjo's name and today he advanced it a day. 'Call me back in fifteen minutes once you've talked to British Airways,' Funmi orders. 'Then I'm off to Lagos. Whilst the cat's away, the mouse must play.' 'What do you mean?' I asked, puzzled. 'My boss is away. I'm off for fun in the big city.' 'Oh, I get it.' 'I'll meet you tomorrow. I'll be in a green Kampala. You'll stay tonight at the farm at Ota. While I'm in Lagos I'll book you on the flight to Abuja at 6.50 in the morning.' My heart sank twice, once at the early hour, the second at flying with some badly serviced Nigerian airline, with the world's highest accident record. 'Then Obasanjo's right-hand man, Otumba Fashawe, will meet you and take you out to meet him at Abuja airport that evening when he arrives back from his round Africa trip.' I just wish Funmi ran the airline. 'Are you sure you'll be there when I arrive?' 'As sure as Christ's second coming,' she shoots back. How am I supposed to take that? I'd forgotten, beneath the corruption and violence that pervades and overwhelms Nigerian society, how moral and religious ordinary Nigerians are. Away from official responsibilities – in personal life, with family, aged parents, sick relatives – they live (and laugh at) the command to be their brother's keeper.

18 MARCH

The crowd of returning Nigerians surge off the plane into another crowd of Nigerians. White men are few and far between. Surely Funmi will have no trouble in recognizing me. There are plenty of people holding up cards with people's names on them. But mine is not amongst them and I obviously give the impression of looking lost. A young man rushes up to me. 'I was waiting for you. My name is Paul.' 'Jonathan Power,' I say, shaking his hand. 'Where is Funmi?' 'She couldn't come. Mr Power, come this way.' We walk down past the luggage carousel to the customs officers. 'Give the man £20,' he says, *sotto voce*. My jet-lagged brain slowly starts to wake up. Would Obasanjo, the politician who campaigned as whiter than white, have a driver who asks me to dish the customs £20? The customs man asks me what I have. Then, as is usual in Nigeria, asks me if I 'have a little something for him'. 'No,' I smile. 'These are new days. Obasanjo won the election, didn't he?' He laughs and lets me through. Paul is waiting, urging me on to his car. 'Where are we going?' I ask. 'To the Sheraton,' he says. But Funmi had said most definitely I'd be staying at the farm. I decide to play for time. If he is the legitimate driver, I don't want to insult the first African I meet after ten years away. 'I must change some money.' I wait in the queue at the bank. A lady in purple uniform sidles up to me. 'We have a taxi for you,' she says. I decide to do some gentle intimidation. 'I'm a guest of General Obasanjo. I'm expecting his car. Could you phone him for me?' I'm not sure what her relationship to Paul is. Or, indeed, his deal with the customs men, who allowed him into the carousel area. But I can see that at least she has a formal job and wouldn't want to lose that by crossing a friend of the president-elect, for the sake of a few thousand *naira* bribe from Paul. She comes back and tells me that the secretary said: 'Funmi is on the way. She'll be there any minute. She probably got held up in the rush hour.'

I walk over to the bar and order a Coke. The menu is up on a big board. 'Chicken parts, goat meat, snail, gizzard and yum yum.' I begin to wind down. Ten minutes later a large lady with a green turban, accompanied by a younger woman, heaves into view. She recognizes me immediately and I give her a great hug of relief. 'And this is Bimbola, General Obasanjo's daughter.' We drive off and I tell them of my encounter with Paul. 'You're lucky to be alive,' Funmi says. 'These types rob you, knife you and throw you out on the road.'

The traffic is chaotic. It's rush hour. Yellow buses, minivans and cars hustle for space. The light is failing and the owners of stores that stretch endlessly along the road light little lamps to illuminate their paltry stock. One sells white bread, another vegetables, another peppers, another pots and pans. There are churches, hundreds of them. 'The Redeemed Christian Church of God.' 'The Kingdom of Heaven Mission on Earth.' The buses, too, have their slogans. 'In Thy Hand, Oh Lord.' And most telling of all, 'Triumph of the Insignificant.' I look at the crowds packed into the buses, people battling their way home, hours on the road after hours of hard work, only marginally better off than the cripples begging hopelessly on the street corner we just passed. And what is this? A man bending over, bleeding. A woman pouring water over his wound. A policeman looking concerned, standing by. Was he hit by a rogue driver? They all seem to be rogues. Driving as if there was no tomorrow. Our driver is the fastest of them all. This is Obasanjo's campaign Land Rover and driver, Funmi explains. There's nothing I can do, just accept I'm in another world. The driver accelerates. We weave in and out, from one side of the road to the other. The pedestrians appear to hurtle by my windows. In the evening gloom, I can see the courtyard of a church. A hundred or so men, all dressed in white, are drawn up in neat semi-circles, listening to a preacher. 'Pray for me,' I whisper.

I sleep well on Obasanjo's farm. I'm fed well, and surrounded all evening and all morning by the sexual and religious banter of Funmi, Bimbola and their friends, who remind me why it is I've long had this love affair with Africa. Life, to them, at least on the personal level, is seamless. It is whole and it is rounded. There are no sharp corners, no mental compartments. Companionship is the most important thing of life, giving you, my friend or neighbour, all humour, warmth and goodwill that I'm able to offer.

At 11, not 5.30 as I feared, I'm rushed to the airport from the farm, this time accompanied by Bimbola and a couple of her friends. Funmi stays behind to man the phone and line things up for me to be met and looked after. I'm dropped off at a charter service and told to wait for the vice-president-elect who will travel with me. Two hours on, his entourage phone and cancel. I'm taken over to the main airport and put on board 'Bellevue Airlines', a company that is a spin-off from a hard-pressed ex-Yugoslav airline. I'd quickly asked the oil man who'd been sitting with me in the lounge which airlines to avoid. This, fortunately, was not one of them. I'm always full of fear, flying. Can I ever be more nervous? It doesn't seem so – perhaps there's only so much nervousness the human mind can accept. After all I have flown with the Tanzanian air force and, on another occasion, battled without radar, through stormy dark rain clouds, at night, getting totally lost on the way, high up, I hoped, in a small Cessna, above the Southern Highlands in Tanzania. Once I had to show the befuddled pilot where the airstrip was. Another time to tell him that the lights ahead were *not* Dar-es-Salaam. He'd gone too far to the left but, fortunately, not to the right where the mountains were.

19 MARCH

I'm in Abuja, Nigeria's capital, by mid-afternoon. A town set in the middle of nowhere, it was chosen as the federal capital only twenty years ago in a sensible attempt to decompress the wildly overcrowded Lagos. Surrounded by little villages of mud walls and conical thatched roofs, it is – what an opportunity missed – full of nondescript modern office blocks and hotels. If only their architects had been ordered to take their cue from the villages and the bold, rocky topography around. But Abuja has its charm too, a lack of crime not least, but also a towering cathedral in mid-construction whose cross can be seen for miles, and an even more magnificent mosque with a golden dome, at least as large as Istanbul's Blue Mosque, that absorbs the equatorial heat and gives the visitor or worshipper a profound sense of earthly tranquillity.

I'd met up quickly with the Obasanjo crowd of intimates and campaign workers, and at 9.30 p.m. we drove in a long cavalcade to the airport to meet Obasanjo on his return from Paris, an add-on stop at the end of his African safari. Suddenly, there were the lights of the plane in the African night. We all surged forward – a crowd of a good fifty, led by his now arrived vice-president – on to the tarmac. The presidential jet drew up, the stairs dropped and a few moments later Obasanjo appeared, draped in a deep reddish-brown toga. He took a momentary pause at the top of the steps – I remember that same gesture, exuding self-confidence and authority, made by Gorbachev when he returned to Moscow after the failed coup – and then slowly descended.

His vice-president seemed decidedly awkward. I felt the same. Obasanjo always carried his authority well. Now he radiates an old schoolmasterly severity that, if one did not know the natural self-effacement and easy humour of the man, you might take for arrogance. I lingered at the back of the crowd, a lone white face, hoping he might look twice. He didn't. I had no other choice but to propel myself forward before he got into the car. Obasanjo smiled, and we gave each other a brief hug. I felt constrained. Perhaps he too. Old friendship though it is, I thought, he will not want to show too much affection for a white man in front of such a crowd, all in their own way competing for his attention – and for jobs. Nevertheless, a journalist in this situation only has twenty seconds at the most. 'When can you fit me in?' 'Tomorrow at 4,' and that was it.

We rejoined the cavalcade, which, on reaching Abuja, did not break up as I expected. Instead we followed Obasanjo's car up the long unguarded driveway to a large white house. 'This used to be Abacha's house,' someone whispered to me in the dark, as we slammed the car doors shut and rushed into the house behind Obasanjo, fearful, in my case at least, that some guard would spring from nowhere and shut me out.

We walked into a large room. Obasanjo and his vice-president were sitting side by side. Silently we circled the walls and were handed fruit juices by waiters in starched white suits and bottle-green buttons, the national colour. It was plush. So was the retinue of hangers-on, sliding from one conversational partner to another, elegant in their rich, woven, gold-braided cloth, which hung from their shoulders with an effortless grace down to their expensive leather shoes. It was a serious crowd, all male, not a woman in sight. There was no raucous laughing, but one could hear an occasional earnest conversation into a mobile phone. From time to time the in-coming call on someone's mobile was handed to Obasanjo. He read his mail and most of the time ignored us.

Abba Dabo, whom I'd befriended in the car ride, a former press secretary of the deposed and last democratically elected president, Shehu Shagari, pushed me forward. 'Show him that column you wrote in 1984,' he said. That was the one after the coup, which argued that the generals one day would be compelled to bring Obasanjo back to power if the country were ever to stabilize. I pulled it out, walked over and gave it to Obasanjo. He read it slowly. 'You were always ahead,' he said, and took my hand. 'How long do you need, will an hour do?' 'Not really. Perhaps I could travel back on your plane to London and we could finish it then?'

I retreated to the crowd. Slowly, around one in the morning, people drifted away. I thought it time to go. I hadn't wanted to disturb him again but, with Abba prodding once more, I called out 'goodnight' and started for the staircase. 'Jonathan,' I heard a big voice. 'You haven't told me how your love life is!' I turned and laughed. 'Not here, in front of your friends,' I pleaded in mock earnestness. 'Come and sit down and fill me in. I'm so out of date. You were never lucky with women, Jonathan,' he laughed. 'But you are looking very good, something must be going on.' I told him of my marriage to Jeany and our 8-year-old daughter. His eyes grew big and he smiled. He was happy for me. 'She must come and sing here.' The ice was broken again, or so I thought.

20 MARCH

The interview started well enough – Obasanjo talking about how he'd been physically reduced by his imprisonment but spiritually strengthened. Always a God-fearing man, I knew, but this was a different degree of religiosity.

Forty minutes in, however, the mood changed. I was pressing him on his plans for privatizing the national oil company, notorious for its corruption and inefficiency. His voice, usually soft, rose by degrees. His eyes tensed, 'Why should we give away what no one has yet put a price on?' We continued, but I could see that I'd rattled him. There is an Anglo-Saxon way of asking questions that is essentially adversarial. Third World politicians, even enlightened democratic ones who, like Obasanjo, enjoy nothing more than a good intellectual argument in private, find it unsettling. I'd questioned him about army excesses during his last presidency and about allegations that the funding of his campaign came from rich generals of the old order. But the question of oil, its use and misuse, is the most sensitive of all issues in Nigeria. In fact, he has a nuanced and thoughtful point of view that came through at the airport press conference later that day.

At the moment, however, he was definitely annoyed, made some remark to the effect that an ambassador was waiting for him and ambassadors were 'much more bloody important than this' and left. I decided I had nothing to lose but to follow him, calling out, as if nothing untoward had happened, 'Could we finish it on the plane tomorrow?' 'We'll see,' he said non-committally, and disappeared. I decided to wait. I had a very incomplete interview, not one that was marketable for what I had in mind, a full-page Question and Answer, and perhaps it never would be if I got pressed out of the timetable by the army of visitors waiting their turn. Half an hour passed and my spirits started to sink. We'd really not had time to settle into our old ways.

Suddenly Funmi appeared, miraculously transported from the farm at Ota. 'The general wants you to eat dinner with us.' I was led into the large dining-room where there were a good twenty people around the table, and plonked at the far end. I was clearly an afterthought, for they were all tucked into their first course. 'We've known each other for twenty years,' he told everyone and we immediately launched across the length of the long table into a dissection of the journalistic art. It was a public conversation, full of laughs and merriment. Old stories told and scores settled, on both sides. I think the company were bemused as we slipped into our old repartee. I made some error of English pronunciation and he picked it up. 'I get nervous when you raise your voice,' I explained. 'I was getting angry,' he said. 'Your question made you sound like you want me just to give away my country. Anyway, if you're my friend I can shout at you.' 'As long as I can shout back!' 'But not in public.' 'My mother brought me up to have manners.' And so we went on, telling stories of our wanderings around Moscow and Hiroshima. 'We are non-conformists, you and me,' he said. 'That's why our friendship has lasted.'

Now we're airborne together, on the presidential jet. I'm the only white man front or aft. The Nigerian air force captain, over the intercom, briefly welcomed the president-elect, bade us all to fasten our seat-belts and told us the flying time to Heathrow was six hours and five minutes (only four to Spain). The heart of Africa is closer than New York. We've passed over the Savannah, out beyond Kano, the northern city of Nigeria, and now we begin the long traverse of the Sahara.

Obasanjo likes to hold my hand – this is the custom I've met all over Africa between good male friends. I no longer find it odd, though once back in my own culture I immediately revert to type. Thus I sit on the armrest of his seat, he with his arm round me or, when the interview slows down or we take a breath, taking my hand in his.

It's good. I've got what I wanted, and more, from this plane ride. His sense of fun as he walks down the small plane (it has only sixteen seats and one toilet, and they're going to circle the world in three weeks) shortly after take off to say hallo to everyone. 'Good morning, I'm Obasanjo, this *may* be your president.' His sense of confidence as we talk after the tape is switched off, about old friends like Helmut Schmidt, whom he thinks the world of ('but he can be very rude'), or David Owen, the clever ex-wunderkind of modern British politics, whom he thinks 'doesn't have a real sense of direction about the world', of Bill Clinton and what's going to happen to his marriage after he leaves office. We digress to discuss our first wives. 'If you met my first wife you would think she were an angel. But she's a demon,' he says very seriously.

We talk a lot about Nigeria. I'm convinced, I tell him, that if real progress is made in the next four years in restoring ethnic harmony, moving the country forward economically and maintaining democracy, it will have a profound effect on the rest of Africa. A number of African countries are already making tremendous progress. Some of the problems elsewhere that now seem insoluble will begin to fall into place. Nigeria itself can easily be another Malaysia. He concurs. 'I feel that too. But will I live to do it? Sometimes I doubt it. There could be a coup. It could come from the military; it could come from some civilian group. Even in my immediate entourage there are people whose motives I doubt, whom I cannot really trust.' 'Why do you have them around you, then?' I ask. 'Because of politics. They represent certain regions, or political groups. It can't be avoided.'

We talk on. Africa slips away. We start to cross the Mediterranean. Europe beckons, but I bring part of Africa back with me. Obasanjo interrupts my reverie. 'Why don't you come to live in Nigeria?' 'Why?' 'Then we could always be talking.' He pauses. 'I don't suppose your wife would want to.' 'I'll ask her,' I say.

Out of Heathrow, where in the VIP lounge they didn't even ask to see my passport, I find a quiet corner in a London café and listen to my tape. For the life of me I can't think why he got so nerved up:

JP: You've only been out of jail for nine months. Have you recovered?
O: Yes. I think when you are in jail, you lose materially, you probably lose physically. It depends on how you have occupied your time in jail, you may or may not lose spiritually. Physically, I believe I am fairly recovered.
JP: You said you didn't lose spiritually. What did you mean?
O: I meant that when you are in jail, you do reflect and meditate on the word of God and on God.
JP: You wrote some books of spiritual reflections.
O: Two have been published, one is on prayer. I have come to be confirmed in my belief in the mystery and power of prayer and I put that into a book form.
JP: You weren't tempted to cry out: 'Oh God, why has thou forsaken me?'
O: Not really, because I know that God really never did forsake me when I was in prison. One thing I knew and believed (that is also

by the grace of God): I would come out of prison. But what I did not know was when and how.

JP: You never felt the dark night of the soul? You never got depressed?

O: Not really. You can see from letters I wrote to friends and loved ones and their replies. Some of them I can show you. They say: 'You seem to have something that we outside the prison do not have.'

JP: Amnesty International campaigned for your release, as they did for all the other hundreds of political prisoners in Nigeria. Did it do much good?

O: It's like constant drips of water on a stone. It seems to make little difference, but over time it does. I think it did three important things: it gave a lot of prisoners who didn't have a well-known name a lot of hope; it wore at the nerves of the jailers and senior policemen, so when change came they were more or less ready for it; and it helped keep awake Western governments on the job of pushing Nigeria. But, in the end, it was probably divine intervention that changed things. [Shortly after his release, Obasanjo, on a visit to London, asked for a meeting with Amnesty International to say thank you.]

JP: When you were in prison I went to talk to your old friend, the former West German Chancellor, Helmut Schmidt, about what could be done to get you out of prison, and he said: 'We have tried everything, nothing is going to happen until someone bumps off Abacha.' Did someone bump off Abacha?

O: I think God did it.

JP: The *New York Times* published a story that some dissenting army officers brought over four Indian prostitutes, sent them to him with poison and as soon as that was delivered they were quickly spirited back to India. Do you give any credence to this story?

O: Well, I think that he died in the company of prostitutes. That is an open secret now. That those prostitutes played any foul game, I don't know anything on that.

JP: I remember when you were president twenty years ago, you once accused your countrymen of callousness and sadism. Why?

O: Why should any human being take delight in the suffering of the innocent? Why should any human being oppress the innocent, except for callousness and sadism? So what I said twenty years ago is now very evident in the life and the action of Abacha and those who cohorted with him. So I wasn't wrong.

JP: But if it is this ingrained and you first spoke about it twenty years ago, how are you going to get it out of the system?

O: Well, it is human beings, and it is not only Nigerians. If you go through the Bible you will see stories of leaders and people who are sadistic and who are callous, who are wicked. I think you need God in your life to really be drawn away from being bad to being good. That's why you find some people have a pessimistic view of human beings. You have those who say the glass is half empty rather than the glass is half full. I also believe that human beings have certain capacities to be cruel. If you read the book which I wrote, *Animal Called Man*, you'll see how I discuss the innate capacity of man to be bad and the possibility of his being good also at the same time.

JP: Are your own hands clean? Your critics recall the time when you were president before, when there were bloody crack-downs on students and your prosecution of the anti-establishment singer Fela. It is said that your soldiers threw his 77-year-old mother from the top floor of her house and she died.

O: As the leader at the particular time, the buck must stop at my table. But a military policeman was on duty, traffic control duty, not too far from Fela's house. Fela wounded that policeman deliberately and intentionally. The soldiers were enraged. And before anybody could put the soldiers to order they took the law into their own hands and attacked Fela's house. I am not condoning the action of the soldiers, but I am also not approving Fela's action.

JP: But the buck, as you said, stopped with you when it came to the discipline of the army.

O: Yes, so what I then did was to carry out an inquiry into the murder, and punish those that needed to be punished.

JP: How are you going to deal with the army that has come to depend on patronage, to depend on the fruits of the oil economy?

O: Well, it's not only the army. Some civilians are in the same sort of form and shape and the same frame of mind and same condition. You must show that the practices you want to get rid of are punished. When they know that you mean business about it – it will take some time – sooner or later you will achieve success.

JP: So you are going to crack the whip from the beginning?

O: I will more than crack the whip, I will use the whip.

JP: People of the oil-rich Niger Delta have watched billions of dollars flow out of their soil as they have grown poorer. One of the leaders, the novelist Ken Saro-Wiwa, a great human rights campaigner, was executed by Abacha. Do you have a plan for repairing the moral and political damage wrought by your predecessors?

O: Yes. I have talked to the Ijaw people and the Ijaws are quite rightly bitter because of real, terrible injustice, which you can see all along the Niger Delta. The insensitivity that some parts of Nigeria have exhibited is just unbelievable. Yes, the first thing is to understand what has gone wrong and what is going on in the Niger Delta. Then devise what will work, because the problem of the Niger Delta can be put in one word: under-development.

JP: Your Nobel Prize-winner, Wole Soyinka, said: 'We may be actu- ally witnessing a nation on the verge of extinction.'

O: Which nation is he talking about?

JP: Your nation.

O: OK. I don't believe this.

JP: And another human rights activist, Beko Ransome-Kuti, has said that if we can't live as one people we are better off living separately. Are these the voices of people you listen to or people you dismiss?

O: Well, I listen to all voices, and after I have listened, I determine what voices are relevant and what voices are not.

JP: Do you worry about the pressures within the Federal Republic from people who want to go their own way?

O: I don't. When some groups of Nigerians have expressed the feeling of wanting to go it alone, it has been when there are signs of injustice. When you go back and you remember that the Ibos fought a war of secession less than thirty years ago, then you will not be so worried. Then you will see that what is important is justice, fairness, equity and democracy. The Ibos and the rest of Nigeria reconciled a long time ago.

JP: Do you expect that because you now have a democratic system, that the stresses and strains can be more easily contained?

O: Naturally. That is what democracy is all about. First, there will be more discussion and more dialogue, more explanation, and people will understand more why certain things are done and why certain things are not done. Second, they will have greater opportunities to express and vent their views.

JP: Let's talk about the rest of Africa for a while. Democracy is now returning to Nigeria, but in many parts of Africa (in Angola, Sudan, the Congo), democracy is very circumscribed. There is an enormous amount of tension, there is fighting, there are terrible human rights abuses, there is corruption, there is disequilibrium. I notice that many observers in the West are now saying there is nothing we can do to help Africa in this predicament. The old order is crumbling; Western intervention of any kind is almost counter-productive. Do you look at it in that way?

O: Yes and no. Yes in the sense that most of the things that will endure in Africa must come from inside Africa. They must be internally generated, like in Nigeria. Our democracy is internally generated. Of course we do need assistance, understanding, co-operation, from outside for the sustenance of democracy, for the deepening and widening of our democracy. Because we must never make the mistake of thinking that once an election takes place that is the end of democracy. I wonder at the number of so-called international observers who go into a country for the election. The election is just one small event in the process of democracy. Then after the election all the assistance and the help that those countries need are neglected and ignored, and then we are accused of not sustaining our democracy. Let's take Nigeria. There is no way Nigeria can sustain its democracy under the present burden of debt. We must have the ability to satisfy the high expectations of Nigerians, particularly in the social and economic areas. If we are not able to do that, two years down the road Nigerians will be asking: 'Hey, what is all this about, what are we getting, our situation has not changed, there is still no food on our table. The farmers have not got anything to help them run their farms.' This then gives room for somebody or a group of people to stage a coup. It could be the military or it could be a combination of military and civilian; it could even be just civilians.

I believe that the success of democracy in Nigeria will have implications for the advancement of democracy in Africa. In the first instance, it means straight away that 20–25 per cent of the population of Africa south of the Sahara are under some form of democratic rule. South Africa is there, Nigeria is there. You have other smaller countries that have been bastions of democracy for a long time. Then Nigeria can also be in a position to help other African nations. To me the kind of help that Nigeria can render to other African nations is to help them democratize, and by helping them democratize it will help them to prevent conflicts which come out of real and perceived injustice. Most of these real injustices can be prevented through striving and working to fashion democracy.

JP: To preserve a government, supposedly to preserve democracy, Nigeria is very directly engaged in the civil war in Sierre Leone. Is this a fruitful way of trying to spread democracy?

O: I don't know. I will not go into how Nigeria found itself in Sierre Leone, but having found itself in Sierre Leone, Nigeria is under obligation not to abandon Sierre Leone without bringing some form of order and security and peace into Sierre Leone.

JP: As you know there has been a United Nations Human Rights report about the behaviour of Nigerian troops in Sierre Leone, accusing them on occasion of severe brutality. This is very counter-productive for an army that's trying to bring peace.

O: Well, those who write these reports are of course accusing Nigerian troops of bad behaviour and acts of indiscipline, and I would hope that when such acts do occur the normal military process of dealing with them will take place. We should also understand that for soldiers deployed away from their country to defend another country for a cause that may not even be clear, some of them must be asking: 'Why are we here?' I am not saying that they should not be condemned, but try and put yourself in the position of these people.

JP: Are you going to be more rigorous than your predecessor on the use of courts martial and disciplining those who are accused of severe human rights abuses like shooting children?

O: Oh, naturally, why should you shoot children? They are frightened. Apart from anything else I hope the soldiers will have a certain code of conduct that will guide their behaviour in the operation. Even in the Nigerian civil war, we had a code of conduct that guided our behaviour and our operations, in addition to the normal military rule and military order and military regulations and military law.

JP: The UN has just pulled out of Angola. The Western powers seem to have thrown up their hands in despair with the massacre of the Tutsis three years ago. In fact President Clinton went to Africa last year and made an apology for not being more interventionist at the time. Where do we go next? Where does the world community go next with the many civil wars that are now raging in Africa?

O: We should know what is fundamentally wrong in each case. When we establish what is fundamentally wrong in each case, then we take a collective action to do what is right, to help that country. I was in Paris a few days ago, and President Chirac and I went over almost all the conflict areas of Africa. I was satisfied at the end of our discussion that the situation in Africa is not a hopeless situation. It is also not a situation where we should expect an overnight wonder. Again, I talked to President Nyerere of Tanzania [now deceased], who has been involved with the Rwanda issue for quite some time now. We all felt some progress is being made, and we should encourage the progress that is being made. The idea of expecting progress overnight should be forgotten; the idea of thinking that a solution should be imposed, I do not believe. We should be ready to be consistent and even-handed. I believe that this is what will lead us out of it. So Rwanda, Congo, Angola, particularly Sierre Leone, I still don't believe that it should all be abandoned. We should consistently and steadily work in that direction. If the world decides to go at a problem and solve it, I believe that in time it will be solved. What will be dangerous is for the world to say they are powerless and we should abandon these countries.

JP: The UN has pulled its troops out of Angola. Was that a mistake?

O: I believe that is a mistake. Remember that it was UN withdrawal that led to the massacre in Rwanda. The UN has to accept that when you send troops into a place, it also will involve a certain amount of loss. If sending UN troops is regarded as a quick fix, then UN troops are not required. To my own way of thinking, you might as well send in boy scouts.

JP: Now as you have just mentioned, the UN did pull out of Rwanda at a crucial moment. Savage massacres followed. When President Clinton went to visit Rwanda briefly at the end of last year he apologized for that decision.

O: I did commend President Clinton for apologizing over Rwanda, but it is already too late, lives are lost, and we have to learn the right lesson from that, and not allow a similar situation to develop anywhere else.

JP: So what's your feeling on how America will take its stand the next time that such a serious situation arises? Do you expect Clinton next time to be more forthcoming?

O: It comes down to what I have said. If the UN wants to prevent massacre and deaths in a country which are preventable . . .

JP: They are preventable?

O: Yes, it must be ready to put its money where its mouth is.

JP: So you are convinced that even in a situation as serious as was Rwanda before the genocide, that, with the right degree of deployment by the UN, those massacres could have been substantially avoided?

O: I think that it was the fault of everybody who looked the other way. They could have been avoided.[1]

*

[1] This is a shortened version of an interview that appeared in the *Los Angeles Times* and *Prospect Magazine*, London.

The sea-change in Nigeria that brought Obasanjo, ex-Amnesty International political prisoner and democracy campaigner, to power has a large number of causes and reasons, and to single out Amnesty International's influence, whether it be in Nigeria or elsewhere, would be regarded by many as simplifying what has been a complex and subtle evolution in society that can be traced through many phases and, indeed, through many cultures back thousands of years.

Yet in modern times it is not unfair to see that since its foundation in 1961 Amnesty has been a catalyst that has transformed, invigorated and even transfigured the debate and the values that contemporary societies put on human rights. So profound has been its resonance that its influence has spread far beyond the confines of Western democratic culture and now reaches deep into the Islamic, Buddhist, Confucian and even communist worlds where men and women of many different political and religious persuasions have made its principles and its concerns part of their own daily credo. As Obasanjo observed of his own country, 'Amnesty drips like water on a stone,' and now clearly in Nigeria one can start to see the image it has defined on the paving stones of contemporary life and the hole it has dug in the consciousness of both high and low.

Typical of the many critiques that Amnesty published during the years of military dictatorship in reports and letters to Commonwealth, European and North American leaders was its 1998 report on Nigeria, the last before Abacha's death. 'Hundreds of political prisoners,' it read,

including human rights offenders were detained during the year. Most were detained without charge or trial: others had been convicted in unfair political trials. There were reports of ill-treatment of prisoners, and at least two prisoners of conscience died as a result of prison conditions so harsh as to amount to cruel, inhuman or degrading treatment. People with links to the political opposition or human rights groups were attacked and threatened. At least forty-three prisoners were sentenced to death and thirty-three executed.

Amnesty could not guess that Abacha would suddenly die, but when he did the transition was probably smoother than it might otherwise have been because the country had been prepared for change. Diplomats, politicians, businessmen and journalists, even *ancien régime* supporters, knew somewhere at the back of their minds there was another more honest way of having their country run.

Amnesty had assiduously worked the Commonwealth front. This organization, a voluntary club for ex-members of the British Empire, carries a certain aura of prestige and exclusiveness, not least easy access, without necessarily waiting for a formal invitation, to each other's corridors of power. In 1995 Nigeria was suspended from the Commonwealth. Similarly, the European Union imposed an arms embargo on Nigeria in 1995, again following sustained Amnesty lobbying. Amnesty also worked on commercial companies doing business in Nigeria, in particular the oil companies. Amnesty now has its own business group and they persuaded Shell Oil, the biggest company in Nigeria, to rethink its codes of practice and ethics in terms of human rights.

Journalists in Nigeria found themselves regularly on the front line, often arrested, beaten and tortured.[1] Amnesty adopted many of them as prisoners of conscience. Nosa Igiebor, the courageous editor-in-chief of *Tell*, was given Amnesty International's Special Award for Human Rights Journalism Under Threat at a ceremony in London. 'From the start the magazine refused to call Abacha "head of state",' he said at the ceremony. 'It was illegal, so we always wrote "junta" or "dictator".' Mr Igiebor spent two periods in prison and his journalists dared not use their office. Copies of the magazine were regularly seized. Most of *Tell*'s journalists had been recruited from Nigeria's first news magazine, *Newswatch*, that had been tamed by constant brutal treatment. Its editor, Dele Giwa, was killed by a letter bomb.

Nigeria produced many heroic human rights campaigners. One such courageous person was Beko Ransome-Kuti, chair of the Campaign for Democracy, which maintained through Nigeria's darkest days a campaign of civil protest. He was detained over thirty times and adopted as a prisoner of conscience by the Amnesty group in Canterbury, England.

---

[1] According to the US State Department's Human Rights Report for 1999, 'Murder remained the leading cause of job-related deaths among journalists worldwide.'

Amnesty also organized a vigil at the Nigerian High Commission in London in 1995, in an attempt, unsuccessful, to prevent the execution of human rights campaigner Ken Saro-Wiwa. Later, it projected a larger-than-life portrait of him on to the building's façade.

Amnesty was able to marshal many of its groups (150 in the UK alone) around the world to work on Nigeria. Letters, e-mails, lobbies and protests were continuous. Did it have an effect? No one can measure it. Nigeria has long had a 'now you see it, now you don't' quality. It has certainly changed beyond recognition, in terms of the way the country is run. Nigeria, two years after Obasanjo's return, may now have its judicial, democratic and individual freedoms, at least in principle if not always in practice, but day-to-day life is still very much as Ben Okri caught it in the convulsing novel of his homeland, *The Famished Road*:

Everywhere there was the crudity of wounds, the stark huts, the rusted zinc abodes, the rubbish in the streets, children in rags, the little girls naked on the sand playing with crushed tin-cans, the little boys jumping about uncircumcised, making machine-gun noises. The air vibrating with poisonous heat and evaporating water from the filthy gutters. The sun bared the reality of our lives and everything was so harsh it was a mystery that we could understand and care for one another or for anything at all.

In the rough and hard reality of the day-to-day existence for ordinary working people, what do human rights freedoms mean? How do the authorities, even if they are willing, as they are now in Nigeria's case, make sure that grand principles of human rights trickle down to ordinary people who are totally caught up in the struggle for their daily bread? It is even more difficult than ensuring a supply of clean drinking water to every village – and that has been an elusive enough goal, despite it being given lip-service by every government since independence, in this oil-rich country.

The biggest problems in Nigeria today can be summed up simply: corruption, an abuse of human rights and a propensity to anarchy. The first is pervasive and has been for thirty-five years, to my knowledge. I remember while working in Tanzania receiving a letter from a friend teaching in Nigeria soon after the country became independent complaining of how widespread the acceptance of corruption was in her school. In Tanzania, at that time, the word wasn't even in the lexicon and all these years later I can still recall how shocked I felt. Even if Obasanjo appoints saints to high positions, which he manifestly cannot, corruption will take decades to root out. Still, he can stop the pillage from the top – Abacha's personal fortune alone has been estimated at $700 million. And this is where he has begun – pulling the snouts out of the oil trough. Within hours of taking power on the last day of May 1999, Obasanjo suspended contracts valued at hundreds of millions of dollars.

With human rights Obasanjo again began at the top, assuming that if he started there, there would be a quick trickle down. Within a week of taking office he began an overhaul of the armed forces, purging virtually all officers who played significant rôles in the corrupt and brutal reign of the military. Next, he appointed a panel to investigate human rights violations committed during the years of military rule with a mandate to identify those responsible for killings and other abuses. The panel was also charged with establishing whether those violations were 'the product of a deliberate state policy or of any of its organs or institutions'.

Nevertheless, the all-too-pervasive near-anarchy that periodically grips inter-tribal relations has all the makings of preparing the ground for future human rights abusers. Only three weeks into his term of office Obasanjo had to send the army into Warri in the Niger Delta to impose a curfew. Around two hundred people were killed by intertribal fighting over confused land ownership. A local newspaper reported that thirty people died in a boundary dispute sparked by a single palm tree. Yet Warri sits poverty-stricken amid oil wells and its violence only underscores the corruption that has permeated the oil industry, skimming the country's wealth away from the populace and giving it to the few. It underlines, too, how weak the state has become as a setter of standards and enforcer of correctness.

Obasanjo flew into Warri himself and started negotiations between the fighting groups. As part of a longer-term programme aimed at redressing the years of neglect of the oil-producing communities, Obasanjo has promised to increase the allocation of revenue accruing from oil to the local producers by 10 per cent. Shortly after, underlining the paucity of skilled manpower capable of putting the Niger Delta region upright, Obasanjo's office took out an advertisement in the *Financial Times*, *The Economist* and elsewhere, inviting tenders from 'regional masterplanners of international standing' to plan out a pathway to the future, to embrace every aspect of development from education to electrification to rural banking. It is a bold step to invite back a sort of localized colonial administration.

The violence in the Niger Delta did simmer down, only to be replaced towards the end of 1999 by tribal fighting in Anambra State in south-east Nigeria and, much more seriously, in the north around the ancient Islamic capital of Kano. (In the 1980s and early 1990s, thousands died in religious rioting in Kano, mainly between Muslims and Christian Ibos from the south-east. In 1966 the massacre of Ibos in Kano was one of the sparks that ignited a bloody civil war and the attempted secession of the province of Biafra.)

In February and May 2000 violence blew up again, this time in Kaduna, the old British administrative centre for the north. Fighting erupted during a demonstration by minority Christians angered by Muslims' calls for the imposition of Sharia criminal law, the strict form of Islamic law which mandates amputations of limbs for theft and stoning for adultery. The ball had been set rolling by Ahmed Sani, the governor of the remote state of Zamfara, who announced he was banning alcohol and would segregate the sexes in schools and on public transport. Mr Sani said he was trying to rebuild a society corrupted under the secular rule of the military. Many saw other motives – an attempt to undermine the southern 'Christian' presidency of Mr Obasanjo or even provide conditions for a comeback by the more northern-orientated army. 'Religion is a very sharp weapon in the northern part of the country,' Shehu Sani, a Kaduna-based civil rights activist, told the *Financial Times*. 'It is being used to subvert the democratic process.' In the ensuing riots in the north hundreds were killed, and revenge slayings followed in the south-east. Reports warned of the conflagration spreading out of control as it had in the mid-1960s, igniting civil war.

Wole Soyinka was quoted as saying, 'The roof is already burning.

Obasanjo thinks it is not. He thinks that some accidental rain, which is the act of God or Allah, will put out the fire.' Obasanjo, despite the chidings, seemed determined to play it cool, refusing the advice of those who told him to stamp on the agitators. In a statement he said: 'Neither the Christian nor the Muslims of Kaduna need to resort to violence in defence of their positions on the Sharia issue since God, whom they both claim to worship, is quite capable of upholding his own causes.'

His quiet diplomacy engineered a compromise and northern governors agreed to hold off introducing Sharia until passions had cooled. Immediately, the violence began to die down. But later in 2000 some of the governors or their legislatures announced their intention to try to push Sharia criminal law to the forefront again. It remains to be seen whether the reassurances they have given that Sharia punishments will not be applied to non-Muslims will be enough to keep the resentment of the Christian half of the country under control.

In the course of 2000 Nigerians began to enjoy their new-found opportunity for free speech, often, as was the custom before the generals seized power, criticizing all and everything. 'The chief challenge is no longer civil and political liberties,' said Olisa Agibakoba, a prominent Lagos-based human rights lawyer. 'The new challenge is economic and social rights, and how they can be more clearly defined.' Basic reforms to improve living standards, said many critics, have yet to be undertaken. Supplies of water and electricity are still sporadic. Roads remain peppered with potholes, and clogged with garbage. Many factories are idle, lacking the equipment and capital to operate. Unemployment is soaring and is rampant even among university graduates.

Clement Nwankwo, executive director of the Constitutional Rights Project, was scathing. 'Heads have rolled, but new heads have stepped in and are not different from the heads on the floor. The reality of corruption is so deep, that you don't just need heads to roll.' He pointed to how in Lagos the best houses in town were still being rented by senior government officials, who also have access to huge fleets of cars. Unnecessary foreign trips by public officials were also becoming the norm again.

Segun Iegede, director of programmes and projects at the Committee for Defence of Human Rights, was even stronger. 'What we have is a civilian government that still has the psychology of a military dictatorship.' He pointed to how little the fundamental ethics had changed under Obasanjo; policemen still demand bribes to waive traffic fines, and attorneys are often forced to pay a series of bribes to get their clients out of custody.

Amnesty itself, towards the end of 1999, started to put out its own critical word. In a press release on 23 November it said: 'There are fears that a military operation in the Niger Delta to seek out and arrest armed youths who have killed twelve police officers in recent weeks has resulted in the killing by soldiers of innocent civilians and the burning of villages . . . Instead of quelling the escalating unrest in the region, the Nigerian government may have opened the door to further human rights violations.'

Obasanjo has little room and less time for manœuvre. He inherited a huge deficit of $2.5 billion from his free-spending predecessors. Oil prices, however, after hitting an unusual low of $9 per barrel, rose in the course of 2000 to over $30 a barrel (although they are now dropping again) and allowed him to budget new funds for development in the Niger Delta, as well as for a rise in civil service salaries and towards making the utilities more presentable for privatization. Still, future fighting, especially in the oil-producing region, could lead to serious cut-backs in production, and that in turn would make Obasanjo's already very difficult task veer in the direction of the impossible. To date the unrest has cost the country well over $1 billion.

Nigeria, under Obasanjo, does have the possibility of going somewhere at last. There are plenty of African countries in these days of economic reform motoring ahead at a steady annual 5 per cent growth in GNP, much different from their decades of losing ground to population growth. There is no reason, with good government, rigorous economic management and reasonable oil prices, why the country should not emulate Botswana and hit the 10 per cent target for a while before settling down to 7 or 8 per cent a year. There is no good reason why within a decade every tiny village should not have clean water and a health centre, and send all its girls to primary school – steps that would not only revolutionize contraception, but would raise life-spans for all, sharply and quickly.

Would this solve Nigeria's political volatility? Not a whit. Rising expectations, we all know, are a combustible material. Obasanjo is probably right to wonder how long he has to live. You don't necessarily win many easy points on earth for trying to achieve what he has set out to do, in a country as tribally divided, violence-prone and economically unsteady as Nigeria is today.

In July 2000 I headed back to Lagos, this time tagging on to an Amnesty International mission sent to examine with a critical eye – as always on their investigations – the situation in the new Nigeria.

2 JULY

My wife had phoned me on the way to the airport and asked me to call her once I found Pierre Sané, Amnesty's secretary-general, who was travelling on the same plane. She wanted to be sure, after my last near fatal incident at Lagos airport, when I nearly allowed myself to be picked up by a would-be throat-cutter, that I was in safe custody. I told her that I wasn't sure I'd recognize him among four hundred Nigerian passengers on a crowded 747, so not to count on it – it was eight months since our only encounter over lunch. In the event, he was hard to miss. As I walked up the corridor to the boarding-gate I saw him on a bench, talking into his mobile, paper on his lap, elegant in powder-blue shirt, pale yellow tie, dark jacket, immaculately polished shoes, brown leather briefcase and a rather expensive gold watch peeping from his shirt sleeve. He looked more respectable than the Pope and I was left to wonder how such appearances would hold up in the heat and dust of equatorial midsummer.

He handed me an Amnesty paper: 'Security Guidelines for High Level Mission to Nigeria.' Under a section 'travel precautions' it read: 'Delegates will be met at the airport and should preferably arrive in daylight. Internal airlines have a high accident rate, but there is no alternative to taking internal flights to visit Abuja and

other towns. There are high levels of armed robbery on the roads –'
and so it went on.

Both of us worked most of the time on the plane. Pierre had his
briefing pages to read and I had a column on Iraq to finish. But,
sitting in the empty row in front of him, my head turned as questions
came into my head. 'I see from the programme you've only got
an hour with Obasanjo. Is that par for the course with heads of
government?' 'An hour is about right,' he replied, 'otherwise I feel
the discussion wanders.' 'I have a lot of points here,' he said, tapping
his sheaves of paper, 'and the Nigerian section of Amnesty will have
their own points, but we must select the main three and focus his
attention on those, otherwise it's just a shopping list.' 'Does he know
what you are going to bring up?' I asked. 'We've written to him and
the ministers we are going to call on.' He passed me the letter to the
foreign minister. A good letter, well written. Hard but polite. 'I think
I'll focus on impunity. His commission to look into human rights
abuses under Abacha seems to be moving very slowly. They haven't
been given much in the way of resources and that's maybe because
Obasanjo doesn't want them to go too far. To be fair to his point of
view, he probably thinks this aids reconciliation.'

He passes me another paper, dated 15 June – an Amnesty press
release on the question of executed foreigners in Saudi Arabia, especially Nigerians. Saudi Arabia, it said, 'has one of the highest rates of
capital punishment in the world and 10 per cent are Nigerians. The
death penalty can be used for a wide range of offences, including
those without legal consequences, such as apostasy, drug dealing,
sodomy and "witchcraft".' But most of the Nigerians on Amnesty's
list were executed – usually by decapitation – for drug smuggling and
armed robbery. 'The Nigerian press gave a lot of space to this release,'
Pierre said. 'So you issued it just before you left on this mission to
warm them up?' 'Sure,' he answered, smiling. 'It's a good idea to
have the local press in a sympathetic mood towards us when we
arrive.'

I see our party is made up of two other people who are already
there – one from Gabon, who is charged with arrangements, and the
other an American, Amnesty's researcher on Nigeria. 'You don't

have a lawyer,' I noted. 'We had planned to have one. And we also wanted a press officer. But we had to cut it. There's no money in the budget.' Pierre, who does one of these missions every month, flies in the back of the plane. 'Do you find', I ask, 'that just being in a country, chatting to the officials and non-governmental organizations, has a catalytic effect, more than work out of London?' 'Oh, yes, often it brings quite a few things to the surface. Or prisoners get let out. But it can work the other way. I've just been on a mission to Nepal and on the first day the communist pro-Chinese guerrillas attacked the police, killing fifteen of them, and the police retaliated. Apparently this was done as a statement to us.'

We start to descend into Lagos, flying over great expanses of fields, dotted with small villages. A quiet river meanders through. It looks neither violent nor cruel, and I don't suppose it is. But within moments the outer reaches of Lagos begin. From the air it looks, at first, tidy and well proportioned, solid-looking houses, faced by straight streets. Then the plane dips and flies low. I see the rusty zinc of the corrugated iron roofs, the crowded balconies of the apartment blocks, the traffic pouring between them, crowds outside a mosque, long queues for the yellow buses at the bus station. I can't from here smell the garbage or touch the violence. But I know it is there, shimmering and moving between the quiet surface of the calm evening light. In a matter of minutes we'll be on the ground in the midst of it.

An efficient foreign ministry woman meets us off the plane. Pierre turns aside her suggestion that we sit in the VIP lounge whilst she retrieves our luggage and gets the passports stamped. 'I want to watch the Euro final,' he smiles a little shyly. 'It's at 7,' she says, nodding, and bustles us down to the carousel. In a few minutes we are through. No phony 'Pauls' around this time, I notice, no one set to abduct disorientated travellers. Everyone inside the airport has an official ID on their shirt or jacket. It's almost tranquil.

It's the same outside. The waiting crowd are well back, as if tied down by an invisible rope, yet there are only a couple of police around. Two men step forward, introduce themselves as the chairman and section director of Amnesty Nigeria, then make a step backward to allow a group of twenty or so supporters to grab our hands, take our photographs and bundle us into a nice red car.

3 JULY

At breakfast, Amnesty's Nigeria researcher, in a half-hour monologue broken by only a handful of questions, succinctly and obviously knowledgeably briefs Pierre on the state of Nigeria. In a word, it's a different world from what it used to be. The difference, she says, between night and day. People feel free. Fear has gone. But, and it's a big but, whenever trouble erupts in ethnic disputes there are often – but not always – reports of army and police abuses. 'Did Obasanjo say "shoot to kill" on one occasion?' asks Pierre. 'Yes, quite publicly,' she answers. (Later, I discover that Obasanjo said 'shoot on sight' those who resist arrest, a rather different formulation – Amnesty researchers are not infallible.)

We drive to what seems to be the other end of this town of eight million people for an early morning television interview with one of Nigeria's new private stations. 'What on earth am I doing this for at eight in the morning?' a grumpy Pierre asks the researcher. The interviewer has done her homework and grills Pierre on everything from the Sierre Leone diamond trade, to the Angolan and Congolese wars, to Liberian killings, to the plight of children in Africa wars (she was just back, she said, from filming child-soldiers in Sierre Leone), to the situation at home. Pierre has a seemingly bottomless store of knowledge. He knows each situation back to front – and how they relate to each other – and I presume he was doing the same thing in Asia the month before.

We drive away, marvelling somewhat at the television company, obviously living on a shoe-string, but professional and fast. 'There is this enormous energy in Nigeria,' says Pierre, shaking his head. I concur. 'Every time I come I'm bowled over by it,' I said. 'If only they had the right institutions they could really go places.' 'About this place you can say one thing: it's not laid back,' concludes Pierre.

Now it's down a scruffy street to the tattiest building, where a corroded sign indicates Amnesty's Nigerian headquarters. It is surrounded by equally down-at-heel shops and offices, many of which, to my surprise, turn out to be computer stores or internet training schools.

Amnesty Nigeria was started in 1968 – by missionaries living in the eastern town of Calabar. By the 1980s it was big enough to start employing full-time staff and now has a membership of 5,500 dispersed in thirty-two groups around the country. Despite their T-shirts carrying a picture of Pierre, the Amnesty committee is terribly formal. An electricity generator grinds noisily in the background, quickly giving me an irremovable headache. It doesn't take long before they tell Pierre their problem is money. Pierre later tells me they're coming to the end of a special development programme, when they are supposed to be self-sufficient. In a month's time an Amnesty team from London will come out for a whole two months to talk them through standing on their own feet. 'All those churches and mosques I see,' Pierre asks, 'where do they get the money?' 'Taking 10 per cent of the people's income – tithing,' replies their chairman. 'Nearly everyone does this.' Pierre tells them solemnly they have no choice but get their members to pay their dues.

Two issues came up in the discussion: the arms trade – where can we get the expertise to deal with this? they ask – and the establishment of the International Criminal Court. Nigeria's Amnesty chairman says the steam seems to have gone out of Amnesty since the statutes were approved in Rome a year ago. 'We're pushing on ratification,' says Pierre. 'Only fourteen countries have ratified it and it needs sixty to be up and going. We've got a new campaign starting on it in two weeks' time. You must get Nigeria to ratify the treaty as soon as possible.'

We drive back for lunch. In the car I read the daily *Post Express*. Some good, eye-catching reporting, I'm pleased to see. 'Lagos is being overwhelmed by mysterious killings, whose products are manifest in the streets. Corpses of people killed by unknown persons dot nearly every street corner in the city of the absurd.' More up our human rights street was a dispatch from Port Harcourt, the oil 'capital'. 'The alleged killing of four school children by a petroleum pipeline surveillance team in Ogale, Eleme Council of Rivers State, has generated outrage,' it began.

In the afternoon we meet some of Nigeria's other non-governmental organizations (NGOs) working on human rights. They all sing the same song: tell Obasanjo when you see him that although he has given us political freedom we still live under the tyranny of the police. 'I was shopping in my local market yesterday,' said one. 'Suddenly young men started turning over the market tables and stealing the market ladies' money. The police arrived after the youths had run off and just arrested the first people they could lay their hands on.' On and on the stories went – of police seeking to kill, not to control a situation; of the Special Anti-Robbery Force that will throw mere suspects into a special prison from which nobody comes out; of magistrates in the lower courts who are ignorant and uninformed.

The sun begins to set and the traffic begins to pile up as we head across this vast city to the nondescript neighbourhood of Ikejin to visit the daughter of one of the richest men Nigeria has ever produced, the businessman/politician Moshood Abiola, the victor in Nigeria's election of 1993. Abacha confined him to a solitary room in a lonely house and there he languished, becoming more and more ill, without the visits of either family or doctor, until Abacha's death. Then there was talk of his release, if he renounced his claim to the presidency. Kofi Annan, the UN Secretary-General, tried to mediate a compromise with the stand-in military president, General Abubakar, but then Abiola had a final heart attack and died whilst still in detention. His wife, Kudirat, who campaigned actively on his behalf, was murdered in 1996. Abacha's son Mohammed is now in prison, awaiting trial on charges that he ordered her murder.

Amnesty had fought hard to save Abiola, albeit unsuccessfully, and Pierre wanted to call on his eldest daughter, Hafsat Abiola, and pay his respects. We wander round the family compound, protected by high walls, the house built more like a factory than a home and furnished expensively with imitation George V furniture and heavy carpets. Hafsat is a charmingly energetic young woman, educated at Harvard, with a sharp brain she used often to dazzling effect on BBC *Newsnight* during the Abacha years. She showed us the family graves in a corner of the yard.

4 JULY

I phone Obasanjo from an airport call box as soon as we've disembarked in Abuja. He tells me to call him from the hotel and he'll send someone to pick me up. At 7.30 p.m. I enter the plush presidential complex for the first time. Built by one of his earlier military predecessors, it looks like the pleasant campus of one of America's smaller, richer private universities, low buildings slung around expansive lawns, broken up with shady trees. It is, as I find with increasing numbers of public buildings in Nigeria these days, spotlessly manicured and clean. The dog-eared, dishevelled and often downright dirty look is not so omnipresent as it was.

I'm ushered into the dining-room, a long table set in another of the *nouveau riche*, heavily curtained, thickly carpeted rooms that seem to have been the taste of military dictators, to find Obasanjo sitting at the head, a range of friends and entourage scattered here and there down its ten-metre length. He is reading a five-day-old *Financial Times* and I ask him if this is his daily fare. 'No, someone just brought it in.' He looks at what I'm carrying, *Prospect* and the hardback of a new novel by Ondaatje, and raises an inquisitive eyebrow, as if to say 'are those for me?' In fact I'd already decided in the car, since I'd brought no present, to proffer them. Obasanjo, as was Senghor of Senegal and Nyerere of Tanzania, is a voracious reader – and writer. One of his three prison books, *The Animal Called Man*, is not only an erudite exposition of Christian belief, it's nicely written too. We often talk religion, as we do later this evening: the doubter who wishes he wasn't and the evangelist whose prison years made him even more fervent.

'So you're travelling with Amnesty. What do they want? I've got nothing to say to them,' he says in the gruff military manner that he uses to intimidate. 'Is it Odi?' 'I think that's high on their list,' I answer. (Odi is a town in the Niger Delta where Amnesty say the military carried out extra-judicial executions in September 1999, after coming under fire whilst arresting armed youths who had allegedly killed twelve police officers.) He shakes his head. 'It seems extra-judicial executions are still going on here and there,' I say.

37

'Amnesty don't know what really happens,' he says. 'So why isn't there a proper inquiry?' I push, wondering how far to go before I trigger his temper. I change the subject. 'I think the other thing they'll bring up is this National Commission investigating Human Rights abuses under the military governments. It seems to be moving very slowly.' 'They should go and talk to Justice Oputa, the chairman.' 'Yes, they are, but you're the man who told me on the plane: "I'm not just going to crack the whip, I'm going to use it."' 'I am cracking it,' and he turns to talk to his other guest, the former governor of Lagos state under Abacha. They disappear into an ante-room.

He returns fifteen minutes later – the old Abacha governor, a seemingly pleasant, articulate man, chats to me a while and then excuses himself and leaves. He explains he is out of politics now and helping run an airline. 'How's it going?' 'Not very well,' he says. 'I noticed at the airport it is a very competitive local market.' 'You're right. We're finding it very hard going.'

'Have you come to any conclusions about how much effect Amnesty had on helping undermine Abacha?' I asked Obasanjo. 'It's hard to pinpoint,' he replies. 'On the surface Abacha seemed as if nothing moved him. But all those pressures from outside had a cumulative effect. There is constant speculation on what caused Abacha's death at such a young age. I'm in no doubt that the cumulative stress of all the external pressure on him had the effect of killing him.' He paused. 'Amnesty is good. The world needs it, but they're not always right.' I tell him the little I know about Pierre Sané. I say he's a tough act. 'People say he fires too much from the hip, but I think he actually fires from the shoulder. Anyway, two or three bullets are coming your way tomorrow,' I add jocularly. He doesn't like my joke. 'I'll walk out, you know, if I don't like it.' His momentary anger flashes briefly, subsides and the conversation drifts. He disappears to come back in shorts and sneakers. 'Come and watch me play. I do this twice a day for half an hour a time.' We walk along to a squash court and he plays a fast and victorious game, against one of his younger staff. 'You intimidate them,' I josh. 'No, I am good. Didn't you see that?' 'You're good.' I reassure him. 'You'd never get a game out of me. I prefer to swim, on my own.'

5 JULY

At 11 o'clock we enter the rather stunning parliament building, with its distinctive green dome, and clamber up one staircase after another in search of the office of the Chairman of the Senate Human Rights Committee, Senator Sodangi. Out of breath, hot and bad-tempered, we are then told he has cancelled the committee meeting with Amnesty in favour of one with visiting ex-president Jimmy Carter of the United States. Pierre fumes quietly, rejects the offer of a quiet chat later with him alone in his office and decides to write him a strong letter.

At 3 o'clock that afternoon we cross our fifth checkpoint into the corridors of the presidential offices. Mahogany-panelled rooms, marble floors and staircases make me think with every step how many villages could have had running water or how many young girls could have been given a good primary education if the money had not gone on this. Perhaps this crosses Obasanjo's mind too, but who could he sell the building to?

We sit in a rather formal room. Obasanjo enters, we are called to stand and he sits himself with four advisers at the head of the table. I purposely sit apart. On the other side of the table sit Pierre, with Amnesty's Nigerian researcher and two members of the Nigerian section. Simeon Aina, the local chairman, briefly introduces everyone and then Pierre gives an introduction, careful to underline how open the country now feels, how the sense of fear has gone. 'I realize', he says, 'that democracy doesn't solve all the problems overnight: you have inherited a legacy of massive human rights abuses. We are here to talk about both the abuses of the past, but also those that continue under a similar justice system that hasn't much changed.' He then runs through the evidence of continuing extra-judicial executions, torture, the abuse of women in prisons and police behaviour. Obasanjo starts: 'I don't have much time, but I want to say I have a high opinion of Amnesty. I've always commended your work . . .' Then for an hour Obasanjo takes the bat and the ball, he runs, hits, ducks, lowers his voice, raises it, tells anecdotes, and firmly knocks away any suggestions the Amnesty team makes for review, reprimand or change, although to be fair, he tells them if they have any evidence on prisons that practise torture to pass the information on to him.

It was all done with great charm and magnificent use of his warm voice, but, on the essentials, he was unbudgeable. On the crucial issue of the behaviour of the army, Obasanjo was, as Pierre put it, 'thinking as a soldier'. 'You have to think about the morale of the army, yes, but you also have to think about the wrong things the army does.' 'Have you ever been shot at, Pierre?' countered the president, who in the war in Biafra was shot at many times. Pierre shook his head modestly, although I know his life has been threatened repeatedly. 'Unfortunately,' Obasanjo added smiling, 'there's nowhere here where we can send Pierre to be shot at!' Only right at the end, when Pierre raised the question of the abolition of the death penalty, did there seem to be a modest meeting of the minds. 'Don't push me to run, I'm crawling, sometimes walking. That's how I want to do it.' No, he would not declare a moratorium,

because the trouble with moratoriums is they come to an end. And it's a wasted opportunity if one has to go back. I want to abolish the death penalty. I'm working towards it, but I have a lot of educating to do. Even when I was a military president I did not sign any death warrants and I won't do it now. But this is a decision each governor has responsibility for, so I can't interfere. But you in Amnesty work to uncover miscarriages of justice so the people can be educated to the flaws in capital punishment.

Pierre and his team have done their forceful best. No one fluffs their lines. They are concise, to the point and they know their stuff. I look across at Pierre after an hour of this. I see his eyelids are heavy, almost closed, out of character. He hasn't won a point and it shows.

Obasanjo, tough old soldier that he is, has a vulnerable side. At the end of it, as he walked past me, I remarked, 'As always, a good performance.' 'You thought so?' he asked his eyes meeting mine for approval. 'Yes, you always put your case superbly. But I can't say I agree with it all.' 'I know you don't, Jonathan,' and he grabbed my arm. 'Come with Pierre for dinner tonight.' We walk down the corridor and I feel the levity in the group. Indeed, I feel it myself. 'We saw him, and the door is open,' said Pierre. 'We can write to him and follow it up. We have built a relationship,' said the Amnesty researcher. 'There was no hostility. It gives us something to work with.' They had fallen under the same spell as I did years ago. Obasanjo is so straightforward, so unduplicitous in argument, with a manner so assuringly authoritative that even the critic translates himself into Obasanjo's shoes and starts to see things from his point of view.

5 JULY

Today we have appointments with the Ministers of the Interior and of Defence. Neither are there when we arrive. The former offers another time which clashes with the supposed appointment with the Minister of Defence. In the event we see neither. Pierre and his researcher conclude that seeing Amnesty is not high on their list of priorities. 'Perhaps we made a mistake,' confides Pierre. 'We shouldn't have waited so long. The air has gone out of the human rights balloon here. We should have come six months after the election, while things were still fresh. We did that in Brazil and South Korea and everyone wanted to see us, high and low. And the media followed us everywhere.'

We drive north to Kaduna, capital of the Muslim-dominated state of Kaduna. Nigeria has a network of good arterial roads and we cover the 180 kilometres on a dual carriageway rapidly, passing through an Africa that hasn't changed in hundreds of years, simple mud houses, some tin-roofed, others thatched, no sign of electricity or even schools for most of the journey.

We drive right to the house of the widow of Obasanjo's deputy head of state from the days when Obasanjo was military president. They were close friends and he was arrested at the same time as Obasanjo. But he died in prison, and it is suspected – there is a court case in process – that he was poisoned. Again, we were to pay our respects. I walk into the room last. The others are seated. She beckons me to sit next to her and once the formalities are over I find myself in conversation with an astute and sensitive woman. 'I didn't know where these riots came from. [1,000 were killed in February and another 300 in renewed Christian/Muslim rioting in May.] Kaduna

41

has been a peaceful town, as long as I can remember. Christian and Muslim have lived side by side for decades. Parts of Sharia law have long been practised in Nigeria. Sharia law has a place in the constitution. We've always had Sharia courts for Muslims – it's an alternative system of jurisprudence. The upset came when the members of our state assembly started pushing for Sharia criminal laws and punishment – amputations and so on. I don't think the governor explained it to the public very well, because it won't apply to non-Muslims.'

6 JULY

We drive along the burnt-out streets – homes, small workshops, mosques and churches, almost side by side, gutted and charred. We climb the steps up yet one more ramshackle building, housing this time the Kaduna branch of Amnesty. Outside hangs a banner with the Pepsi slogan affixed: 'Kaduna Amnesty welcomes Pierre Sané.' An elderly lady walks me to the balcony. 'You see those large patches of discoloured tar on the road. That's where they built bonfires and burnt people alive. I had to stand here and watch it. I couldn't get out. I didn't dare go down on to the street.'

Pierre, now dressed in full-flowing northern Nigerian desert garb, addresses a meeting of the local Amnesty branch and a large number of non-governmental organizations' representatives. The room is crowded and everyone wants a chance to speak. Amazingly, nearly everyone is brief and to the point. I notice there's hardly anyone in the room over 40. But they aren't students either. Politics in Nigeria, alas, seems to be for the old school and NGO activity for the young, educated professionals.

'The purpose of this meeting is quite enormous,' declares the chairman in the heavy cadences of Nigerian English. 'People have been burnt out and don't have the wherewithal to rebuild their businesses or their homes. The state should compensate them,' says the first speaker. A Muslim from the Inter-Faith Mediation Centre says, 'We Nigerians are notoriously religious. For most of the time we respect each other. A few people used this freedom we have under democracy to stir things up.' 'Why doesn't the governor sweep the town of arms?' asks another. 'After the Biafran war they went house to house and confiscated every gun and every bullet.' Pierre concludes the meeting by telling them: 'The NGOs must continue to discuss these problems. The community won't progress until the NGOs progress. NGOs can be a powerful force for change if you assert yourselves.'

We head for the governor's office. He's in his late thirties – an exception to the rule? – a Muslim, of course, and perhaps a tolerant man – there has been no effort to erase the graffiti scribbled on the outside of his office wall: 'Sir, sorry to say, "No" to Sharia.' As with Obasanjo it's all very formal. We sit in a large conference room with microphones. And as with Obasanjo we are called to stand as he enters. Someone whispers to me that he used to have a job with the Abacha regime. Pierre does a succinct job of summarizing the criticisms of the NGOs, and the governor an equally effective and swift job of rebutting them. 'I was glad to see no nation, large as well as small, escaped criticism in your annual report – I saw it discussed on CNN,' the governor begins. 'We are introducing a form of "neighbourhood watch" – drawn from various interest groups in each neighbourhood. We'll investigate their nominees are responsible characters and then we'll give them a monthly allowance. But we want them to be responsible not just for security, but for maintaining the environment too.' Then he went down through Pierre's checklist: compensation – no, but assistance; arms – we are looking for them; NGOs – 'they are welcome to come and see me'; Sharia – 'we can't solve problems by fighting. We have to have a civilized dialogue.'

The meeting lasted all of half an hour and then we rushed to the airport to catch the only plane of the day back to Lagos. Pierre said we couldn't miss it. Tomorrow he was going to be made an honorary Yoruba chief by the Alaafin (king) of Oyo, for services to human rights.

7 JULY

The Yoruba kingdom of Oyo used to extend in pre-British days half-way across the width of southern Nigeria and into Benin. Today it is a pale shadow of its former glory – power and wealth passed long ago to the bourgeoisie and – for a long period – to the army. Still, the old traditional leaders retain the affection of their people, especially out in the more remote corners of the country where we are today.

We arrive at the king's house – more rusted corrugated iron than gold leaf – on the edge of the small town of Oyo. There is a salute by toothless old men, dressed in black, firing home-made muskets. The king and Pierre walk under a parasol, embellished with the logo of the Gulf Oil Company, up to the reviewing stand. A succession of elderly men and women come to prostrate themselves full-length before the king. A child dressed as an African carved doll dances. Pierre himself is dressed in the russet red robes of a chief. He kneels before the king, who puts red beads around his neck and a walking-stick in his hand. The king speaks, calling him 'one of the illustrious Sons of Africa'. Then it is Pierre's turn to answer. The crowd of about two thousand press closer to hear. 'Amnesty International has reached deep into the heart of Africa,' he says, 'deep beyond the cities of Africa, deep beyond the politicians of Africa, deep into the people of Africa.'

That, indeed, is the amazing conclusion I've reached myself. An organization begun forty years ago in the mind of a Catholic English lawyer of Jewish descent now is known – and appreciated – in the back of beyond, in darkest Africa.

1

Guatemala – 'Only Political Killings'

In Guatemala there has been no paramount leader[1] in the struggle for human rights and democracy to single out. Indeed, there is no defining moment when one could say that things started to get better after a particular event. Guatemala is simply one of the contemporary world's worst horror stories that gradually, often enough imperceptibly, got better. Amnesty was in at the struggle from the beginning. Some of its exposés gained world attention, but none profoundly changed the situation for the better. Again, improvement came by the dripping of water on hard stone, incrementally, painfully slowly, but, over time, clearly ameliorating an appalling state of affairs, where not that long ago assassinations and disappearances were as common and as prevalent as cars and motorbikes on the capital's overcrowded streets.

Guatemala is part of the isthmus that links the great continents of North and South America. In the 1970s and early 1980s it was, along with El Salvador and Nicaragua, the part of the world where human rights were most violated. Proportionally to its population, more people were tortured and killed for their beliefs than anywhere else on the globe. For centuries, since the Spanish moved their initial interest in Central America to the vast continent to the south, these

---

[1] The controversial Indian leader Rigoberta Menchú came to prominence late on in the events I describe, although she was active from the early 1980s, but only as an exile. She became both world- and Guatemala-renowned when she was awarded the Nobel Peace Prize in 1993. She has been a major figure in creating sympathy around the world for indigenous peoples, and also for the guerrilla movement within Guatemala.

countries have been a backwater. (Costa Rica and Panama, also Central American countries, have different histories, the latter because of US occupation of the Canal Zone and the former because of its lack of feudal history and its distinct, liberal political culture.) They have all been feudal, reactionary states *par excellence*, long used to the writ of the local strong man. In the 1970s they became the focus of superpower interest. In each of these countries anti-establishment guerrilla groups were formed with discreet support from communist Cuba – but also from Venezuela, Panama, Costa Rica, Mexico, Peru, Ecuador and Bolivia and, it was said, without any evidence, from Moscow. The USA, long the passive supporter of the status quo, became increasingly an active participant, not always on the side of the dictators, but more often than not.

In 1981 I made my first visit to Guatemala, struck by an interview I'd recently done with Thomas Hammarberg, who was then Amnesty's secretary-general, in which he had singled out Guatemala as Amnesty's no. 1 priority. The organization, I learnt, was just about to publish a report in which it concluded that 'the selection of targets for detention and murder, and the deployment of official forces for extra-legal operations can be pinpointed to secret offices in an annexe to Guatemala's National Palace, under the direct control of the President of the Republic.'

Before I left, Hammarberg cautioned me: 'Guatemala is not a typical Amnesty country – there are no political prisoners, only political killings.' Amnesty's usual practice of dealing with human rights violations – the adoption of prisoners – was fruitless in the Guatemalan case, he explained. Most of the time, news of an arrest arrived after the prisoner was dead. When the notification had been immediate and Amnesty had been able to intervene within hours of the arrest, there had been a handful of successes. But, he added, no more than ten or fifteen in the whole of the preceding ten years.

Surprisingly, to enter Guatemala was not difficult. Passport control was lax and it was easy to disappear into the airport throng with only a tourist visa. There were a few soldiers lazing in the sunshine. Even a visit to the press spokesman for the army, Major Francisco

Djalma Domínguez, whose predecessor had been murdered by guerrillas a year before, was made without inspection of papers and with
only a pleasant middle-aged secretary to question my purpose. The
single soldier on the doorstep was day-dreaming.

All this was deceptive. Guatemala, I soon found, was a country in
the grip of fear. Government critics, with very rare exceptions, would
not be seen talking to a foreign reporter inside Guatemala. To do so
was to court assassination. Every day the morning newspapers had
more of the same: ten or a dozen bodies discovered, another wave of
killing. The bodies of the victims were found piled up in ravines,
dumped at roadsides or buried in mass graves.

Since 1944 the Guatemalan ruling class had been living in fear of
a left-wing revolution. In that year a military rebellion broke the grip
of fourteen years' dictatorial rule by Jorge Ubico. A university
don, Juan José Arévalo, was given the job of sorting out the long
legacy of misrule, social deprivation and economic inequality. He
stepped down in 1951 and in free and fair elections his defence
minister, Colonel Jacobo Arbenz Guzmán, took over the reins of
government.

Guatemala, at that time, was a classic 'banana republic'. Arbenz,
a determined reformer, decided to end once and for all the United
Fruit Company's control of vast estates and its near monopoly of
banana production. The first beneficiaries were to be the Indian
population. Despite the spectacular cultural heritage of the native
Indians – their direct ancestors, the Mayans, built mammoth temples
and houses and pioneered major breakthroughs in astronomy and
mathematics – they were a people who had experienced worsening
poverty right through the twentieth century. The Indians made up
half of the population and they were becoming increasingly overcrowded on their traditional territory, the mountainside fields. Their
infant mortality rate was high, their diet was deteriorating annually,
and younger sons were reduced to scraping a living on precipitous
slopes that barely held the soil to the mountainside.

Arbenz issued a decree expropriating parts of large estates – in the
main their uncultivated portions. In doing so, he took on imperial
capitalism at its crudest. The United Fruit Company had for decades

had its way throughout Central America, much of the Caribbean and parts of South America. By the 1950s United Fruit's investment in Guatemala accounted for almost two-thirds of the country's total foreign capital. It owned 2,500,000 square kilometres of territory and the country's single railway line, and had great influence in many of Guatemala's most important institutions.

Arbenz's experiments not only threatened United Fruit, they aroused Washington's fears. At the height of the Cold War, the US government was afraid of anything that smacked of communist influence. No matter that Arbenz himself was clearly not a communist and that only four out of fifty-six Guatemalan congressmen were self-confessed communists at that time. The CIA was asked by President Eisenhower to help overthrow Arbenz, using as a cover a group of mercenaries and exiles.

The deed was done, United Fruit retrieved its estates, Arbenz and his sympathizers were hunted down and killed or went into hurried exile. Arbenz's successors ruled largely by decree. Occasionally there were street demonstrations led by students and trade unionists. But nothing really disturbed the status quo until 1960. Then a small group of nationalist army officers attempted an uprising. It came to nothing in itself. It was the start, however, of a guerrilla campaign which waxed and waned for most of the next forty years.

By 1966 the guerrillas' strongholds in the mountain ranges of Sierra de Las Minas and Sierra de Santa Cruz seemed a genuine threat to the government, which, with the aid of paramilitary civilian groups, moved ruthlessly to suppress them. Colonel John Webber, the US military attaché, was reported by *Time* magazine on 26 January 1968 to have acknowledged that it was his 'idea' to mobilize these groups,[1] which were the precursors of the 'independent' civilian death-squads that still exist today. In June 1966 the first leaflets of the Mano Blanca (White Hand) appeared. (Mano was the acronym for the Movimiento Anti-comunista Nacional Organizado (National Organized Anti-communist Movement).) The guerrilla movement

---

[1] US government documents now made available to the public make it clear that this was official government policy.

did not re-emerge until the mid-1970s, when a group surfaced calling itself, disarmingly, the Guerrilla Army of the Poor. By 1981 there were another three groups at work in different parts of the country, concentrated in the highlands and mountains of the north – the People's Armed Organization, the Revolutionary Armed Forces and a breakaway branch of Guatemala's communist trade union.

Their members were few – the army told me only two hundred, sympathizers said one or two thousand. But they were multiplying fast and, to the surprise of observers of the Latin American scene, were winning a great deal of support and membership from the Indians. (When Che Guevara was hunted down and killed by the Bolivian army in 1967 it was widely observed by both left and right that he made the mistake of thinking the Latin American Indians and mestizos would be willing supporters of the guerrillas. In fact, they were too apathetic and fearful and he was quickly isolated. It was Guatemala that became the first country in Latin America where significant numbers of Indians were politically active to the point of lending their support in measurable terms to a guerrilla effort to overthrow the government.) However, while the guerrilla movements' activities were sporadic, the right-wing pro-government death squads operated on full throttle.

Amnesty International from the beginning always maintained that the association of the death-squads with important key government and political figures was close enough to cause serious concern. In its 1981 annual report covering the year 1980, it talked of the 'political murder' encouraged by the Guatemalan government. But it stopped short of saying that the killings were directed by the government. Amnesty at that time was still awaiting irrefutable evidence to confirm its suspicions.

The nuanced approach was discarded on 18 February 1981. In one of the most outspoken reports ever issued by Amnesty, it stated unequivocally: 'People who oppose or are imagined to oppose the government are systematically seized without warrant, tortured and murdered. These tortures and murders are part of the deliberate and long-standing programme of the Guatemalan government.' The government, for its part, denied having made a single political arrest or having held a single political prisoner. The 'disappearances',[1] senior government officials told me, were brought about by right-wing and left-wing death-squads. That Amnesty report is an accumulation of horrors that pointed a firm finger at the government. My own conversations with exiles in Costa Rica and with the vice-president of Guatemala, who fled the country in late 1980, backed it up.

Nearly 3,000 Guatemalans were seized without warrant and killed in the years immediately following General Lucas Garcia's accession to the presidency of Guatemala in 1978. (And thousands more subsequently.) Many of them were tortured. Death for some had been quick and clean, a bullet in the head. Others had died slowly and painfully, suffocated in a rubber hood or strangled with a garrotte. One letter received by Amnesty International described a secret grave in a gorge, used by army units who had seized and murdered the leaders of a village earthquake reconstruction committee (Guatemala was rocked by an earthquake in 1976; 20,000 people died):

More than thirty bodies were pulled out of the 120-foot gorge ... but farmers who live near the site told me there were more bodies, many more, but that the authorities didn't want to admit as much or go to the trouble of dragging them out. They said vehicles have been arriving at the edge of the gorge at night, turning out their lights, engaging in some mysterious activities.

We went down to the bottom of the ravine the next day ... About halfway down the ravine the stench became unbearable. Barely visible in the dim light were piles of bodies. Most were in extremely advanced states of decomposition, but still with remnants of tattered clothing.

The people killed were often, like these villagers, simple peasant folk, but ones who had shown some initiative like running an earthquake reconstruction committee that badgered the government for help, or a co-operative or church leadership training group. Overwhelmingly it was the incipient peasant leadership that had suffered the most.

---

[1] The now well-used word 'disappearances' was first coined in Guatemala.

The next sizeable group to have been penalized were students and labour leaders. After that, a whole range of professional people disappeared – journalists, clergy, doctors and educators and the cream of the Social Democratic and Christian Democratic parties. Anyone who spoke out and complained, much less organized a formal opposition grouping, was the target for assassination.

How did Amnesty arrive at its conviction that the government were in charge of the killings? A series of violent events, observed and recorded by reliable witnesses, all suggested government involvement. The most widely reported mass killing by regular army forces took place on 29 May 1978. One hundred Indians, including five children, were shot dead in the town square of Panzos. The Indians had been protesting about land rights. They were cold-bloodedly shot down by soldiers positioned on rooftops and inside buildings. Townspeople have told Amnesty that mass graves were dug two days before the killings. In January 1980 a group of Indians occupied the Spanish embassy to protest against this and other abuses carried out by the army in El Quiche province. The government, outraged by the protest, ordered the army to attack the embassy. One peasant, Gregorio Yuja Xona, and the Spanish ambassador were the only survivors. Yuja Xona was held under police guard in a hospital, then, without explanation, the police allowed him to be removed. His body was later found, mutilated.

There were a number of occasions when prisoners officially acknowledged to be in police custody were later found dead – for example, thirty-seven killed by garrotte in 1979 and dumped in a ravine. Or the twenty-six labour unionists who, in June 1980, were arrested by plain-clothes men while the street was closed to traffic by uniformed police, and have not been seen since. The government denied holding them.

There is evidence from one of the very few who have escaped after being picked up. Amnesty International published a taped interview with the former prisoner. He described how he was held in Huehuetenango Military Base and tortured by being pulled up by his testicles and hooded with a rubber inner tube of a tyre lined with quicklime. His testimony was terrifying in its simple directness:

Before my very eyes they killed three people; they strangled them. The way they killed them was with a piece of rope, a kind of noose, which they put around the neck and then used a stick to tighten it like a tourniquet from behind and with their heads held down in the trough. When they came out, their eyes were open; they'd already turned purple. It took at most three minutes in the water. I also saw that one of these three, a boy, when they threw him down on the floor with his clothes wet, was still moving and one of the officers ordered them to put the tourniquet on him again until he stopped moving.

They just showed me the other six bodies and said the same thing would happen to me if I tried to lie to them.

On other occasions, plain-clothes men have been overpowered and found to possess identification papers associating them with the intelligence services. One such event occurred when Victor Manuel Valverth Morales, student representative on the executive committee of the Universidad de San Carlos, was seized at gunpoint on 10 June 1980 by two men in plain clothes inside the university school of engineering in Guatemala City. His assailants did not identify themselves as law enforcement officers or produce a warrant for his arrest; when he tried to escape they shot him several times. Other students then came to his assistance and overpowered the attackers, one of whom, Adán de Jesús Melgar Solares, was murdered by students when a force of uniformed army troops attacked his student captors inside the university precincts.

Students took the dead man's identification card, which showed him to be a military intelligence agent from the 'General Aguilar Santa Maria' army base in Jutiapa Province. The second man, who was not harmed, carried an identification card issued by the Guardia de Hacienda (Treasury police) for 'Servicio Especial' (Special Service), in the name of Baldomero Medoza. The government denied that either of the two men who attacked Víctor Valverth were members of the security services, but the dead man's widow later confirmed his identity to the press.

I spent four hours in Mexico City with the researcher for Amnesty International, Mike McClintock, cross-examining him on how

Amnesty garnered such a wealth of information and established its truth. It was clearly an exhaustive process. External organizations – church, union and political – who had live networks inside Guatemala fed him with information all the time. He and other members of the small Amnesty team had to evaluate it carefully, learning over time who could be trusted, who had a propensity to exaggerate and who they could ask to double- and even triple-check. When it came to the crucial indictment – that these killings were organized from an annexe to the central palace – Amnesty's method of verification and double-checking indicated to me, an outside investigator, the difficulties and complexities that confront Amnesty.

Amnesty research on the matter required a visit to Washington in 1979 to look at the records and files of US government agencies. With access granted under the Freedom of Information Act, they enabled Mr McClintock to pinpoint key developments in the Guatemalan security apparatus. A 1974 document described the Centro Regional de Telecomunicaciones at Guatemala's principal presidential-level security agency working with a 'high-level security/administrative network linking the principal officials of the National Police, Treasury Police, Detective Corps, the Presidential House and the Military Communications Centre'. This organization had built up a sophisticated filing system, listing anyone who might be a potential leader of anti-government movements or a critic of the government. Amnesty also knew from reliable sources that the agency was directed by the joint head of the presidential general staff and military intelligence, Major Hecht Montalván. How could Amnesty confirm, however, that the organization was something more than a records agency? The research team answered by pointing to the lines of command under Major Montalván, which led directly to some of the killings described above, the capture by dissidents of papers on agents they had overpowered, and denunciations from people who were well known and trusted and who had friends and relatives who worked in the presidential palace.

Montalván's headquarters were situated in the presidential guard annexe to the National Palace, adjoining the presidential house. I walked around it. Next door, innocently sandwiched into the same block, is the office of the Obras Pontificias Misionales (Roman Catholic missionaries). For a moment I assumed I was at the wrong building, but only yards further on a soldier peered over a balcony and caught my eye; and to his right a television camera monitored the street. On top of the roof were three large telecommunications masts and around the side of the building was the main entrance. In this side street, which on the other side had the door to the president's house, heavily armed soldiers stared at passers-by. Cars with foreign plates or without licence plates at all were parked alongside.

A slip of the tongue in a later conversation confirmed that this was indeed the centre of intelligence operations. I was interviewing the head of press information of the army, Major Domíguez. In an aside, he told me he knew that a distinguished Social Democrat politician had been bumped off by a rival. I asked him how he knew. 'You see, I used to be military intelligence. But don't tell anyone or the guerrillas will kill me.' Casually as I could, I said, 'Oh yes, you had your office in the presidential annexe.' Surprised, he nodded: 'Yes, but remember, don't tell anyone what I've told you.'

My loyalty to secrecy in such a situation is, I regret, non-existent. The only task left to do was to confirm the Amnesty investigators' conviction that the intelligence operation did do the killings. Since in Guatemala it is impossible to talk to anyone about politics frankly, I flew to Costa Rica and met some of the Guatemalan exiles who live there. In the relaxed atmosphere of this green and pleasant land – Costa Rica has been democratic for all but a year since it gained its independence from Spain in 1821 – it was possible to talk to people who underlined Amnesty's findings. Frustratingly, they were still secondary sources. They insisted that they knew soldiers or officials who had links with the intelligence agency. But only one person I met said he had sources right within the heart of the operation centre.

Some of them knew Elias Barohona y Barahona, who had been the press spokesman of the minister of the interior until he resigned in September 1980. He had told them (and Amnesty had his statement) that blank letterhead stationery of the alleged 'death-squads', Ejercito Secreto Anticomunista and Escuadron de la Muerte, was stored in the office of the minister of the interior. According to him, the lists of people to be eliminated were prepared from the records of military intelligence and the national police. They included the names of trade union leaders and peasants provided by the Department of Trade Unions, by the Ministry of Labour and by a number of private enterprises. He also said that an officer in military intelligence had told him that the definitive lists of those to be killed were approved at meetings attended by the ministers of defence and the interior and the chief of the general staff of the army.

Again, it could be argued that this was still a secondary source. Neither Amnesty nor I were able to talk directly to people involved in the command structure of the intelligence agency. A visit to Washington, DC, however, brought me close to doing so. I called on General Lucas's former vice-president, Francisco Villagrán Kramer, now living in exile in the USA. He had just finished reading the Amnesty report and although it had been written without any consultation with him, he said it was 'absolutely accurate'. While he was in power, he said, he learnt how the system worked and was in no doubt that the overwhelming majority of killings were decided in the presidential palace. Nevertheless, he argued that the independent death-squads do play a role, a point which Amnesty in its report seemed to play down.

Whenever he wanted to intercede on behalf of a person who had 'disappeared', he went to one of three persons – Montalván, the chief of the president's staff and of intelligence, the army chief, or the minister of the interior. These were the three, working through Montalván, who were responsible for deciding who should be picked up and killed. The fact that Villagrán was successful half a dozen times proved to him that those arrested were in the hands of those under their command. There was also the telling fact that others who had been picked up in the same swoops never reappeared.

His conclusion was reinforced by the scores of army officers who came up to him privately and said: 'Mr Vice-President, you're a friend of so-and-so. Do your best to get him out,' or 'Let him know they're after him.' Only if the army were intimately involved in the assassinations could this happen. There was even a man known to him personally, Villagrán told me, who was phoned by President

Lucas himself and told to get out while the going was good. Although ideological opponents, they were old school buddies and the President was moved to short-cut the normal process of his governmental machine.

The final piece of evidence presented by Villagrán was the information given to him by a military officer. According to Villagrán, he was senior enough in the military hierarchy to know how the system functioned. The senior army officers were a clique with an *esprit de corps* developed over the years of intimate contact. Villagrán, who says he became convinced against his will that the government was responsible for the killings, had no reason to doubt what he was told in confidence by this man.

After a series of conversations in Guatemala about who had killed whom, why and where, it became difficult to keep a sense of perspective and to remember that the deaths were not simply a total to be compared with, say, deaths in neighbouring El Salvador. Moreover, conversations with senior army officers and government officials quickly lulled one into false feelings of security. Their hospitality and bonhomie was disarming. Often enough, probing questions were turned aside graciously and without rancour. Of course, they did not have much to do with the soldiers and intelligence officials who actually carried out the tortures and killings. They gave the orders and the lower ranks implemented them. Blood never touched their hands: it was an antiseptic world that allowed them to make their decisions with the required single-mindedness and ruthlessness.

After a morning of such meetings, I decided to drive the 140 kilometres from Guatemala City to Lake Atitlán, a silver sheen of water lying below three cloud-covered volcanoes. I chartered one of the local fishing boats. It took eighty minutes to reach the village of Santiago Atitlán on the far side. Described by one tourist I had talked to as a 'Shangri-la', it certainly gives that first impression. Small houses, inhabited by Indians, rise up the hillside from the water's edge. The men were dressed in broad-striped white trousers cut off just below the knees, the hems decorated with coloured birds laboriously embroidered by their womenfolk. The women had skirts, blouses and shawls of an intricate weave, combining deep reds, browns and yellows, so that when, as I arrived, they poured out of the village church after a mass, there was a riot of colour down the street to the water's edge.

I found the American missionary father, an elderly man who told me he was standing in for the young parish priest who had returned to the United States after the governor of the province had warned him that his life was in danger. Six months earlier, twenty-five Indians had been murdered. Four of them ran a small radio station established by the parish; the others were active in the agricultural co-op. 'Anyone who shows any leadership potential gets wiped out,' the priest told me – an opinion that echoed the Amnesty report.

Did Amnesty itself have any influence? Superficially, one could say, quite the reverse. The killings escalated after Amnesty sent its mission to Guatemala in 1979. Francisco Villagrán, for one, felt that Amnesty's pressure in the short run might have been counter-productive. Government officials were obsessed about Amnesty, hardly letting a week go by without denouncing it, just as they made President Carter's human rights policy an object to be scorned and repudiated.

Yet over the long run Amnesty may have been more effective than Carter, who liked to see himself as the 'human rights president'. For many years, because of the pressure on Washington from Britain, worried about Guatemalan threats to neighbouring Belize, there had been a gradual reduction of arms sales to Guatemala. By the time Carter and his restrictive arms sales policy came on the scene, Guatemala, not having much left to lose, itself decided it would be better off with US arms. Apart, then, from resisting suggestions from the US embassy to try and woo the Guatemalans to better behaviour by dangling the possibility of renewed arms sales and counter-insurgency training, Carter's pressure didn't add up to very much. The occasional critical speech and an attempt, which Guatemala resisted, to send them a liberal ambassador was the sum of it.

Amnesty, on the other hand, had succeeded in alerting a wide constituency to the violence and horror of Guatemala. To take one example, on the basis of Amnesty reports church, liberal and union groups in Europe mounted a boycott action over the behaviour of the local bottler of Coca-Cola. In the United States, where the threat of such a boycott was obvious, US labour, liberal and other groups held talks with Coca-Cola management, and eventually put sufficient pressure on the company to force it to buy out its franchise holder on human rights grounds. The manager, apparently, was a personal friend of Colonel German Chupina, director of the national police, and allegedly would simply ring him up if he had a labour problem, and the security forces would be sent in to eliminate the leadership of the local union. (Several union secretaries-general are said to have been killed in this way.) The publicity produced by the Coca-Cola affair in Europe and the United States, together with other reporting, often Amnesty-inspired or at least containing a hard core of Amnesty facts and figures, created an atmosphere that hurt Guatemala economically.

Press reactions to the Amnesty report on Guatemala, following its publication in February 1981, make one understand why the Guatemalan government felt it was the victim of a co-ordinated and widespread attack. The report received blanket coverage: two articles I wrote on the editorial pages of the *International Herald Tribune* and the *New York Times*, a front-page report in the London *Times* and Mexico's *Excelsior* and a long article in *The Economist*. One can perhaps forgive the outburst of the Secretary for Public Relations of the Presidency who told the Guatemalan City daily, *El Imparcial*, that Amnesty 'had set out to undermine the prestige of Guatemala'a institutions and headed up an orchestrated campaign to damage the image of Guatemala for the simple reason that its government is not disposed to permit the activity of international communism'.

The consequence of this kind of bad publicity – there had been a lot before – was that the bottom fell out of the tourist market, once the third largest export earner. Nor was there much foreign investment. A number of US banks closed down their Guatemalan offices, although publicly they gave non-political reasons for doing so. None of this, it must be admitted, had any discernible impact on the government's thinking, so single-minded and determined was the regime. Nor did it influence the Reagan administration in Washington. However, Amnesty's human rights initiatives gave a great deal of succour and support to the opposition. All of the exiles I talked to gained an enormous psychological boost from the Amnesty campaigns. Here they were, citizens of a small country, vulnerable and expendable, being given international attention. Although, unlike other countries where governments hold people prisoner rather than kill them, it was impossible to mount campaigns to release people, the Amnesty publicity did give a sense of assurance to those who were determined to bring about a major change in government policies.

A few years later, in June 1984, I returned to Guatemala, anxious to see if the work of Amnesty had had a cumulative effect. It clearly hadn't. The Guatemalan government cared nothing about its pariah image in most of the world. As long as its relationship with Washington was reasonably good – and with Ronald Reagan as president it was more than that – it felt it had nothing to worry about and had all the latitude it wished for to do what it believed had to be done. The new president of Guatemala, General Rios Montt, visited Washington. 'We have no scorched earth in Guatemala,' he said in an official address, 'only scorched communists.' In fact, at this time tens of thousands were killed in the counter-insurgency campaign. In July 1982 Amnesty published a paper entitled 'Massive Extrajudicial Executions in Guatemala's Rural Areas'. In official Washington no one cared, although the *New York Times* published an editorial saying that if even 5 per cent of what Amnesty was saying were true, it would be a scandal.

Reagan was obsessed with communist influence in Central America, to the point that most moral considerations were ruthlessly relegated to the back-burner. Reagan felt it was essential *realpolitik*. As he said on more than one occasion, the close relationship between the guerrillas of Central America and Moscow (never proved) and Havana meant that the red legions (wherever they were supposed to come from) were 'only two days' drive to Harlinen, Texas'. The Reagan administration persistently tried in its early days to persuade Congress to lift its embargo on military aid to Guatemala (imposed in 1977). It finally gave up after two Guatemalans who were working for the US Agency for International Development in a local project were assassinated. Only in 1985 did it finally manage to persuade Congress to allow military aid to go through, although it is suspected the CIA continued to keep the pipeline open all along. (And Washington actively encouraged right-wing regimes in Argentina, Israel, Taiwan and South Africa to keep the arms flowing.)

On this trip I decided to retrace the steps of my previous journey to Santiago Atitlán. There had been fragmentary reports of clashes between the guerrillas and the army and I wanted to reconnoitre the terrain first-hand. I decided to walk the 107-kilometre circumference of the lake, following Indian paths that sometimes took me along the fertile, low-lying lakeside strips, carefully terraced, growing onions, tomatoes, cabbages and avocados in profusion. Sometimes they veered high up in the mountains, where steep cliffs and impossible gorges made cultivation possible only on the upper slopes.

In fact I saw nothing, apart from realizing that this was perfect guerrilla country where hideaways would be hard to discover. No one wanted to talk, apart from the Catholic missionary priests with whom I lodged at night. They told me of what had happened to the young priest I'd heard about in Santiago Atitlán on my previous visit. About six months later he had returned from Oklahoma and, true to all his fears, had been murdered. Violence hung in the air. The priests feared it, both for themselves and for their parishioners. They said at the moment things were quiet but it could not last. They were right. Over the years there were many clashes between guerrillas and the army. Nine years later, in December 1990, the army opened fire on a village protest march in Santiago Atitlán, killing eleven people.

Only as late as 1995 did the beans of Guatemala come to be spilt. The trigger was a Congressional enquiry into the circumstances surrounding the murder of an American hotel owner in Guatemala. Richard Nuccio, a State Department official, surprised everyone with his frank testimony that the CIA had been aware all along about this, and other political killings in Guatemala. The CIA, he said, had in fact been present in Guatemala, contrary to official US policy, all through the 1990s. President Bill Clinton immediately announced he was opening an investigation to find out why and on whose authority the CIA had been present. Yet the White House did nothing to protect Nuccio, who, having lost his high-security clearance, found himself jobless.

Over the next couple of years more US diplomatic cables and intelligence were declassified. But a breakthrough in getting the full picture did not come until April 1999, when the UN-appointed Guatemalan Commission for Historical Clarification presented its report to Secretary-General Kofi Annan. (The report received most of its financial underpinning from the US and European countries.) A peace agreement between the government of Guatemala and the principal revolutionary movement, the Unidad Revolucionaria Nacional Guatelmalteca, signed in Oslo in June 1994, along with Clinton's decision to open American archives, had made it possible to delve into what had really happened. The Commissioners wrote in the preface that although before they came to write the report 'we knew in general terms the outline of events . . . none of us could have imagined the full horror and magnitude of what actually happened'.

The commission estimated that the number of persons killed or who 'disappeared' 'as a result of the fratricidal confrontation' reached a total of 200,000. Seven per cent of the acts of violence were attributable to the guerrillas, 93 per cent to the state. Both the guerrillas and the established institutions of government were blamed for the intensity of the insurgency, the guerrillas for receiving 'political, logistical, instructional and training support' from Cuba and for treating those 'who sought to remain distant from confrontation with profound mistrust and even as potential enemies'; the state, for its part, was condemned for its 'repressive response, totally disproportionate to the military force of the insurgency . . . At no time did the guerrilla groups have the military potential necessary to pose an imminent threat to the State . . . The State deliberately magnified the military threat of the insurgency . . . The vast majority of the victims of the acts committed by the State were not combatants, but civilians.' Worst of all, 'a large number of children were among the direct victims of arbitrary execution, force, disappearance, torture and rape, often [being beaten] against walls or [thrown] into pits where the corpses of adults were later thrown. A quarter of all victims were women.'

Much of the report reads like Amnesty reports written twenty years earlier, not least in its pinpointing of the supreme role of Guatemala's intelligence system in being 'the driving force of a state policy that took advantage of the situation resulting from the armed confrontation, to control the population, the society, the state and the Army itself'. 'The majority of human rights violations occurred with the knowledge or by order of the highest authority of the State,' the Commission concluded. The report's condemnation of US involvement, however, is perfunctory, merely alluding to how 'US military assistance was directed towards reinforcing the national intelligence apparatus and for training the officer corps in counter-insurgency techniques, key factors which had significant effect on human rights violations during the armed confrontation.' (It omits to mention that for much of the time this military aid was never approved by the US Congress.) Nevertheless, it was enough to prompt President Clinton to make a public apology during a visit to Guatemala in March 1999 for past US involvement in abuses. At a forum with Guatemalan leaders, Mr Clinton said: 'For the United States, it is important that I state clearly that support for military forces and intelligence units which engaged in violence and wide-spread repression was wrong.' And it led the *Washington Post* to editorialize: 'We Americans need our own truth commission.'[1]

Yet, if it wasn't for independent work done by the non-governmental organization, the National Security Archive, we would still be in the dark as to what went on, particularly during the Reagan years, when human rights abuses sharply escalated (see Fig 1). The Reagan administration's ambassador to Guatemala, David Chaplin, often prompted his Washington superiors as to what was going on in the country. If less exacting than Amnesty, his embassy's monitors

[1] In March 2000 the highest ranking CIA official, dismissed in 1995 for failing to inform Congress about CIA ties to a Guatemalan colonel linked to two murders, was awarded one of the agency's highest honours, the Distinguished Career Intelligence Medal.

Figure 1. Total number of human rights violations and acts of violence, by ethnic group. Guatemala (1962–96)

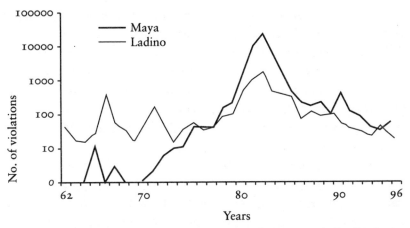

Source: CEH Database (Guatemalan Commission for Historical Clarification)
Notes: The lines of the vertical scales – number of violations – follow a progression of multiples of ten. Ronald Reagan was US president 1981–89

recorded much of the horror of the time. In February 1984, only one day after Chaplin had sent one of his regular cables to Washington alerting the State Department to Guatemalan government involvement in recent abductions, he was taken aback to hear that the Assistant Secretary of State for Human Rights, Elliott Abrams, a Reagan hard-line appointee, had signed off on a secret report to Congress in which he had argued that human rights were *improving* in Guatemala and that Congress should no longer be inhibited about a resumption of US security assistance. 'The Mejia government', Abrams wrote,

has taken a number of positive steps to restore a constitutional, electoral process and to address the practice of extra-legal detention ... Failure to provide some politically meaningful sign of support for the efforts being undertaken to return the country to democratic rule and to reduce the human rights violations, will only increase the chance of further political instability. In addition, the US has other strong interests in Guatemala and the region which necessitate a solid, bilateral relationship, including a positive relationship with the Guatemalan military.

Typical of the State Department cable traffic of the early Reagan years is a cable that reads: 'If General Lucas García is right and the government of Guatemala can successfully "go it alone" in its policy of repression, there is no need for the US to provide the government with redundant political and military support.'

All during the Reagan years the bureaucracy of the State Department's human rights division waged a ferocious propaganda war of its own – to discredit the human rights lobbies. One confidential State Department cable, dated October 1982, observed: 'After analysing human rights reporting from Amnesty International, the Washington office on Latin America, the Network in Solidarity with Guatemala and the Guatemalan Human Rights Commission, the US Embassy [in Guatemala City] concludes that a "concerted misinformation campaign" is being waged against the Guatemala government in the United States, by groups supporting the Communist insurgency in Guatemala.' The cable accuses the groups of assigning responsibility for atrocities to the army without sufficient evidence, abuses which may never have occurred or may have been propagated by the guerrillas. While the cable concedes that the army has committed violations, it concludes that many of the accusations of the human rights groups were unfounded and that their sources are highly questionable, since they come from 'well-known communist front groups'.

A month before, Abrams's predecessor as Assistant Secretary of State for Inter-American Affairs, Thomas Enders, had written to the head of Amnesty's Washington office arguing that 'many of the incidents [mentioned in the 1982 Amnesty report on extra-judicial executions in Guatemala] cannot be corroborated by other sources such as the press, the army, the police or intelligence information. In fact, the town where one incident allegedly took place (Covadonga) doesn't appear on any map of Guatemala available to the embassy.' Amnesty's Guatemalan researcher later said it was 'a marvellous occasion' when, during a briefing for a visiting delegation from the Organisation of American States (OAS), she could point to the village on the big map she'd brought from her office.

It was also a sweet if modest revenge when these same activists from non-governmental organizations could call a press conference

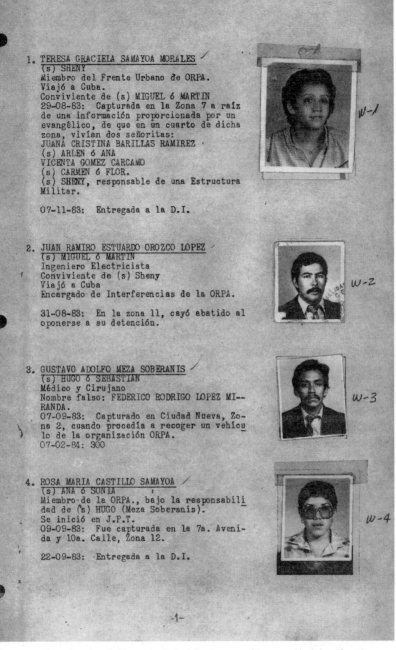

1. TERESA GRACIELA SAMAYOA MORALES
   (s) SHENY
   Miembro del Frente Urbano de ORPA.
   Viajó a Cuba.
   Conviviente de (s) MIGUEL ó MARTIN
   29-08-83: Capturada en la Zona 7 a raíz
   de una información proporcionada por un
   evangélico, de que en un cuarto de dicha
   zona, vivian dos señoritas:
   JUANA CRISTINA BARILLAS RAMIREZ
   (s) ARLEN ó ANA
   VICENTA GOMEZ CARCAMO
   (s) CARMEN ó FLOR.
   (s) SHENY, responsable de una Estructura
   Militar.

   07-11-83:   Entregada a la D.I.

                                           W-1

2. JUAN RAMIRO ESTUARDO OROZCO LOPEZ
   (s) MIGUEL ó MARTIN
   Ingeniero Electricista
   Conviviente de (s) Sheny
   Viajó a Cuba
   Encargado de Interferencias de la ORPA.

   31-08-83: En la zona 11, cayó abatido al
   oponerse a su detención.

                                           W-2

3. GUSTAVO ADOLFO MEZA SOBERANIS
   (s) HUGO ó SEBASTIAN
   Médico y Cirujano
   Nombre falso: FEDERICO RODRIGO LOPEZ MI--
   RANDA.
   07-09-83: Capturado en Ciudad Nueva, Zona 2, cuando procedía a recoger un vehícu
   lo de la organización ORPA.
   07-02-84: 300

                                           W-3

4. ROSA MARIA CASTILLO SAMAYOA
   (s) ANA ó SONIA
   Miembro de la ORPA., bajo la responsabili
   dad de (s) HUGO (Meza Soberanis).
   Se inició en J.P.T.
   09-09-83: Fue capturada en la 7a. Aveni-
   da y 10a. Calle, Zona 12.

   22-09-83: Entregada a la D.I.

                                           W-4

-1-

Figure 2. Log-book of Guatemala's 'disappeared', compiled by the Guatemalan army. (The Guatemalan Project for the National Security Archive)

Figure 3. Forces responsible for human rights violations and acts of violence. Guatemala (1962–96)

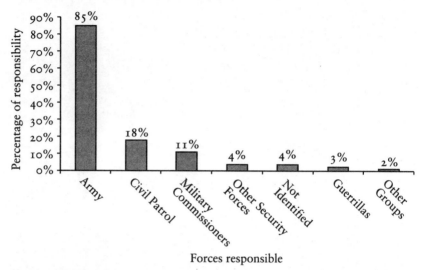

Source: CEH Database

Notes: The columns indicate the percentage of responsibility by different groups, whether acting alone or in conjunction with other forces, with regard to the total number of human rights violations and acts of violence committed. Consequently, the 'Army' category accounts not only for the violations committed by this force when acting alone, but also for those committed in conjunction with civil patrols, military commissioners, death-squads or other members of state security forces. In the same way, the civil patrol category records the violations committed by its members, acting alone or together with another force. This logic holds true for all of the categories, therefore the sum total of the percentages is greater than 100.

in Washington on 20 May 1999 and disclose the existence of an internal log-book compiled by the Guatemalan military that was a detailed record of its death-squad operations. The army log revealed the fate of scores of Guatemala citizens who were 'disappeared' by security forces in the period between August 1983 and March 1985, precisely the period when Elliott Abrams had testified that things were getting better. Replete with the photos of 183 victims and coded reference to their executions, the fifty-four-page document was smuggled out of army intelligence files and put into the hands of human rights advocates.

Figure 4. Responsibility for human rights violations and acts of violence. Guatemala (1962–96)

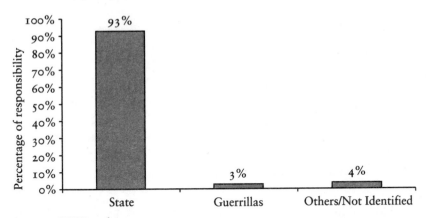

Source: CEH Database
Note: The categorization of group responsibility yields the following data: 93% rests with agents of the state, including in this category the army, security forces, civil patrols, military commissioners and death-squads; 3% rests with the guerillas, the remaining 4% rests with the other unidentified armed groups, civilian elements and other public officials.

How change finally came to Guatemala is not easy to document. It was almost imperceptible. It had many turns and setbacks along the way. Some highlight the end of nearly twenty years of military rule in January 1986. Incoming President Vinicio Cerezo Arévalo immediately committed his government to returning the country to the rule of law. Briefly, there was an improvement, but not many months elapsed before Amnesty noted that 'Guatemala is now experiencing a steady escalation in human rights violations' (see Figures 1–5). The death-squads, maybe no longer under direct presidential authority, were still active and still in the main composed of police and military agents. Indeed, the amnesties granted by the outgoing military government and then by President Cerezo's government appeared to have facilitated further human rights violations.

It was not until 1993 that Guatemala began to face both its own dark history and the fact that it had isolated itself from a majority of world opinion. Most important, it no longer had an ear in Washington. The turning-point was President Jorge Serrano Elias (Cerezo's

Figure 5. Principal human rights violations and acts of violence. Guatemala (1962–96)

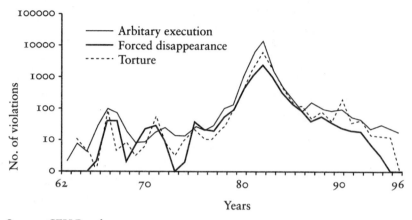

Source: CEH Database

Note: The lines of the vertical scales – number of violations – follow a progression of multiples of ten

successor) and his attempt to seize dictatorial powers. Guatemalan public opinion was enraged and it turned even the army against him. Into the presidency in 1993 stepped a well-respected governmental human rights advocate, Ramero de Leon Carpio. Again, despite its initial promise, the military continued to be recalcitrant and there were a series of high-profile assassinations. Importantly, however, the government signed an accord with the guerrillas, paving the way for a United Nations human rights monitoring team.

Carpio also, it can be said, paved the way for his successor, Alvaro Arzú, to negotiate a peace settlement with the guerrillas. The peace accord was signed in December 1996. Arzú brought solid progress with a series of land, fiscal and constitutional reforms. He established a fund to help the poor buy land. Arzú also sacked thirteen of the twenty-three generals and replaced them with younger officers. Yet by the end of his term of office it was clear that his reforming zeal had run out of steam.

Why, exactly, the situation changed for the better in the 1990s is hard to pinpoint. It was more the confluence of events than any single person, either in Washington DC, or in Guatemala City. With

Figure 6. Total percentage of human rights violations and acts of violence, by department. Guatemala (1962–96)

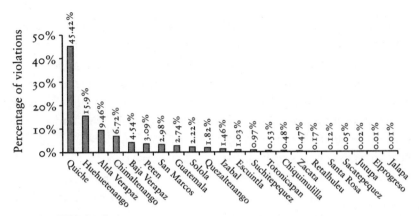

Source: CEH database

Reagan's term of office at an end and the Cold War winding down, there was certainly a new way of looking at Central America in Washington. The new president, George Bush, had moved quite quickly, once in office, to end the polarization in neighbouring Nicaragua and the clandestine support, against the wishes of Congress, for the right-wing guerrillas, the so-called Contras. This change of tack also sent a clear signal to the military in Guatemala that Washington would not for much longer turn a blind eye to atrocities, although there is no doubt the Bush administration did continue clandestine military support.

Parallel with the change of mood in Washington, but also influencing it, was the Soviet president Mikhail Gorbachev's decision to withdraw Soviet military and economic support for Cuba. This rapidly led Havana to cut back its support for the guerrillas in Guatemala.

Yet beside these major currents of *realpolitik* there was, within Guatemala itself, the process of a generational change. Both in the military and in business, younger elements wanted to end Guatemala's isolation and become accepted by the world outside. At the same time, the ageing guerrilla leadership was attracted by the idea of being welcomed into mainstream politics. The vision of perpetual guerrilladom, ensconced in some hideaway, part sun-baked, part rain-sodden, depending on the season, had less allure as the years slipped by.

Under Alvaro Arzú Guatemala had a government, democratically elected, that claimed it wanted to put the past behind it. Centrally directed governmental activism in death-squad murders appeared to be quiescent. Nevertheless, dissatisfied groups, in or close to military intelligence, still took their revenge, whenever they could – as with the brutal murder in 1998 of Bishop Juan Geradi, who had led the Catholic Church's major project to attempt to document all the human rights abuses over the previous twenty years.

The government, moreover, had been cautious in its welcome of the recommendations of the United Nations Historical Clarification Commission. President Alvaro Arzú made the decision not to receive the report directly, although the previous year he did seek the pardon of the Guatemalan people in a special 'Day of Forgiveness'. Despite the Commission's charge that the Guatemalan army perpetrated genocide against the country's indigenous people, the government, according to Amnesty, has responded to only about half of the suggestions put forward by the Commission and made few – if any – concrete commitments. Amnesty wrote to the government and singled out, as crucial Commission recommendation, the need to:

- establish a special commission to investigate and take appropriate measures concerning the conduct of military officials involved in the armed conflict;
- establish a government exhumations programme to assist in excavating hundreds of mass grave-sites;
- create a commission to establish the fate of all those who 'disappeared' during the conflict, including numerous children (some of whom may have been illegally adopted);
- pay reparations to victims of human rights abuses and their families.

The government did not respond to Amnesty's letter. Amnesty was to observe that 'experience throughout the world, including elsewhere in Latin America and post-war Europe, has shown that when questions of responsibilities and accountability for past human rights violations are not adequately addressed, they will not just disappear. They will resurface at later stages, presenting the risk of renewed violations and further pain and suffering.'

Mrs Tracy Ulltveit-Moe, Amnesty's long-time researcher on Guatemala, commented:

It is not enough to say 'I'm sorry.' Under the Peace Agreements, the government committed itself to adopting measures beneficial to national peace and harmony. It also promised to preserve the memory of victims, promote a culture of respect for human rights and strengthen the democratic process. Those of us who have been following events in Guatemala for some time [and Mrs Ulltveit-Moe has held the Guatemala portfolio for over twenty years] cannot help but think of the words of philosopher Jorge Santayana, who said that those who forget the past are condemned to relive it.

In her opinion, if the authorities once again simply bury the past, there will before long be another upsurge in violence. 'In Guatemala cyclical violence and state-sponsored human rights violations have occurred over and over again.'

The elections of November 1999, the first since the formal end of the thirty-six-year civil war, did not at first sight appear to realize the promise of the peace accords. Indeed, the result appeared to be a set-back for those who thought the peace process might accelerate. The victor was Alfonso Portillo, candidate of the right-wing party, the Guatemalan Republic Front. Although a left-winger, a scholar of Marxist thought in his youth, who spent much of the war in exile in Mexico (where, he admitted, he had shot two men to death seventeen years ago – in what he says was self-defence – in a brawl), he ended up attaching himself to the party created by the brutal ex-dictator General Efrian Ríos Montt. Many believe that Ríos Montt, as leader of Congress, will run the government from behind the scenes.

There are, however, two or three hopeful omens that Portillo may carry out more of the reforms promised in the peace agreement than his predecessor. By appointing a relatively junior colonel, Juan Estrada, who has a clean war-time record, as his defence minister, he automatically won the retirement of nineteen generals and one vice-admiral who outranked him, freeing jobs for younger, more reformist officers. Another sign of hope was his speech at his swearing-in on 14 January 2000, when he said that the failure to find the killers of the murdered bishop was 'a national disgrace'. He said he would ensure the murder was solved, no matter where the trial led. A week later, in fact, the police arrested two military officers, a father and son, colonel and captain, and charged them with the killing. Then in June in a statement President Portillo admitted the state's responsibility for atrocities during the civil war and vowed to prosecute those responsible. 'We are doing this today so that the dramatic history we have lived through isn't repeated,' he said.

If it is difficult to locate with precision the exact reason or particular personality that triggered positive change in Guatemala, it is even harder to follow the thread of Amnesty's influence. Amnesty has been active in Guatemala for over twenty-five years. For long enough it was a lone public voice for winning whatever attention was given by the outside world to the horrendous events there. From the 1970s on Amnesty was monitoring and recording events in Guatemala, at a time when few other outside organizations were interested and press coverage was minimal.

A number of clear consequences of its involvement do stand out in any retrospective analysis. Amnesty gave enormous emotional support to the persecuted and bereaved in Guatemala. Amnesty provided financial assistance to those in need, such as trade union members. Amnesty often supported families who had lost their breadwinner. German Amnesty groups, in particular, 'adopted' many families. Amnesty provided both cash and psychological help for those who had suffered from torture. Amnesty was instrumental in setting up mutual support groups formed by the families of the 'disappeared'. Often such families were ostracized by their neighbours, who, understandably, were frightened of the repercussions if they offered support. Over the years Amnesty had extended its support to many individual cases, such as the 4-year-old boy who was shot and paralysed in an attempt on his father's life. Amnesty arranged for him to be sent to a hospital in Boston, where he was photographed in a Boston Red Sox basketball cap visiting the mayor and, later, the governor of Massachusetts. Amnesty also used its contacts in the embassies of Guatemala City to arrange for diplomatic escorts for those it felt ought to leave the country. Not least, by providing the UN Human Rights Commission with information which it had neither the staff nor resources to gain for itself, Amnesty stimulated the UN into making Guatemala a high profile concern.

The chemistry of Amnesty's precise relationship with the authorities in Guatemala has always been opaque. Cause and effect have been, except in individual cases, impossible to determine. Take, for example, the surprise invitation Amnesty received from the Guatemalan ambassador to France to visit the country in 1985. The government had said for years it had nothing to hide, yet for more than a decade Amnesty had received no substantive response from the authorities to its repeated submissions of detailed documentation of human rights violations.

The delegation was led by Rear Admiral Dam Backer (Retired), president of Amnesty's Dutch section, who, given his military past, was the ideal choice for the meeting. The authorities appeared to go out of their way to open the doors, setting up meetings with the chief of the military forces, the ministers of the interior and foreign affairs, the attorney-general and the president of the judiciary and the Supreme Court. The delegation was also invited to meet the commanders of various police and military installations throughout the country. Tracy Ulltveit-Moe has a good recollection of what happened on that extraordinary mission:

We travelled first of all in two armoured cars, one of which broke down. We thought at the time that this was maybe an attempt to make us vulnerable to a kidnap attempt, but in retrospect, I'm pretty sure it was just the general state of repairs of the military equipment of the time. In fact, later in the same trip we went up on a military plane to the special forces training school in the jungle in Petén, and there was an explosion on take-off. The military on the plane with us apologized for the incident, saying it was just a tyre blowing off, but that, of course, it was Amnesty's fault that their planes

73

were in such bad nick, because our work exposing human rights violations in the country had affected military aid packages.

There were also other funny (in retrospect) incidents at the hotel. First we arrived to find armed guards outside our doors, supposedly to protect us. Nigel Rodley [Amnesty's long-time legal adviser] made a huge fuss as only he can, insisting it would rather interfere with our work. It took ages for the types to go far enough up the command chain to get permission to withdraw. Meanwhile, Nigel said we should refuse to enter our rooms. For their part, the soldiers refused to go till they had the instructions to do so, so they stood rigidly to attention on chairs outside our room and we stood rigidly in front of them, refusing to enter. Not funny at the time, because we had just completed the 14-hour or so trip to get there, and I wanted to sleep! Finally, they got permission to 'withdraw', so they saluted smartly and marched off down the corridor. We marched into our rooms!

But back to the funny aspects of finding the secret cells: First, when we arrived the commander was literally caught with his pants down (he was with a girl) and came hurrying out, zipping up as he went, to try to block our entry. He was a gorgeous ladino guy with blond hair and super-green eyes, so I'm not surprised he was scoring with the local girls, but he was also scary, saying he now knew who we were and what we looked like and we would be hearing from him. An obvious threat, but he was probably surprised by our reaction, as opposed to what the locals must have reacted like when getting similar threats, because Nigel just said, 'Shall we record that as an official threat?' He backed off.

There was also the amusing spectacle of our two delegates, Dam, the admiral and Nigel, going around surreptitiously kicking at the dirt at various places in the [military] post where the maps we had been provided [with] said there should be a cell, trying to discover the pit, while myself and the interpreter we took along for Dam tried to engage the soldiers' attention elsewhere so Nigel and Dam could engage in earth-kicking to their hearts' content. They eventually did find the pit. While Nigel went down into it to inspect it, Dam tried to draw the soldiers elsewhere. That's how he found the secret below-ground-level passage that linked the base and the cemetery, so they could take prisoners in and out without anyone seeing.

The then Chief of the Army Chiefs of Staff and the real strong-man at the time, Lobos Zamora, whom we saw in Guatemala City upon our return from this most amazing excursion and discovery, was not at all pleased when he learned what had happened (via a phone call that came in while we were actually with him, sipping tea from a very delicate rose-patterned china service). You could feel the atmosphere freeze.

Nevertheless, in each of the cases Amnesty raised they were able to discuss the safeguards against human rights violations in the legal system and codes of practice in the military and the police. Moreover, they were able to meet with the relatives of victims of past abuses. An Amnesty report of the visit shows a telling photograph of a long line of people queuing up to present evidence on human rights violations to the visiting team. Yet, when the delegation submitted a concluding memorandum in December, neither the outgoing military government of General Mejìa Victores nor the newly elected government – and the first civilian one for twenty years – of Vinicio Cerezo Arévalo replied.

In June the following year, Amnesty's secretary-general Thomas Hammarberg wrote a telling but courteous follow-up to President Cerezo. He carefully pointed out that Amnesty had noticed that human rights violations had abated since he took office, but that there were still continuing 'disturbing numbers' of apparent extra-judicial executions and 'disappearances'. Although the letter was couched to elicit a response – 'Amnesty International has been favourably impressed by certain recent legislative developments' and 'Amnesty International would appreciate the opportunity to learn more about the measures taken thus far' – no reply was received. A look at the graph of atrocities (Figure 5 on page 68) shows that this was a reformist administration, if still one that tolerated a high level of human rights abuse.

Whether Amnesty helped the internal discussions within the new administration is not yet known. But one can surmise from the fact that the invitation to visit was received and that the delegation could work freely while in the country that Amnesty as an organization was taken rather seriously by some would-be reformist elements in the government.

Today, as the violence winds down, Amnesty sees its major task as bringing the perpetrators of massacres and violators of human rights to justice. It is able to help with exhumations and in providing documentation and encouragement for the prosecution of the human rights criminals. Amnesty's long involvement is paying dividends. Amnesty knows the history of Guatemalan human rights abuses better than any other organization and its knowledge is invaluable both to the UN and to local political and legal authorities.

None of this answers the question of how much Amnesty's influence counted in tilting the scales of contemporary Guatemalan history. It is, by its nature, a contribution we cannot measure. What we do know is that without Amnesty and the other organizations that followed in its footsteps, the rest of the world would have heard little of Guatemala, and done less.

Nevertheless, although the drumbeat of violence is diminished, Guatemala's indigenous people – two-thirds of its eleven million inhabitants – remain downtrodden and common crime is soaring. Even after being reduced in size, its army remains over-mighty and remains capable of calling too many of the shots, the judicial system is usually ineffective, with communities resorting to lynchings in the absence of the rule of law, business is too much in hock to Mafia elements and active citizenship remains a right exercised only by a minority. To remedy all this is the work of another generation.

2

Bokassa, the Dead Children and the Lessons Unlearnt

Tolstoy wrote in *Anna Karenina* that all unhappy families are unhappy in different ways. So it is with the stories Amnesty has collected about children. This is an African story; it has its own very sad conclusion. If there had been no one in recent memory who walked on the world stage quite like the Emperor Bokassa of the Central African Republic, tales could be told of children on other continents which have a similar heart-rending conclusion.

The Emperor Bokassa was a wilder creation than could ever have been dreamt up by John Updike or Evelyn Waugh even in their most satirical moments. A man who cut off the ears of his prisoners, murdered his former finance minister in the privacy of his palace cabinet room, engaged the full facilities of the French diplomatic service in tracking down an illegitimate daughter in Indo-China, conceived while he was a wartime sergeant in the French forces, who would receive the French ambassador in his underwear and would conduct a serious conversation with him in an empty room in the palace, furnished only with a mattress. No novelist could have created such a character. Yet this was only a part of him.

According to a Commission of Inquiry consisting of five senior African jurists, sent into the Central African Empire in the wake of Amnesty's revelations, 'riots in Bangui [the capital city] were suppressed with great cruelty by the security forces and in April 1979 about a hundred children were massacred at the order of Emperor Bokassa, who almost certainly participated in the killings.'

No one will ever know the precise truth of the degree of Bokassa's bestiality, a man who considered himself the 'father protector of children', who had himself crowned emperor with a golden crown and a golden throne specially made in France with French 'aid'. Nevertheless, there is no good reason to doubt eye-witness reports that he kept pieces of his victims in his refrigerator and feasted on them in private orgies.

The discovery and exposure of the child-murders was one of Amnesty's major breakthroughs. No great detective work was necessary, just diligence and persistence, putting together the pieces of an incomplete picture. But no one else had either the facilities or the interest to do it. It was, indeed, typical of the diligent, time-consuming method of attention to detail used every day by Amnesty researchers. In the end not only did Amnesty reveal one of the most horrible events of the last decade, the disclosure also provoked the French government into sending in paratroopers to depose a tyrant who had become an embarrassment.

Amnesty had been watching the Central African Empire for some time. A number of happenings over the years had caused alarm and persuaded Amnesty researchers to give more than passing attention to unusual pieces of gossip or small items of news carried by the wire services, such as the beating of thieves and cutting off of ears, and a report by an Associated Press journalist, Michael Goldsmith, on appalling conditions in Bangui prison. Amnesty also over the years had received a trickle of letters. But not until 1979 was there enough information to prove a systematic pattern of abuse.

Bokassa, whose father was assassinated when he was 6 and whose mother committed suicide a week later, seized power from his cousin in 1966. Since then judicial standards in the country had declined fast. There had been many 'disappearances', with relatives uninformed of the fate of their loved ones. Imprisonment was harsh, with a high mortality rate among political prisoners – mostly high civilian and military officials suspected of trying to overthrow Bokassa, or ordinary people suspected of trying to organize opposition movements. The Porte Rouge section of Ngaragba prison in Bangui had earned itself a notorious reputation. It contained three cells where political prisoners were herded in almost on top of each other. Food was inadequate, medical aid insufficient and prisoners were denied any contact with their families.

Cruel and inhuman punishments seemed to have become Bokassa's speciality. In July 1972, President-for-life Bokassa (this was in the days before he had been crowned emperor) decreed that thieves should have their left ear cut off. Three thieves were immediately dealt with. When thefts continued, Bokassa reacted by ordering that forty-five suspected thieves, who were being held awaiting trial, should be severely beaten by soldiers. Bokassa joined in himself, hitting prisoners with a big stick. Three of the thieves died. The corpses, along with the other beaten prisoners, were put on public display in the town. When he was told that Dr Kurt Waldheim, the UN Secretary-General, had protested, Bokassa, bursting into one of his frequent rages, called him 'a pimp, a colonialist and an imperialist'.

Bokassa hit the headlines every so often. But by and large, the world passed him by. The French government, which kept itself well-informed, kept its information to itself. The press was not greatly interested in his African backwater. Amnesty maintained its watch, almost alone, as it does on dozens of other seemingly unimportant countries.

The Amnesty alert began in January 1979. Bokassa had issued an order compelling all students in the empire to wear special uniforms, costing about $30 each, way beyond the means of most parents. Besides, the government and its multitude of agencies rarely paid its employees with anything approaching regularity. The students began to protest and then to rampage. In the Bangui suburb of Miskine, sympathetic crowds joined in. Shops were vandalized, including one called 'Le Pacifique', owned by Bokassa's beautiful wife, Catherine. Bokassa sent the soldiers in. Armed with machine pistols, they began shooting indiscriminately. They were met by a bow-and-arrow attack in which maybe as many as a hundred soldiers died. Bokassa asked President Mobutu of Zaire to send in troops to help quell the unrest.

An Amnesty International representative in Paris got the first wind of what had been going on from brief press reports. The information was enlarged upon when she went to a meeting of the

Union Nationaledes Étudiants Central Africains. Apart from the communist deputy-mayor of Montreuil, hers was the only white face in the auditorium. She approached the students after the meeting. They were sceptical of Amnesty, with some reason. Amnesty had not in recent years given their part of the world much detailed attention. Nevertheless, they told Amnesty's representative that their estimate of the deaths was around four hundred.

As more information came out, based on interviews with travellers and businessmen, press estimates also climbed to four hundred. Although the journalistic reports were thin, Amnesty became concerned; experience had shown that when demonstrations are put down, arrests are likely. The research department set to work to contact people who had recently been in the country or might know what was going on. They spoke to the relatives of prisoners, Central Africans living abroad, particularly in France, who had contacts in Bangui, and foreigners who had visited the Central African Empire. The aim was to contact as many independent sources as possible and to cross-check the details in each account.

In mid-February, Amnesty was receiving reports suggesting that important heads of schools and *lycées* had been arrested, as well as an unknown number of students and some civil servants from the Ministry of Education. During February and March Amnesty worked hard to try to get names. It was difficult, as it often is in this kind of situation. Even people living outside the country were frightened, fearful that to give a name to Amnesty, which might then publicize it, would result in retribution. The prisoner could be killed and the family persecuted. Iran, Uganda, Ethiopia and Equatorial Guinea were all countries in which Amnesty had a similar problem. Eventually, however, Amnesty was given the names of three prominent headmasters who were in prison. It was felt their reputations were sufficient to give them a measure of protection.

By the middle of March Amnesty still had the names of only a handful of prisoners. It knew there were many more but it was hard to get hold of reliable information as there was no free press, no foreign news reporters based in the country and no normal means of communication to transmit information. Amnesty's suspicions were aroused that Bokassa was engaged in a particularly nasty piece of repression, but they had insufficient facts to go public. There could clearly be much error, exaggeration and sheer misinformation in the material they had collected so far.

Nevertheless, Amnesty sent a cautiously worded telegram to Bokassa on 14 March. Amnesty expressed its concern at the reports of detainees held since 1973 and new prisoners detained since January. They asked Bokassa to grant a general amnesty to all those detained for their beliefs. The cable read:

Amnesty International, a movement independent of all governments and political parties, which intervenes on behalf of prisoners of conscience throughout the world . . . has the honour to communicate its serious concern about the fate of military and civilian detainees, some of whom have been held for several years and a considerable number of whom have been detained since the events of January 1979. We ask for special amnesty for people detained for reasons of conscience.

Ten days later Bokassa replied. He said that everyone imprisoned had been released on his fifty-eighth birthday, a month before. Amnesty, he said, could come to Central Africa to confirm this. Amnesty attempted to see if there was any truth in his reply. Contacts did confirm that there had been prisoners released in early March. Yet, there were many cases where families had had no contact with imprisoned relatives. Moreover, this was not the first time that Bokassa had announced an amnesty, only for news to filter out later that political prisoners were still locked up. Amnesty decided to step up its investigation.

They learnt that further arrests had taken place. This time it was the parents of the students who had participated in the January demonstrations. Then, on 21 April, Agence France Presse reported that these parents had been put on trial. According to the dispatch, the ruling Central Committee had 'examined the retrograde character of the events that had occurred in the capital and condemned the disorder, hate and subversion organized by students and supported by an occult force'. The report, however, did not say what the events were. About this time Amnesty learnt of the arrest of the Minister of

Information, Barthelemy Yangono, and others, accused of distributing tracts on behalf of an illegal opposition group, the Front Patriotique Oubangien.

In early May Amnesty's Paris office was approached by a number of people who had stories of events they said occurred between 17 and 20 April, relating to the arrest and disappearance of a group of children. The Amnesty representative in Paris admitted, with some embarrassment, that if she hadn't been away on holiday, Amnesty would have started to receive the critical information some days earlier. One important informant was waiting on her doorstep for her to return. This often happens to Amnesty. After it becomes known that Amnesty is working on a case, people who think they have information get in touch. Sometimes they are private individuals who have accidentally run across an event or piece of information. On occasion, they are high officials, ashamed at what their colleagues are up to and seeking to unburden themselves. On 8 and 9 May Amnesty received information from four sources in Paris, each independent of the other. Some were old and established contacts.

Again, as is often the case, there were discrepancies in the information. Some alleged that the children, once arrested, had been taken to the Imperial court in Barengo. Some said that all the children had been taken to the central prison, Ngaragba. Some said the arrests had taken place in four districts; another said five districts. All said the children were of school age, not university students. Some said a few were as young as 8, with most between the ages of 12 and 16. Others said they were between 10 and 15 years of age. There were also differences in pinpointing the cause of the arrests. In London, Amnesty set to work to try and sort out the conflicting stories.

While in the middle of this they were visited by a new contact, a priest, Joseph Perrin, who had lived in Bangui between 1971 and 1976 and who returned there for a week's stay just after the killings had taken place. Father Perrin talked to more than fifty people about what had happened and passed on the information in the form of a detailed letter to Amnesty International when he returned to Europe. Father Perrin had a wealth of detail – from people who had heard the screams of young voices in the prison; from a family who had had five sons taken away; about a boy killed with the pocket-knife he was carrying. He'd also talked to some children who had been arrested, imprisoned and then released. One of them told him that they had seen sixty-two dead children.

This report seemed to flesh out the earlier testimony. The situation was serious enough to go public. On 11 May Amnesty sent a telegram to Bokassa expressing its deep concern. It also alerted the International Year of the Child Secretariat in New York. Three days later Amnesty issued a news release which was both direct and circumspect. Amnesty was careful not to describe the context of the incident since they were unsure of it. Nor did they publicize the allegations that Bokassa himself had been personally involved. These were not, in Amnesty's view, satisfactorily corroborated. Nor did Amnesty say that the children had been taken to the Emperor's court and killed. The details of the transfer from prison to court seemed too murky. For Amnesty, it had been a piece of investigation in the normal line of business: the slow, sometimes arduous, sifting of facts. The press release, in fact, was a model of restraint. Only in paragraph four did the bombshell explode:

On 18 April more than one hundred children are known to have been taken to Bangui's central Ngaragba prison where they were held in such crowded conditions that between twelve and twenty-eight of them are now reported to have died from suffocation. Other children are reported to have been stoned by members of the Imperial Guard to punish them for throwing stones at the Emperor's car. Some have been bayoneted or beaten to death with sharpened sticks and whips.

Amnesty said it had received reliable reports that between fifty and a hundred children had been killed in prison. A witness said the bodies of sixty-two dead children had been buried by government officers during the night of 18 April alone.

To Amnesty's surprise, the press leapt on the story. Bokassa, the child-murderer, was page one news. The French foreign minister, Jean François-Poncet, was more cautious. He talked of 'conflicting reports' and his colleague, the minister of co-operation, referred to what he called 'pseudo-events'. Information now began to pour into Amnesty offices in Paris and London: reports from foreigners who had been there, first-hand testimonies by people who had been at the prison. By June Amnesty had built up an authoritative picture that nobody has credibly disputed.

The trouble had begun in January with the beating-up by some schoolchildren of two security guards sent to spy on them following their protests about wearing school uniforms. The repression had been more severe than realized in January 1979. Between 400 and 500 people had been killed. The arrests of the schoolchildren had begun three months later on the morning of 18 April. Most of those arrested were boys between the ages of 12 and 16, but some of the children were as young as 8, 9,10 and 11. Any who attempted to resist arrest or shouted anti-government slogans were beaten up and in some cases killed on the spot.

The children were flung into the backs of trucks, and beaten with rifle-butts, whips and sticks with nails in them. By the time the trucks arrived at the prisons, many of the children had died, some from their wounds, some from being crushed alive by the weight of the others on top of them. When the children reached the prison of Ngaragba the guards began hurling stones at them. Several more died. As many as thirty children were crammed into each cell, which was only two metres square and had tiny windows letting in only whiffs of air. The heat was overpowering. There was no food and no water. By next morning twenty-two of the children in one cell were dead. According to a survivor of this cell, more children were pushed into the cell and a further eleven died.

Other children were tortured and killed. Some of the survivors claimed that they saw Emperor Bokassa inside the prison personally directing and participating in the killings. Another survivor described how a group of twenty boys was taken outside Bangui and killed when stones were dumped on top of them. Amazingly, forty or so survivors were let out of the prison on 20 and 21 April. It is they who gave much of the information that Amnesty's investigation was built on.

At first the French government was loath to recognize the Amnesty charge. Then, as the accusations gathered strength, it sought to defuse them. The chosen vehicle for this was the meeting in late May in Rwanda of the Francophone African heads of state, including President Valéry Giscard d'Estaing. They decided to send a team of five respected African jurists, from the Côte d'Ivoire, Liberia, Rwanda, Senegal and Togo, to investigate the atrocities. It would have been difficult, given the unanimity of the Francophone states, for Bokassa to have refused their request to investigate. It was, however, the first time the African nations had done anything of this kind, and it set a precedent which African nations, led by Nigeria and Senegal, have built on, seeking to establish an African Human Rights Commission, with the power to investigate and criticize. The Commission of Inquiry was a very successful first effort. It managed to interview Bokassa himself as well as senior ministers and the prime minister. It took testimony from the local Red Cross, priests, teachers, students and schoolchildren. Its report also contains interviews with ten children who were incarcerated in the Ngaragba prison, but who survived. Two of these survivors had been presumed dead by their captors and had been taken with a truck-load of dead bodies to the cemetery. In the confusion they managed to escape before being buried alive.

The Commission, besides confirming Amnesty's principal findings, also described a number of events which Amnesty had not publicized: how local Red Cross officials were fired on by soldiers in January; reports on the personal participation in the killings by Bokassa and also by General Maimokola and Colonel Inga, senior members of the Central African Empire's armed forces. It also explained how the dead bodies were disposed of – some were taken to the cemetery, others to military camps and others thrown into the Ubangi river, which flows past Ngaragba prison.

The report was made public in August. By that time several of those who had given evidence to the Commission had been executed or arrested. In September 1979 the French sent in their paratroopers to overthrow Bokassa. For a long time France's close friend and ally, Bokassa had finally become an impossible embarrassment. No one criticized the invasion, not even the most anti-French of the African countries. There was, it seems, a crude element of self-interest in the French decision to go into the Central African Empire. President Giscard d'Estaing, when he had been minister of finance, had formed a close personal link with Bokassa. The French journal, *Le Canard Enchaîné*, revealed in its issue of 10 October 1979 that it had documents proving that Giscard had accepted a present of diamonds from Bokassa, to the value of $250,000. (Today's value would be nearer $1 million.)

Giscard did not deny it at first. His press statement was an ambiguous declaration that amounted in the eyes of some observers to a confession. It said that it was usual for presents to be exchanged when members of a government visited foreign countries but that they 'never had the character nor the value of those mentioned in the press'. What the communiqué did not mention was that when such gifts are exchanged in the course of foreign visits, they are donated publicly. Bokassa's gift, however, was not made during a public visit. It was a private present sent by special messenger. Later, just before the 1981 May election, Giscard announced he had sold the diamonds and that they were worth much less than had been said, and he had sent the proceeds to a Central African Republic charity.

The scandal gave rise to a theory, as French scandals always do – that Giscard sent in the paratroopers not only to depose Bokassa, but to hijack his papers and correspondence before Bokassa could blackmail him any more. While the French paratroopers were sorting out Bokassa's soldiers, other troops were removing Bokassa's archives to the French embassy. This was witnessed by a number of French correspondents.

Whatever the truth in these allegations, which were to haunt Giscard right through his re-election campaign in the spring of 1981 and contributed to his defeat, there is no gainsaying the fact that Giscard's relationship with Bokassa had been unusually close and Bokassa was adept, politically at least, at exploiting it. Giscard loved to hunt in Bokassa's private hunting area, a large tract of jungle in the east of the country, accessible only by private plane. It was Giscard's *chasse gardée*. Accompanied by Bokassa, he could shoot elephants, giraffes, and the rare white rhino. (Bokassa claimed, in an interview in the *Washington Post* just before the French election, that he gave him a 3,000-square-mile hunting preserve.) Giscard's family also had close connections with the country. His cousin, Jacques Giscard d'Estaing, represented French interests in Bokassa's attempt to get uranium mining started. Another cousin, François, had banking interests in the country. Both have been accused by *Le Canard* of having received diamonds.

Giscard made things worse by choosing Central Africa for his first presidential visit to Africa, by being the first president to congratulate Bokassa after his crowning, and calling his host during a visit 'a cherished relative', an endearment which Bokassa used to love repeating. Take this 'imperial press release', for example: 'On October 2 the head of the French State, M. Valéry Giscard d'Estaing, left Paris to visit his relative in the Château de Villemoran (one of the emperor's four estates in France). The Central African monarch and President Giscard d'Estaing met at a family lunch. Gifts of Central African *objets d'art* were given to the French head of state by His Majesty Bokassa I, thereby combining business with pleasure.'

Bokassa's strength in the French government's eyes was that he was staunchly anti-communist. In the context of mid-African geopolitics, this was an important consideration, particularly when the support for the West nearby appeared rather precarious. Zaire, although also pro-West, had long been subject to unpredictable upheavals. Congo-Brazzaville had been hostile to the West. Chad was continuously in a turbulent state (and in early 1981 was effectively taken over by Libya). Outside powers have long shown an interest in the Central African state. The Soviet Union had a large embassy and Bokassa enjoyed teasing France and upping the French economic commitment by doing deals with the Soviets. With Libya, too, he had played fast and loose. In 1976, when Colonel Gaddafi visited Bangui, Bokassa announced he'd become a Muslim – again, a reminder to France of his real worth.

It was Charles de Gaulle who began the serious courting of Bokassa. Bokassa was given a grandiose official visit to Paris, complete with a wreath-laying ceremony at the Tomb of the Unknown Warrior, a triumphal drive down the Champs-Elysées, a gala night at the theatre and a ceremonial dinner at de Gaulle's residence. De Gaulle's dinner speech was sycophantic. He lauded the Central African government's achievements and added, 'Mr President, I insist on saying that this is the case more than ever and that your personality has contributed much of it.'

Eight weeks after his visit to France, Bokassa liquidated his former finance minister, Alexandre Banza, in circumstances, according to *Le Monde*, 'so revolting that it still makes one's flesh creep'. The *Le Monde* report continued:

Two versions concerning the end circumstances of his death differ on one minor detail. Did Bokassa tie him to a pillar before personally carving him with a knife that he had previously used for stirring his coffee in the gold-and-midnight blue Sèvres coffee set, or was the murder committed on the cabinet table with the help of other persons? Late that afternoon, soldiers dragged a still identifiable corpse, with the spinal column smashed, from barrack to barrack to serve as an example.

The French press did its best to highlight these allegations and Bokassa was furious, convinced that French diplomats had leaked the story. He slapped France across the face by nationalizing the diamond mining company. A little later, France's foreign minister, Maurice Shumann, attempting to placate Bokassa, sent him a carefully worded message: 'You have understood quite well that there is nothing in common between what some more or less well-informed journalist thinks he can print and the brotherly respect in which the French government has always held the Central African Republic and its head.'

After France's invasion, Bokassa at first fled to exile. In exile on the Côte d'Ivoire, he was sentenced to death *in absentia* the day before Christmas 1980. Eight years later, to everyone's surprise, he voluntarily returned from exile. He was tried again and received the death sentence. This was later commuted to life imprisonment. In 1993 he was released. Three years later he died of natural causes.

Optimists would have expected that France would have learnt its lesson from this. Optimists would have hoped that Africa's political class would have been so stunned by the revelations that children would have been ensured a special protected status in future political upheavals. Neither have come to pass. Amnesty's power, it seems, does not extend to changing the fundamental *realpolitik* of France's African policy. Amnesty can have an impact on events when they have exceeded what even the hardest diplomats and political practitioners can tolerate. But it can have only marginal influence on the political relationship that nurtures and gives refuge to such behaviour.

Twenty years after the terrible events in the Central African state, President Jacques Chirac made a visit to Africa in July 1999. He said he was carrying a message emphasizing the importance of democratization and the rule of law. Yet he ended up publicly attacking Amnesty International and defending President Gnassingbe Eyadéma of Togo, who has held a tight grip on power for thirty-two years, making him the longest-ruling head of state in sub-Saharan Africa.

Just two-and-a-half months before Chirac's visit Amnesty had published a report on Eyadama's government, giving the evidence for extra-judicial killings, disappearances and torture extending back over three decades. The government responded by arresting one Amnesty International worker and by barring three others, including its African-born secretary-general, Pierre Sané, from entering Togo. 'It is probably, to a large extent, an attempt at manipulation,' Mr Chirac said of the Amnesty report at his news conference in Lomé, the Togolese capital. He added that Mr Eyadema had been right in deciding to sue Amnesty International. Shortly after, Mr Sané received a summons to appear before an investigating magistrate in Togo for a possible indictment for 'contempt, incitement to revolt, dissemination of false news and conspiring against the external security of the State'. 'Instead of helping put an end to the culture of impunity in Togo,' Amnesty said in a statement issued to the press, 'the French president is supporting a regime which has never brought to justice those responsible for human rights violations.'

Amnesty did not then leave matters alone. In August it persuaded the United Nations Sub-Commission on Prevention of Discrimination and Protection of Minorities to set up an internal commission of inquiry into extra-judicial executions during the rigged presidential election the previous year. In September Amnesty also made representations to the Francophonic Summit in Canada 'to press the Togolese authorities into taking concrete measures to prevent any further human rights violations'. Then in June 2000 came an important breakthrough – the UN and the Organization of African Unity announced the setting up of a Commission of Inquiry into hundreds of alleged extra-judicial killings in Togo. All this was grist for the French media mill, but whether President Chirac is any more embarrassed than his predecessor, Giscard d'Estaing, is not clear. In the intervening twenty years France has gradually changed its African policy to favour democracy and is less prepared to use its military presence in Africa to prop up all and every pro-French tyrant. However, as was clearly revealed by this episode, it remains an unclear, imprecise policy change, and one that seems oblivious to painful lessons learnt a short twenty years ago. *Plus ça change.*[1]

Change on the human rights scene comes incrementally. In recent decades it has been two steps forward and one step back, as with France's African policy. Yet with the protection of children the reverse has been more apparent than the advance. The burgeoning problem of child soldiers, a phenemonon practically unknown two decades ago, has become one of the burning questions of our time and one that is peculiar to Africa. In no other part of the world is the issue drawn on such a massive scale.

In countries as diverse as Sierre Leone, Angola, the Sudan and Uganda, children have been at the forefront of the fighting. Amnesty International is part of an organization called the Coalition to Stop the Use of Child Soldiers. In a report published in April 1999 it estimated that more than 120,000 children under 18 years of age are

[1] In July 2000 an independent panel assembled by the Organization of African Unity harshly criticized Security Council members, in particular France and the USA, for not preventing and later stopping the 1994 genocide in Rwanda that took the lives of up to 800,000 people. The report found that France had 'unrivalled influence at the very highest levels' of the Hutu-led government in Rwanda and chose not to exercise it to derail well-laid plans for the genocide.

being used as soldiers across the African continent. When not actively engaged in combat, children are often used to man checkpoints. The adult soldiers stay back so that if bullets start to fly the children will be the first victims.

Children can become so hardened to combat that there have been many reports of them committing atrocities. In Algeria, one report tells of boys who decapitated a 15-year-old girl and then played 'catch' with the head. Some children do volunteer to join the armed forces, but tens of thousands are forced to join up, at gunpoint. Many of the worst abuses have been committed by armed anti-government groups. During the civil war in Burundi in 1994 the Hutu militias recruited both boys and girls under 15 years of age. In Sierre Leone, during the civil war that has raged since 1991, rebels have recruited children, some as young as 7.[1]

In northern Uganda, thousands of children are victims of a vicious cycle of violence, caught up between the Ugandan government and a brutal rebel group, the pseudo-religious Lord's Resistance Army. Although the LRA say their purpose is to overthrow the government of Uganda, they are in political terms only a fringe force – but one that appears driven (with their religious fanaticism that makes them believe they are immune to bullets) to raid villages, loot stores and homes, burn houses and schools, and rape, mutilate and slaughter civilians unlucky enough to be in their path.

When the rebels move on to the next village to be raided, they leave behind the bodies of the dead. But they always take away some of the living, in particular young children, often dragging them away as they cling to the dead bodies of their parents. They tie the children to each other and force them to carry heavy loads of looted goods, as they march them off into the bush. Children who cannot keep up the fast pace or who try to escape are killed. The deaths are not quick. It is not a bullet in the head – it is death by a thousand cuts, of a machete or club, inflicted by other abducted children who know

---

[1] At the end of July 2000 the USA asked the UN Security Council to establish a special international court to try the Sierra Leonean rebel leader Foday Sankoh and others accused of atrocities.

if they don't do this they will be killed too. One girl, Susan, aged 16, sobbingly told an investigator this story:

One boy tried to escape, but he was caught. They made him eat a mouthful of red pepper, and five people were beating him. His hands were tied and then they made us, the other new captives, kill him with a stick. I felt sick. I knew this boy from before. We were from the same village. I refused to kill him and they told me they would shoot me. They pointed a gun at me, so I had to do it. The boy was asking me, 'Why are you doing this?' I said I had no choice. After we killed him, they made us smear his blood on our arms. I felt dizzy. There was another dead body nearby, and I could smell the body. I felt so sick. They said we had to do this so we would not fear death and so we would not try to escape.

I feel so bad about the things that I did . . . it disturbs me so much – that I inflicted death on other people . . . When I go home I must do some traditional rites because I have killed. I must perform these rites and cleanse myself. I still dream about the boy from my village who I killed. I see him in my dreams, and he is talking to me and saying I killed him for nothing, and I am crying.

And Timothy, aged 14, recounted his war experiences, with a remarkable, if frightening, detachment:

I was good at shooting. I went for several battles in Sudan. The soldiers on the other side would be squatting, but we would stand in a straight line. The commanders were behind us. They would tell us to run straight into gunfire. The commanders would stay behind and would beat those of us who would not run forward. You would just run forward shooting your gun. I don't know if I actually killed any people, because you really can't tell if you're shooting people or not. I might have killed people in the course of the fighting . . . I remember the first time I was in the front line. The other side started firing, and the commander ordered us to run towards the bullets. I panicked. I saw others falling down dead around me. The commanders were beating us for not running, for trying to crouch down. They said if we fall down, we would be shot and killed by the soldiers.

When the rebels return to their bases in the impoverished south of neighbouring Sudan, the children are forced to serve the rebels.

Smaller children may be made to fetch water and cultivate the land. Girls as young as 12 are given to rebel commanders as 'wives'. All are trained to march, use guns and be prepared to fight. Most of the food and arms in the camps comes from the Sudanese government in the north, which has enlisted the LRA in its own fight against the long-standing rebellion in the south by the Sudanese People's Liberation Army. The Sudan government, however, maintain they only help the LRA because the Ugandan government first provided military support to the Sudanese People's Liberation Army.

Graça Machel, the wife of Nelson Mandela, who headed the United Nations study on 'The Impact of Armed Conflict on Children', argues that 'the reality is that children have increasingly become targets, and not incidental victims of war, as a result of conscious and deliberate decisions made by adults . . . War violates every right of the child . . . The injury to children, the physical wounds, the psychosocial distress, the sexual violence, are affronts to each and every humanitarian impulse that inspired the Convention on the Rights of the Child.'

Amnesty International and their coalition partners in the campaign to stop the use of child soldiers – Human Rights Watch, Save the Children, UNESCO and the German Ministry of Foreign Affairs – constantly lobby African governments to seek to end the use of children as soldiers. In April 1999 they brought together in Maputo, Mozambique – Graça Machel's home town – the largest-ever gathering of African governments, non-governmental organizations and representatives of the UN and the Red Cross. The issue, at least, is now on the political map. What for years was perceived as, at best, an undefined, poorly researched subject, at worst, an ignored problem, is now seen as a central concern by responsible African governments. South Africa, as a token of its commitment to the efforts of the coalition, has decided to raise the minimum age of recruitment to its armed forces from 17 to 18.

The abuse, torture and ill-treatment of children in the name of political cause has become in a relatively short period a continent-wide issue. What seemed two decades ago as peculiar to the psychopath Bokassa is now pervasive, extending its poisonous reach to too many parts of Africa. It is but the worst manifestation of the breakdown of many African societies under the pressure of ill-government, the personal pursuit of untrammelled power, constant and unrelieved war, growing poverty and a deteriorating environment. All these issues have to be tackled together if progress towards a solution is to be possible. Amnesty's contribution is a vital but, in the end, small part of it. What Africa needs, perhaps, is rather more of President Obasanjo and a little less of President Chirac.

3

The Pinochet Case

The arrest in London of the former Chilean strongman, Augusto Pinochet, was a bolt from the blue. Not even the most well-informed Amnesty supporters considered it a possibility.[1] It can be said with near certainty that it never crossed the mind of senior members of the British judiciary, who were soon to be landed – quite unprepared – with untangling the legal intricacies. Indeed, it was such an impossible idea that until almost the very last moment it never occurred to the ex-dictator himself that he could be vulnerable in the very country where his great friend and supporter, Margaret Thatcher, had been prime minister.

Pinochet's mistake was to mention to a reporter for the American highbrow magazine, the *New Yorker*, that he would soon be in London. By word of mouth, the news reached Baltasar Garzón, an extraordinary, intelligent and diligent Spanish magistrate, who had already made a reputation for himself in Madrid by hounding Felipe González, the former Socialist prime minister, for having been party to the use of a police cell to assassinate leaders of the violent Basque independence group, ETA. Garzón, not a member of Amnesty, but one who had been influenced by their public campaigns, was a man seized with a mission – to put behind bars those in Chile and Argentina who had led the military coups and the bitter repression that followed.

The climate was right. In the summer of 1998, 120 nations of the

[1] Amnesty had tried, but failed, on Pinochet's previous visits to Britain to persuade the authorities to investigate the case.

world had given their massive approval (with only seven opposing or abstaining, including the USA, China and Israel) to the creation of the International Criminal Court, to enable those accused of 'crimes against humanity' to be tried and, if convicted, sentenced. In Britain, too, there had been a change of government and the Conservative party, natural allies of Pinochet, were out of office.

Pinochet had visited London many times before, receiving red-carpet treatment, especially by the Ministry of Defence, and invariably been invited home for a drink or tea by Margaret Thatcher. This time he was the guest of a British arms maker, Royal Ordnance, and the Foreign Office arranged for him to receive VIP treatment at Heathrow airport. Garzón seized the moment, and made a request for Pinochet's arrest under the European Convention on Extradition. Very much against its own wishes, the Spanish Conservative govern-ment felt it could not intervene to stop the application and the relevant paperwork was passed along via the Spanish embassy to London's Scotland Yard. Somehow, Pinochet had got wind that something was afoot and, recovering from an operation on his back in a Harley Street clinic, decided to flee on the 7 a.m. flight to Santiago on Saturday, 17 October 1998; but at 11.25 p.m. on 16 October anti-terrorist police officers sealed off the clinic and arrested him. The next day Margaret Thatcher attacked the police publicly for disturbing the rest of a 'sick and frail old man', while Peter Mandelson, Prime Minister Tony Blair's closest confidant in the Cabinet, said that many British would find it 'pretty gut-wrenching' if he were now to be set free. Battle-lines were firm right down the dividing line of the political spectrum and it was now up to the courts to decide the outcome.

The Pinochet affair was a momentous event in the human rights struggle. As the British lawyer Geoffrey Robertson has written: 'The great play of sovereignty, with all its pomp and panoply, can now be seen for what it hides: a posturing troupe of human actors who when off stage are sometimes prone to rape the chorus.'[1] The rulings – first by the High Court, then by Britain's highest court, the House of

---

[1] *Crimes Against Humanity*, by Geoffrey Robertson (Penguin, 2000), p. 374.

Lords, and later by the London magistrate – crystallized half a century's debate on the legal and political problems of accountability for crimes against humanity. For the first time in a high court anywhere it had been decided that sovereign immunity must not be allowed to become sovereign impunity. For that we have to thank most of the nations of the world, including Chile and Thatcher's Britain, who in the late 1980s and early 1990s put their signatures to the UN Convention Against Torture and thus laid the legal basis for the British ruling.

The doctrine of immunity was first challenged successfully by chief prosecutor, US Supreme Court of Justice, Robert Jackson, at the Nuremberg trial of Nazi leaders. But afterwards the notion appeared to lapse, 'and remained for decades a talking point in university common rooms . . . Until the Serb and Croat blood feuding it had no practical application other than as a legal lasso for old Nazis like Eichmann and Barbie.'[1]

Had Pinochet flown to New York rather than London and taken tea with Kissinger rather than Thatcher, the legal net would probably never have closed, argued Robinson. Even if he had been arrested his fate would have been determined by politics rather than law. The State Department would have probably sent the court a 'suggestion of immunity', reasoning that Chile was a friendly state and wishing to avoid the publication of details about the US role in Pinochet's *coup d'état*. Likewise, in most of Europe the issue would have been rapidly settled by the government weighing up the costs to alliances and trade, as indeed the Spanish have done.

But the British government, for reasons not yet totally clear, decided for most of the way to let the law take its course. In the end, however, partly bowing to powerful influences, it did allow Pinochet to return home, released, the government said, on 'humanitarian grounds'. The pressures upon the British government to call it a day and issue a humanitarian reprieve were immense. The law had made its point, it was said. A shot had been fired across the bows of all present and future dictators and mass torturers who will know from

[1] Robertson, *Crimes Against Humanity*, p. 374.

now on that they cannot behave like this at home and expect to travel thereafter. Pinochet is very old and his ordeal had been punishment enough. And anyway if he were sent to trial in Spain and was convicted, according to Spanish law he can't be sent to jail at his age. Did a humane Britain then have to insist on the *coup de grâce*? Enough is enough.

All this was to miss the main point. Pinochet's crimes were no ordinary crimes of the maintenance of political authority in a time of turbulence. They continued until 1990, long after Pinochet announced in 1978 that the 'communist threat' to Chile had ended. 'The rituals of torture were intended to send horrific whispers throughout the populace,' says Robertson. Pinochet, the smiling, stately, grandfather figure, is also the man who, it is alleged, personally supervised the torture operations, with the boss of the torture unit, General Manuel Contreras, reporting daily and directly to him. He is also the man who on occasion joked that the 'disappearance' had saved bereaved families the cost of coffins.

The determination made by the British government to release Pinochet on 'humanitarian grounds' was arguably the most important single legal ruling that was made by any government since the decision to execute German and Japanese war leaders. Compassion cannot be offered to someone who showed not one iota of compassion to his victims. To allow Pinochet his freedom was to fudge a major turning-point in the world's maturing understanding of jurisprudence. Seen properly to its conclusion with a trial in Spain, it would have laid down a marker for all time. No wonder that Amnesty decided that the case had to be fought practically all the way to the airport.

Amnesty has been at the heart of this battle ever since Pinochet, in a military coup in September 1973, overthrew the democratically elected government of Chile and proceeded to round up, incarcerate and torture, sometimes to death, anyone he conceived might be a possible opponent. Not even pregnant women and children were beyond the reach of the barbaric apparatus of the torture chamber. It was for years a classic Amnesty case-load like any other, and not even the most far-sighted or optimistic of Amnesty staff members ever thought the day would arrive when Pinochet would appear in the dock in a court a fifteen-minute taxi ride from Amnesty headquarters.

When the case was effectively first thrown out by the Chief Justice – who refused the Spanish government, the plaintiff in the case, an adjournment to prepare the case and then argued that an ex-head of state had sovereign immunity for every crime he committed in exercising the functions of office – Amnesty's legal team went into high gear. The case then proceeded to the House of Lords, and Amnesty worked hard to provide the evidence to show that recent developments in international law had not been appreciated in the lower court.

Later, when the Home Secretary announced in January 2000 he was 'minded' to allow Pinochet to be released because an examination by doctors had found him not fit to be tried, Amnesty, along with other human rights organizations and the Belgian government, challenged the British government in yet another series of High Court hearings.

Like all good stories, one must begin at the beginning to get the measure of its full impact.

During the 1960s Chile had been the special focus of US policy towards Latin America. The Alliance for Progress, begun under Eisenhower and expanded under Kennedy, provided Chile with more economic aid per caput than any other country on the continent. Even then, with an almost unbroken continuous democracy since independence in 1818, its political and economic success was held up as a model of what could be achieved in a turbulent continent of worsening income distribution, Caudillo-prone politics and continuous army intervention. But in the presidential election of September 1970 a Marxist socialist, Salvador Allende Cossens, surprised Washington by winning 36.2 per cent of the vote in the first round. The State Department and CIA analysts took it in their stride, despite the knowledge they had that in a previous election Allende had received a good amount of financial help from communist and communist-front organizations with ties to Moscow. The CIA, in a formal Intelligence

Memorandum, observed that the USA 'has no vital interests with Chile – an Allende victory would not pose any likely threat to the peace of the region.'[1] But President Richard Nixon and his National Security Advisor, Henry Kissinger, hit the roof. Kissinger was minuted as saying: 'I don't see why we need to stand by and watch a country go Communist due to the irresponsibility of its own people.' For Kissinger there was the worry that an Allende victory would send the wrong message to Italian voters, who were being wooed by the Euro-communists.

Nixon, who had no time even for the incumbent Christian Democratic, but left-leaning, president, Eduardo Frei, gave the order that Allende must not be allowed to come to power. In a series of hectic White House meetings, every tool was considered, even a proposal to assassinate Allende.

Much has been made of the role of big US corporations in getting rid of Allende. Undoubtedly ITT, Anaconda Copper, General Telephone and Electronics and Pepsi Cola were involved in the effort to undermine him, even in the latter's case offering to put up substantial sums to supplement the CIA's effort. For Nixon the welfare of US corporations operating in Chile was an important concern; for Kissinger much less so. But both were obsessively driven by the idea of a communist toe-hold; they had no faith that the sophisticated Chilean electorate would itself in time get rid of Allende if he went too far to the left. In fact, the matter was regarded as too important to be left to the American business sector.

Thus, on 15 September Nixon personally gave Richard Helms (the CIA chief) the widest possible authority ('a marshal's baton', Helms later called it) to prevent Allende's presidency by any means available, at whatever cost or risk of failure.[2] From mid-September 1970 to mid-October a small CIA task force based in Santiago made plans that focused on the removal of Chile's chief of staff, General René Schneider, who was known to be not only a staunch upholder of the constitution but strongly opposed to military intervention.

[1] *Price of Power*, by Seymour Hersh (Summit, 1983), p. 270.
[2] *A Tangled Web*, by William Bundy (Hill & Wang, 1998), p. 201.

Although the US Ambassador, Edward Korry, came to Washington and strongly argued to Nixon himself that a military coup would not be in the best interests of Chile, and although Kissinger later claimed he had called off the CIA operation, Schneider was duly murdered by the very conspirators that the CIA had funded earlier. As Thomas Powers in his book on the CIA[1] observed, 'If the CIA did not actually shoot General Schneider, it is probably fair to say that he would not have been shot without the CIA.' William Bundy, a former senior foreign policy official in the Kennedy and Johnson administrations and author of the most authoritative book to date on the Nixon administration, observes: 'In legal terms, a US judicial proceeding would surely have concluded that US agents (acting on presidential authority) had been at least accessories before the fact and co-conspirators in the kidnapping and thus in the killing that resulted from it.'[2]

The result, in the short term, was immediately counterproductive. There was almost universal outrage in Chile. Allende easily won the run-off election two days later. Nevertheless, with Schneider out of the way, it was only a matter of time before the right would strike again. Nixon stoked the furnace, cutting off all US government financial support and pressuring US corporations to cut back their interests in Chile. All World Bank aid ceased. At the same time CIA activity – fronted by the Australian secret service – was stepped up in an attempt to further the process of political and economic destabilization. Inevitably, this worked to push Allende in an authoritarian direction. In the summer of 1973 riots broke out in Chile.

The US embassy had been neutral during the turbulent weeks of middle-class rioting over the summer. But the work had already been done. Two years of severe US economic squeeze had helped produce the middle-class malaise that gave Pinochet his opening. On 11 September 1973, as commander-in-chief of the Chilean army, he ordered the bombing of Allende in the presidential palace.

---

[1] *The Man who Kept the Secrets – Richard Helms and the CIA*, by Thomas Powers (Knopf, 1979), p. 201.
[2] Bundy, *A Tangled Web*, p. 203.

Defiant to the last, Allende broadcast to the nation, and then took his own life. (Pinochet's determination to drive ahead with the coup took many of his colleagues by surprise – he was not regarded as unusually ambitious or particularly political. Moreover, he had been promoted by Allende himself, who considered him a politically neutral general.) All along, however, the CIA had been active with an elaborate disinformation and propaganda programme which reached into the heart of the army. All the actors in Chile knew that the USA would not oppose a coup, and that was confirmed when the administration moved rapidly not only to recognize the Pinochet regime but to start talks on renewed financial help. This was despite Pinochet's immediate decision to round up and imprison thousands of Allende supporters, including quite a few US citizens.

Two years later, after thousands had been tortured, murdered and 'disappeared', Kissinger, in a conversation in Washington, told Patricio Carvajal, Pinochet's foreign minister: 'I hold the strong view that human rights is not appropriate for discussion in a foreign policy context. I am alone in this. It is not shared by my colleagues in the State Department [by then Kissinger was Secretary of State] or on the Hill.'[1]

Amnesty International had not lacked diligence in putting into the public arena a full accounting of what was going on. Those who were prepared to hear, heard. Those like Henry Kissinger and Margaret Thatcher who didn't want to, didn't. Amnesty's first report on Chile was published four months after the coup. In the interim it had sent a delegation to Chile composed of two distinguished American lawyers, one the presiding judge of the Supreme Court of Orange County, California, the other an expert on human rights. Much to Amnesty's surprise, the government did nothing to impede their visit and Amnesty was, it said, 'well received'. The Pinochet government seemed steeped in a protective cocoon of self-righteousness (a trait seen still alive in Pinochet in old age, when he complained of being 'England's only political prisoner' and appealed, successfully, to his

---

[1] Official transcript.

close friends in the Vatican to persuade the Pope to intervene with the British government on his behalf). Even while the delegation was in Chile, summary executions continued unabated.

In January, Amnesty went public with a damning report. In a covering letter to Pinochet, Amnesty's secretary-general, Martin Ennals, wrote: 'The report of our delegation has convinced us that torture has taken place on a large scale.' The report said that electric shock and beating had been employed during the interrogation of prisoners and that foreign 'experts' had been present. 'Those charged with handling prisoners held in the national stadium readily admitted that Brazilian police had been present at interrogations and that they were there to teach Chilean interrogators their methods.'

A later Amnesty report spoke of the

many hundreds of refugees, both Chilean and foreign, hiding in houses, all over Santiago. No house was secure. Gradually, these people were disappearing, thanks to denunciation by suspicious neighbours, or to the chance movements of the police and military who were systematically searching houses and blocks of flats . . . Embassies which gave refuge to the bulk of asylum cases seem to have been the Argentine and Mexican. The French and British refused to take in anyone except their own nationals. The Finns and Swedes were the heroes of the hour. The Swiss refused to take one of their own nationals, a girl nine-months pregnant, because she refused to be separated from her husband, a Colombian. They later managed to reach the Mexican embassy, where her child was born some hours later.

Altogether about 3,000 people were executed or 'disappeared' during the Pinochet dictatorship. Tens of thousands more were tortured or forced into exile. Most were leaders and members of the Communist and Socialist parties as well as other political and religious groups that supported or took part in the government of Salvador Allende.

Over the Pinochet years Amnesty did its utmost to keep the pressure on Chile – quite simply, to make it in the eyes of the rest of the world a pariah. Interestingly, just before Pinochet was due to make a state visit to the Philippines in 1980, President Ferdinand Marcos, a great human rights abuser himself, cancelled the invitation. Under fire, he had decided that the last thing he needed was to be photographed together with such a man. Rightly, he could read the headlines the sub-editors would cook up.

All through the 1970s, the pressure from abroad increased. Not only was Pinochet shunned by most foreign governments but his armed forces were subject to foreign boycotts. The British Labour government halted its arms sales. Italy refused to appoint an ambassador, the country having been shocked to the core when Pinochet's soldiers had dumped a corpse in the embassy garden a few days after the coup as a warning to the ambassador. In the USA, Senator Edward Kennedy won Congressional backing for a halt to arms sales. Undoubtedly, outside pressure took its toll, even if progress in ameliorating the Pinochet reign was a slow and protracted business. Undoubtedly, too, it gave courage and inspiration to those within Chile who wished to see the dictatorship ended and democracy restored.

Finally, Pinochet, growing old, believing he had done his job by defeating the left and making a dazzling success of the Chilean economy by importing the monetarist, free-market ideas of the University of Chicago, decided to step down. In fact, Pinochet had been aghast when, calling a plebiscite, as he had done successfully before, he had not gained a plurality. On 5 October 1988 the votes were counted and Pinochet had won only 43 per cent. Elections were called for the following year and a coalition of the Christian Democrats and parties of the left and centre nominated as their presidential candidate the cautious Christian Democrat, Patricio Aylwin. He won comfortably. On 11 March 1990, sixteen years after the coup, Aylwin was sworn in. Pinochet remained, for a while, as commander-in-chief of the armed forces with a seat, guaranteed for life, in the Senate. The Senate also had nine senators appointed by Pinochet, ensuring that Pinochet could, if necessary, block the will of the government, and guarantee himself immunity from prosecution in perpetuity.

Aylwin had the difficult balancing act of responding to a widespread feeling that amends should be made for past abuses and not alienating Pinochet and the army, whose power was still considerable. The compromise was the establishment of a National Commission on Truth and Reconciliation. It issued a meticulous report, documenting

957 disappearances. Aylwin sent each bereaved family a copy of the report with a personal letter apologizing on behalf of the state. But unlike a parallel effort in Argentina, the Sábato Commission, it did not refer for prosecution those responsible. Nor did it try to attribute individual responsibility. Hamstrung by the amnesty which the military had decreed for itself before stepping down from power, the commissioners were well aware that Pinochet would mobilize the might of the army again if the government went too far.

Pinochet satisfied himself with an address to military colleagues. 'Its [the report's] content reveals an unpardonable refusal to recognize the real causes that motivated the action to rescue the nation on 19 September 1973 ... The Chilean army certainly sees no reason to ask pardon for having fulfilled its patriotic duty.' The spell within Chile that protected Pinochet was not truly broken until his arrest and arraignment in London. Then, as the Chilean playwright, Ariel Dorfman, wrote:

The events of the past year have drastically reconfigured the Semantics of Pinochet. His confinement, trial and public abasement have led to an extraordinary transformation of that word 'warning', re-signifying it. It is now the petty and grand tyrants of the world who, instead of their subjects, are filled with fear at the thought of General Pinochet ... His image has infiltrated some part of their brains, creeping into their eyes and sinews to remind them of the ominous destiny that could await them. If human rights abuses will not cease because of the general's exemplary punishment, a subtle shift has nevertheless been verified in the way in which the world imagines power and equality and memory.

Even within Chile that change has been noticeable. Clifford Krauss of the *New York Times*, in his dispatch of 14 October 1999, observed: 'The arrest of Pinochet has opened a quiet and long-postponed reckoning in Chile over its years of dictatorship that is finally bringing former military officers to task for the deaths or disappearances of thousands of political opponents.'

The critical factor was the absence of Pinochet from Chile. That, combined with the embarrassing and detailed attention being cast on the past, had put the officer corps – the traditional bulwark of his power – on the defensive. Moreover, a new generation of officers had been taking over senior commands and many of them were prepared publicly for the first time to admit human rights abuses did occur.

The new army commander, General Ricardo Izurieta, was prepared to open negotiations with human rights lawyers to establish the fate of those who disappeared and to identify those officers who were responsible. In July 1998 he insisted that the military hand over to a judge a list of the names of hundreds of former secret agents, together with their code names, to aid an investigation into the 1987 killings of twelve guerrillas. The defence minister, Edmundo Perez Yoma, observed publicly in 1999 that a new attitude towards past abuses was emerging among the military high command. 'You deal with it, or it will never go away. You have to confront it – that's the changed attitude.'

One important evidence of this sea-change was the decision of the Supreme Court to uphold the indictment of retired General Humberto Gordon and Brigadier-General Roberto Schmiedt after their arrest in September for the killing of a labour union leader in 1982. General Gordon had been a member of the original four-man junta and chief of Pinochet's secret police. Another item of evidence was the army's passive acquiescence to the life sentence ordered by the Appeals Court against Alvaro Corbalan, a former head of operations of the dictatorship's secret police, for a 1983 political murder. There was also the critical ruling by the Supreme Court in July 1999 when it upheld a ruling by a lower court that the amnesty declared by the former Pinochet regime to protect military officers involved in political crimes was no longer applicable to cases in which people disappeared. Moreover, in June 2000 the armed forces reached an agreement with the government and human rights organizations under which they have up to a year to produce information on the bodies of around 1,000 people who disappeared.

Perhaps most important, Pinochet's arrest had brought mental release to some of the forty thousand Chileans who were tortured under his regime. 'It was only when Mario Fernandez saw the headline, "Pinochet Under Arrest" that the dam broke and he finally found it possible to talk about the beatings, the electric shocks, the cigarette burns, the terrible sense of humiliation and alienation,' reported Clifford Krauss in the *New York Times*. 'My body froze. I had an intense allergic reaction and I didn't know whether to laugh or cry,' Mr Fernandez said. He ran to his wife and wept on her shoulder, he said, and at long last took her advice to seek therapy. 'I needed to talk about the terror inside, the hood they put on me, of not knowing whether they would kill me from one minute to the next.' Psychologists report that hundreds or perhaps thousands of people like Mario Fernandez have begun to see therapists, to organize group therapy, to share their long-hidden horrors with spouses and children.

While Pinochet was under house arrest near London reports about the torture era had begun to appear regularly in the Chilean press. Newly reinvigorated human rights groups came to victims, first seeking testimony they could use in the courts in London and Madrid, but also urging them to seek help.

Although the government, led by President Eduardo Frei, continuously argued, cajoled and attempted to hatch complex deals with both the British and Spanish governments that would enable Pinochet's immediate return, it significantly changed its position as the months of his detention rolled by. By the autumn of 1999, one year after his arrest, it was saying that he should be tried, but in Chile. A senior Chilean judge even sent him questions about his involvement in various crimes.

Despite the changing arguments of the Chilean government and the obvious unwillingness of the Spanish government to walk in the footsteps made by examining magistrate Garzón, the case wound its way through various levels of court proceedings in London. Geoffrey Robertson wrote that 'the case became the most important test case for international law since Nuremberg.' Amnesty was intimately involved in the case, both institutionally and at the personal level, because of the scandal, as it became, of one of the law lords who ruled on the case, Lord Hoffmann. It was said he had not declared in court his membership of a charitable branch of Amnesty International.

(But it was registered in the House of Lords, for anyone who cared to ask.)

The first round was held before the Lord Chief Justice, Lord Bingham, and two other judges. Pinochet's lawyer won. The Crown Prosecution Service, arguing for his extradition to Spain on behalf of the Spanish state, had not only lost, it seemed the case had little future. Lord Bingham, although giving leave to appeal to the House of Lords, had concluded that Pinochet had committed the alleged offences whilst head of state and that therefore, under the doctrine of sovereign immunity, his immunity could not be challenged. The House of Lords, to most people's surprise, overturned this judgement, deciding by three votes to two that Pinochet did not have such immunity. But nineteen days later Pinochet's defence team announced they were impugning the House of Lords' decision on the grounds that the South African-born judge, Lord Hoffmann, was compromised by his association with Amnesty, an active witness in the case.[1]

In judicial circles it was no secret that Lord Hoffmann was an Amnesty activist. Indeed, as a lawyer, he had argued a case before the High Court about the charitable status in Britain of many of Amnesty's activities. Not only had the House of Lords never questioned its own judgement before, but his colleagues, led by senior judge Lord Browne-Wilkinson, did so without consulting him either formally or informally. In the closed circle of the court, whose membership was only twelve, it seemed a damning personal slight and Hoffmann was deeply wounded.

In a new judgement, a new group of law lords decided to scrap the previous verdict and order a new hearing. This time there were to be seven judges with the senior judge, Lord Browne-Wilkinson, presiding. In the event, the delay allowed the anti-Pinochet forces to marshal world experts on international law and to give them time to make their submission in a more substantial way. Amnesty itself, in a long and detailed disposition (it should be remembered that never before this case had a high court anywhere allowed a non-

---

[1] For a comprehensive legal and constitutional analysis of the Pinochet hearings the reader is referred to Diana Woodhouse (ed.), *The Pinochet Case* (Hart, 2000).

governmental organization to file an argument on such a sensitive political matter), argued that torture was an international crime and there was no immunity. On 25 March the court agreed by a majority of six to one that Pinochet could be prosecuted. At the same time it narrowed its ruling from the Hoffmann court, stating that Pinochet's alleged crimes could only be considered from 8 December 1988, the date by which Chile, Spain and the UK had ratified the UN Convention Against Torture and it had taken effect in British law.[1]

The case now passed to the home secretary, Jack Straw, to decide whether extradition proceedings should continue. He decided affirmatively. Again, his decision had been preceded by intense lobbying from Amnesty, who argued that it was irrelevant that the period under which Pinochet was accused of acts of torture had been reduced. Both Amnesty and magistrate Garzón had found ample examples of torture committed on Pinochet's watch, post 29 September 1988. 'According to the Convention Against Torture', argued Amnesty, 'even one case of torture would be sufficient to a state able and willing to try the person accused. This will be the only way to give a chance to justice, to prove that international law goes beyond the signing of treaties and to offer to victims and relatives of human rights violations in Chile an opportunity to have their claim answered after twenty-five years of waiting.' Amnesty added the point that Pinochet's victims included 1,198 'disappeared' people. Their families will continue to suffer anguish until their fate is resolved.

Amnesty, with its voluntary membership, each person donating a relatively small amount of money, was up against the apparently bottomless resources of the Pinochet legal defence team. The *Independent* reported that his two British lawyers, Clive Nicholls QC and Clare Montgomery QC, were charging respectively £500 and £350 an hour and their ten backroom solicitors were costing £4,500 a day. Pinochet, for his part, spent all his time, except when called before the magistrates court in October (where the validity of the extradition order was upheld), under house arrest in a fine mansion

---

[1] It was incorporated into English law by Section 134 of the Criminal Justice Act, 1988.

in Virginia Water in Surrey. He told a Chilean newspaper: 'In this world they also betrayed Christ.'

Yet, for all their financial and legal prowess, the Pinochet camp realized, as 1999 drew to a close, that if they were going to have any chance at all of winning their man's release they had to switch tactics and pass up the appeal they lodged with the magistrates court due to be heard in March 2000. They played their last card – Pinochet's clearly deteriorating health.

Straw succumbed to their appeal and agreed to appoint a panel of independent doctors to assess whether Pinochet was fit to stand trial. Although only one of the four-person panel spoke Spanish – and Pinochet's English was limited to a few words – they decided that recent strokes and a deteriorating capacity for understanding all but the simplest matters meant that he was probably not up to the rigours of a trial. Their verdict was submitted to Straw, who after a few days' reflection told the House of Commons on 12 January 2000 that he believed Pinochet was unfit to stand trial and he was 'minded' to allow Pinochet's release. But, he added, he was prepared to listen to the views of interested parties.

Amnesty and its colleagues went into battle once again, insisting that the medical report be made available to the parties in this case. Joined by the Belgian government, they first lost their request, renewed it and then won what they had asked for. But their efforts to allow doctors from other interested countries – France, Switzerland and Spain, as well as Belgium – to perform their own independent examinations were turned down.

Then on 3 March Straw finally pulled down the curtain. He announced his decision at 8 o'clock in the morning. Amnesty's legal team perused the order and realized 'within minutes' that an attempt to challenge it would fail. The Chilean government had an air force plane waiting and Pinochet was in the air by ten minutes after one. He'd spent seventeen months in British hands.

Pinochet's plane touched down in a Santiago air base to a red-carpet, full-dress welcome from his successor as armed forces chief. Looking hale and hearty Pinochet left his wheelchair and waved happily to the large throng of well-wishers. The doubters and cynics muttered that he looked more than fit to stand trial and that by staging such a greeting the army had once again thrown down the gauntlet to the government. But the new Socialist government-in-waiting of Chile, elected on 16 January 2000 and due to take office in March, headed by Ricardo Lagos, who had been the murdered Allende's ambassador to Moscow, promised that the end of the road was not yet reached. Only a month after his election, in an interview in the Brazilian weekly *Veja*, in which he was asked 'Are there conditions to judge Pinochet in Chile?', President-elect Lagos replied: 'It's my duty as president to create those conditions. Anything else would mean our democracy is a lie.'

However, he also made it clear, reiterating the point on a number of separate occasions, that the matter is for the courts. Meanwhile, he said, he was going to try to persuade the Christian Democratic-led opposition, whose candidate for president he defeated by only a narrow margin, to agree to change the constitution's undemocratic clauses which give the army and Pinochet himself political power through their permanent representation in the upper chamber of parliament, the Senate. If he fails, said the new president, he would put the question to a plebiscite. On 2 July 2000 the Chilean Supreme Court, although numbering a significant number of Pinochet's appointees, lifted Pinochet's senatorial immunity from prosecution. Ariel Dorfman commented:

The past is not as easily killed as some in power would like to proclaim. The hidden light of the men and women who gave what they believed cannot be extinguished while there is one person in this world who is willing to remember and resurrect them. That is all it takes. 'One person crying out in the ethical wilderness, one person, and then one more, then another' – that is all that is needed to keep the spark of justice alive.

In January 2001, after much legal manoeuvring, Pinochet was finally subjected to a court-mandated medical examination in a military hospital. On 17 January the results were made public. It was clear that the Chilean doctors had done a much more thorough job than their British counterparts. Indeed, Luis Fornazzari, the neuro-psychiatrist on the team, criticized his British colleagues for a lack of expertise. 'The examinations carried out in London were very insufficient for a diagnosis,' said Dr Fornazzari. The Chilean doctors concluded that Pinochet's strokes had been light enough that there was no severe damage to the brain and he was fit enough to follow and understand the course of a trial.

On 29 January Judge Juan Guzman, his interrogation of Pinochet completed, announced that he was formally charging Pinochet with murder. He was immediately confined to house arrest. The streets of Santiago erupted into song and dance. What had seemed impossible became possible. The end was in sight. Everyone, friend or enemy, soldier or ex-dissident, knew that there was a real chance Pinochet would finally come to trial. (A later decision by the appeals court narrowed down the charges to 'covering up' homicide.) The world would be a safer place than it was before, not just in Chile, but everywhere.

Pierre Sané often mused, he told me, about how a number of fortuitous happenings had come together in the most extraordinary way to bring Pinochet to within almost physical reach of Amnesty's headquarters. But in the end, although Pinochet wriggled free of the hook, he was but one fish, albeit a big one, in the new pond of crimes against humanity.

For years Amnesty had campaigned for the UN Conventions on Torture and Genocide[1] and, in recent years, for the war crimes tribunals for ex-Yugoslavia and Rwanda and, most important, for a general court to cover war crimes and crimes against humanity, the International Criminal Court.

In the early 1970s, Amnesty had had a long internal debate before moving into this more political arena. The first question to be answered was whether a broadening of the mandate would undercut the work with political prisoners. The reply to that seemed to be: in the short run, perhaps a little; in the long run, it should mean fewer political prisoners on their books, an eventuality that by the end of the millennium came to pass. The second question was this: was any

---

[1] Although adopted by the UN General Assembly in 1948, the Convention on Genocide did not have real effect until the USA finally ratified it in 1988, after a long campaign by human rights activists.

other organization more competent to campaign for such bodies? In Switzerland, there were the Committee Against Torture and the Geneva-based, long-established International Commission of Jurists, an association of lawyers from all over the world that campaigned for a widening of the law to embrace the outlawing of torture and war crimes. But the answer to that was obvious: Amnesty was not only a world-wide organization, it was the only one with popular appeal, a body which when it spoke got instant media coverage and the quick mobilization of a very sizeable membership. Perhaps Amnesty could move the rocks on the path that others had failed to dislodge.

An affirmative answer to these two questions begged a third. Did Amnesty believe that present-day outbursts of ethnic hatred, and the pogroms, genocide and torture that follow, are due more to leadership manipulation than ancient animosities? The evidence, as events unfolded in countries as diverse as Cambodia, Iraq, Yugoslavia and Rwanda, seemed to be clear. In every case the combustible material was consciously set alight by unscrupulous leaders intent on consolidating and enhancing their own power, prestige and geopolitical reach. It was this that had set Amnesty firmly on the path to fight for an International Criminal Court. From that moment on the risk of future Pinochets, Saddam Husseins or Slobodan Milosevics using unbridled power to squash their opponents or eliminate alienated minorities would be tempered by the realization that they could well end up in the dock of the court. As Richard Goldstone, the former chief prosecutor for the ex-Yugoslavia War Crimes Tribunal, has put it, 'There's only one way to stop criminal conduct in any country. If would-be criminals think they're going to be caught and punished, then they're going to think twice.' Already, Amnesty researchers have noted that the 'Pinochet-effect', as they call it, is working.

The passage of an international law to outlaw torture from idea to convention is one of Amnesty's most important success stories. On 10 December 1972 Amnesty launched a world-wide one-year Campaign for the Abolition of Torture. Chairman Sean MacBride called torture an 'epidemic' perpetrated by regimes 'to control dissent and maintain power'. Amnesty, he said, was setting itself the task of making torture 'as unthinkable as slavery'. He pointed out that the

Universal Declaration of Human Rights in Article 5 stipulated that no one should be 'subjected to torture or to other cruel, inhuman or degrading treatment or punishment'. In his encyclopaedic book *NGOs and the Universal Declaration of Human Rights*, William Korey observes that Amnesty's campaign

was one of the most successful initiatives ever undertaken by an NGO. In the course of a fairly short time-frame, masses of people were involved, along with numerous NGOs, in pressuring governments and, ultimately, the UN General Assembly to brand torture among the vilest of crimes and to erect a set of institutions to combat it. The campaign was impressively orchestrated, with a variety of individual and separate initiatives integrated into the overall effort, each reinforcing the other.

Ironically, it was the coup in Chile that gave an enormous boost to Amnesty's Campaign for the Abolition of Torture. It gave a sense of immediacy and urgency to everything Amnesty had been saying, spilling over into the UN General Assembly, which began its session only days after the coup. At that time most Third World countries were highly suspicious of 'Western' critiques of their human rights behaviour. But Allende was to many of them a heroic figure, and they suspected that the US was behind his overthrow. They willingly made use of Amnesty material in their efforts to blacken Pinochet's name. The number of countries who addressed the subject for the first time in the General Assembly debate made a remarkable jump. Communist eastern Europe joined in too. Bulgaria, not known for its attachment to political liberty, singled out a report by Amnesty on Chile, and the Soviet Union referred to testimony submitted by Amnesty, the International Commission of Jurists and the Women's International League for Peace and Freedom.

Nigel Rodley,[1] Amnesty's chief legal officer, led the campaign himself. A highlight of his work was the Fifth UN Congress on the Prevention of Crime and the Treatment of Offenders held in 1975.

[1] Rodley was the first Amnesty staff member to be knighted, on the recommendation of Prime Minister Tony Blair. In 1993, he became the UN's Special Rapporteur on Torture. In his many years on the staff of Amnesty he drew only the standard Amnesty salary, forsaking the usual rewards of clever lawyers.

Amnesty spent a year preparing for the Congress – lobbying governments, submitting a sixteen-page document with a series of recommendations and sponsoring two seminars on torture at the Congress itself. No stone was left unturned. It had its effect. The Congress agreed on a moving Declaration Against Torture. Amnesty followed it up with a massive world-wide lobbying attempt to persuade the General Assembly to adopt the Declaration. On 9 December of that year, they succeeded – extravagantly so. It was adopted unanimously.

It took another nine years of hard, grinding work before the UN finally approved a legally binding treaty against torture, in 1984. It came into force three years later. The list of those who fought for it in these years includes the expected – Scandinavian governments and Holland – and the quite unexpected – the US administration of Ronald Reagan.[1] But it was Amnesty International, with its combination of attention to detail and zeal of purpose, that carried the day. Without that degree of energy the Convention Against Torture would never have seen the light of day – and Pinochet would never have been arrested.

Already, Amnesty researchers have noted that the 'Pinochet effect' is working. In early August 1999 the former Ethiopian dictator, Mengistu Haile Mariam, wanted in his own country for crimes of genocide and torture, suddenly left Zimbabwe, where he had been given shelter for years. Reportedly, he moved his residence to North Korea, one of the few countries that will not consider a UN demand for extradition. Also in mid-August 1999 Izzat Ibrahim al-Douri, Saddam Hussein's right-hand man, who led the forces that bombed and gassed thousands of Iraqi Kurds in 1988, was spotted in Vienna at the expensive Doeblinger Clinic. A member of parliament, Peter Pilz, appealed to the Justice Department to have him arrested on charges of genocide and torture. While the Justice Department dithered, Izzat Ibrahim made a dash for the airport and safety.

[1] A more detailed description of the vicissitudes of the campaign and the intricacies of the debate can be found in my columns in the *International Herald Tribune* of 6 October 1983, 29 March 1984, 1 December 1984 and 20 May 1987.

Next time, however, with another case the Austrian government will probably feel compelled to move more quickly and effectively. Also in late August of that year the former Indonesian dictator General Suharto cancelled the trip he makes annually to Germany for medical treatment. The journey was more imperative than usual, following a stroke and intestinal bleeding. But the fear of an arrest warrant for authorizing army massacres in East Timor appeared to be an effective deterrent. Indeed, if Pinochet's advisers had had their wits about them, they would have noticed a landmark prosecution in Britain in September 1998. A Sudanese doctor, resident in Scotland, was charged in connection with the torture of detainees at a secret detention centre in Khartoum in 1990. He was charged under 1988 criminal justice legislation which brought British law in line with the UN Convention Against Torture.

The international atmosphere on crimes against humanity has in the short space of three years undergone a pronounced change. The time seems long past when France, in 1986, provided the deposed Haitian dictator 'Baby Doc' Duvalier with a refuge on the Côte d'Azur. Or the ex-dictator of the Philippines, Ferdinand Marcos, was given the right to live out his days in Hawaii. Part of that can be explained by the sheer cumulative horror of the post-Cold War decade. But part is the growing strength and effectiveness of the human rights lobby, in which Amnesty International is a key player.

In December 1999, in a landmark ruling, a seven-judge panel of the Inter-American Court, the judicial arm of the Organisation of American States, made public a landmark ruling on the human rights of children. The case revolved around two Guatemalan police officers who were finally convicted of murdering two teenaged street children after savagely mutilating them. Eyes had been slit, ears and tongues slashed and a boiling liquid poured over one of the victims.

The two officers had been cleared by Guatemalan courts, but the case was taken to the Inter-American court by lawyers briefed by Covenant House, Latin America, an outreach organization for street children in Central America and Mexico. The court, in a sweeping decision, concluded that Guatemala had violated seven articles of the American Convention on Human Rights, including those that outlaw torture and specify the rights to life and to effective and impartial justice. With as many as forty million children living and working on the streets of Latin America, the ruling is a warning shot across the bows to the numerous police forces and vigilante groups who hound, persecute and, on occasion, murder street children. Following the judgement, Guatemala itself is required to investigate, prosecute and punish those responsible for both the crimes and the miscarriage of justice, including judges who have acted negligently. The government is also required to pay damages to the victim's families.

The early months of 2000 also made it clear how the war-crimes movement was gaining momentum, despite the set-back of the USA refusing to vote for a permanent International Criminal Court eighteen months before. The USA itself – along with much of the membership of the UN – was pushing the new, democratically elected government of Indonesia to agree to the setting up of an international war crimes tribunal on East Timor. (East Timor, once a Portuguese colony, had been invaded by Indonesia in 1975 and occupied ever since. On the overthrow of the dictator, Suharto, it had been promised its independence in 1999, only to be threatened by a campaign of massacres and intimidation backed by the Indonesian army.) In the event, the new government of Indonesia rebuffed the international effort, arguing that its own official inquiry into human rights could do the job. The inquiry, in fact, was exceptionally thorough, not only blaming the Indonesian army for much of the violence but forcefully attacking ex-president Suharto, whom the government later charged with massive corruption. The newly elected president, Abdurrahman Wahid, asked for the resignation from his cabinet of General Wiranto, the former head of the armed forces. Nevertheless, the USA and others kept the threat of an international war-crimes tribunal alive, insisting that it be regarded as an option unless General Wiranto and a number of his close colleagues were formally prosecuted. The situation was aptly summed up by the East Timorese resistance leader and Nobel Peace Prize laureate, José Ramos-Horta. 'In this day and age,' he commented, 'you cannot kill hundreds of people, destroy a whole country, and then just get fired.'

All around the world the urge to prosecute war crimes seemed to gather further speed. A Congressional commission in Brazil filed a petition to indict Paraguay's Alfredo Stroessner, the most durable dictator of the twentieth century until his overthrow in 1989, who now lives in exile in a mansion in Brasilia. In Argentina, which briefly jailed its military junta before pardoning its members in 1990, the former dictator Jorge Videla and eight other leaders of the 'dirty war' are back under arrest, facing charges that they stole babies (for adoption) from female political prisoners. In Uruguay, a new commission has been formed to investigate the whereabouts of people who disappeared under the country's former military government. Calling him 'Africa's Pinochet', human rights groups and individuals who say they were tortured during the rule of Hissene Habré, the former dictator of Chad, announced they were prosecuting him in Senegal, where Mr Habré lives in exile.

'Do the principles of international justice apply only to Europe or do they apply in Africa as well?' asked Reed Brody, advocacy director for Human Rights Watch in an interview in the *New York Times*. According to Mr Brody, during Habré's eight-year rule, vigorously supported as a Cold War friend by the USA and France, his secret police killed tens of thousands of people and tortured as many as two hundred thousand out of a population of only six million. At the end of January 2000 a group called the Chadian Association of Victims of Political Repression and Crime, representing 792 people, lodged criminal charges against Habré with a Senegalese court in Dakar. In early February, a judge made a formal indictment. Habré was then placed under house arrest. It was the first time in Africa that a former head of state has been charged in one country for atrocities said to be committed in another. In March, however, there was a change of government in Senegal and the newly elected president Abdoulaye Wade appointed Mr Habré's lawyer as his special adviser. He also removed from the case the judge who had indicted Habré. Not surprisingly, in July the court decided to drop the charges. Pierre Sané felt it almost as a personal blow. He had been overjoyed when Senegal became the first nation in the world to ratify the International Criminal Court. Now, he said, 'My country seems to be going backwards. Nevertheless, I still think the momentum of events is on our side.'

4

Amnesty's Forty Years

Amnesty International has many enemies – and lots of friends. Its membership, now more than a million world-wide, is still increasing. It has supporters in over 160 countries and territories. Thirty years ago the secretariat employed nineteen people and had an annual budget of £35,000. Today, it staff is 357 with an additional 93 volunteers. There are more than 4,200 local groups plus youth, student and professional groups and it has a budget of £19.5 million, none of it sought or accepted from governments. It may still be small compared with most international non-governmental organizations, but its impact on individual lives is perhaps greater than any of them.

Only forty years old in 2001, it was the product of the imagination of one man, Peter Benenson, a Catholic lawyer of Jewish descent, born of English and Russian parents, described by some who know him as a 'visionary', even a saint; a man, however, who, some people think, went through a period of losing faith in the creature he had created, to the extent that he nearly succeeded in destroying it.

Benenson, aged 40 when the idea of Amnesty came to him, had been active with the issue of human rights for a long time. He was defence counsel in a number of political trials, and in 1959 was a founder-member of Justice, an all-party organization of British lawyers which campaigned for the maintenance of the rule of law and the observation of the United Nations Universal Declaration of Human Rights. Then, in November 1960, his imagination was fired by a newspaper report about two Portuguese students in Lisbon during the dark days of the Salazar dictatorship. They had been arrested and sentenced to seven years' imprisonment for raising their glasses in a toast to freedom.

How, Benenson wondered, could the Portuguese authorities be per-suaded to release these victims of outrageous oppression? Somehow a way must be devised to bombard the Salazar regime with written protests. It was, as Martin Ennals, a future Amnesty secretary-general observed later, 'an amazing contention that prisoners of conscience could be released by writing letters to governments'. As Benenson nurtured the idea, it grew roots and branches in his mind. Why, he thought, have just one campaign for one country; why not a one-year campaign to draw public attention to the plight of political and religious prisoners throughout the world? Nineteen sixty-one seemed a good year to launch his effort – it was the centenary of the freeing of the slaves in the United States and of the serfs in Russia.

Benenson approached two people in London whom he thought would be interested in the idea and whose reputations and contacts would help give it momentum: Eric Baker, a prominent Quaker, and Louis Blom-Cooper, the internationally known lawyer. The three men decided to call the campaign 'Appeal for Amnesty, 1961'. Their aims were limited but clear-cut: to work impartially for the release of those imprisoned for their opinions, to seek for them a fair trial, to enlarge the right of asylum, to help political refugees find work, and to urge the creation of effective international machinery to guarantee freedom of opinion. At Benenson's office in London they would collect and publish information on people whom Benenson was later to call 'prisoners of conscience'. The three men spoke to their friends and soon had a nucleus of supporters, principally lawyers, journalists, politicians and intellectuals.

Benenson sought the support of his friend David Astor, long-time editor of the influential liberal Sunday newspaper, the *Observer*, who agreed to provide space for the new group's opening shot. Benenson decided this should be published on 28 May, which was Trinity Sunday, the Christian feast day celebrating God the Father, Christ the Son, and the Holy Spirit. Benenson, always the man for symbol-ism, had conceived a method that was to last for many years – 'A Threes Network': each group of Amnesty supporters would adopt three prisoners and work for their release. One would be from a communist-bloc country, one from the West, and one from the Third World.

The article appeared in the *Observer* spread over a full page. *Le Monde* simultaneously carried its own piece, and the next day other newspapers picked it up – the *New York Herald Tribune*, *Die Welt*, the *Journal de Génève*, Denmark's *Politiken* and Sweden's *Dagbladet*, as well as newspapers in Holland, Italy, South Africa, Belgium, Ireland and India. Even in Barcelona a newspaper, taking a risk with the Franco regime, gave it a mention.

The *Observer* article focused on eight people whom Benenson called 'forgotten prisoners'. Among them was Dr Agostino Neto, an Angolan poet, later to become the first president of independent Angola. He was one of only five African doctors in Angola, but his efforts to improve Africans' health, combined with his political activities, had proved unacceptable to the authorities. He was flogged in front of his family, dragged away and imprisoned in the Cape Verde islands without trial. Another 'forgotten prisoner' was Constantin Noica, a Romanian philosopher who had been sentenced to twenty-five years' imprisonment for 'conspiring against the security of the state' and 'spreading propaganda hostile to the regime'. The others were Antonio Amat, a Spanish lawyer imprisoned without trial for three years for trying to form a coalition of democratic groups; Ashton Jones, a 65-year-old American minister who had been repeatedly beaten up and imprisoned three times in Louisiana and Texas for demanding equal rights for blacks; Patrick Duncan, a white South African jailed for his opposition to apartheid; Tony Abiaticlos, a Greek communist and trade unionist jailed for his anti-regime activities; Cardinal Mindszenty of Hungary, who had first been imprisoned, then made a refugee in his own country, trapped in the US Embassy in Budapest; and the archbishop of Prague, Josef Beran, also jailed because of opposition to his country's regime.

It was an effective piece of propaganda, which touched a wide range of political nerve centres. The reaction was overwhelming: a flood of letters and donations, together with a great amount of information on thousands of other prisoners of conscience. In a piece of inspired improvisation, this concern was channelled by putting sympathizers in touch with others who lived nearby and encouraging churches and schools to set up groups. Each group was to 'adopt' individual prisoners and then start pestering the life out of the governments responsible. They were to make contact with the prisoners' families, send them presents and raise money for them. Above all, they were to write to the prisoner, even if no reply was possible, in the hope that at least one letter would get through and a prisoner would know that someone somewhere cared about his or her plight. This idea, characteristically British – parochial, low-key, frugal, committed to working across ideological, religious and racial boundaries – was amazingly effective on the international scene.

Benenson asked a British artist, Diana Redhouse, to design an emblem for Amnesty based on a candle encircled by barbed wire. The image, which brilliantly illuminated the spirit of the movement, had come to him, Benenson said, when he recalled the ancient proverb, 'Better to light a candle than curse the darkness.' The first Amnesty candle was lit on Human Rights Day, December 1961, on the steps of the beautiful Wren church, St Martin-in-the-Fields, on the corner of Trafalgar Square. Like the square itself, St Martin's has long been the home of great causes that have needed a meeting-room, a concert hall or a pulpit. Benenson asked Odette Churchill Hallowes to light the first candle. Odette, as she is known far and wide, was the most famous British agent in occupied France; she was eventually captured by the Nazis and survived Ravensbruck concentration camp.

Significantly, while Odette was lighting the first candle, a group which included Carola Stern, the head of a large publishing house, and a journalist, Gerd Ruge, was establishing the first Amnesty branch outside Britain, in West Germany. Their first three adopted prisoners were a Soviet poet, a Jehovah's Witness in Spain, and a communist writer in South Africa. This was just a beginning: other national groups began springing up all over the place. It was import-ant to bring the groups together, to exchange and co-ordinate views. Only eight weeks after the Trinity Sunday launching, delegates from

Britain, France, Belgium, Ireland, Switzerland and the USA met in a café in Luxembourg. There was strong feeling on two counts. First, that Amnesty should not be a one-year flash in the pan; it must become a permanent movement. Second, it should change its name to Amnesty International. By the end of that year there were Amnesty groups in Belgium, Greece, Australia, Sweden, Norway, Switzerland, France, West Germany, Ireland, the Netherlands, the UK and the USA.

One critically important person who had offered his services early on was Sean MacBride. Later, because of his role on a UNESCO committee attempting to draft 'A New Information Order', he became almost an object of hatred by the West, particularly in the eyes of press commentators, who saw him as a stalking horse for totalitarian tendencies in the Third World and the Eastern bloc. MacBride, the only man ever to have won both the Lenin Peace Prize and the Nobel Peace Prize, managed to straddle the great East–West ideological divide better than most political figures. He was the son of an Irish Republican Party activist and became a member of parliament. By 1948 he was foreign minister of Eire. He worked with Benenson on much of the early planning of Amnesty, and helped establish high-level contacts. The first of what became regular missions to explore human rights abuses was initiated by MacBride. He and Benenson persuaded the weekly Catholic newspaper, the *Universe*, to put up the money for MacBride to take up the case of Josef Beran.

As a priest, Beran had been imprisoned by the Nazis in Dachau and Theresienstadt. After the communist coup in Czechoslovakia in 1948, he became the archbishop of Prague, but he fell out with the new government. Preaching in St Vitus Cathedral, he delivered a defiant sermon. The police raided his home and carted him away, and nothing was heard of him for two years.

Benenson had put pressure on the Czech authorities through their embassy in London and Amnesty groups in other countries had followed it up. But nothing had happened. MacBride was well enough placed to secure an interview with Jiři Hajek, the Czech foreign minister, although the prime minister refused to see him. MacBride wrote in his report back to London: 'I pointed out that it was in the interest of Czechoslovakia to reassure the world that its new constitution of 1960 heralded a new era of freedom. I found this direct argument had some influence and I left feeling more hopeful about the future.'

Nothing on the surface, however, seemed to move. Amnesty stepped up its campaign with more letters, telegrams and embassy lobbies. Eighteen months later the prison gates opened. Beran and four other bishops were freed – although they were put under house arrest and banned from religious activities. Of course, there was no way of knowing if it was Amnesty pressure or other influences that had brought about the release. But Beran was clear. He wrote to thank Amnesty for help in gaining his freedom. 'I pray for Amnesty International,' he wrote. 'I pray for all who support Amnesty.' Two years later he was allowed to leave Prague for Rome. A year after that he came to London – to light a candle for Amnesty.

Another apparent success in these early days was Louis Blom-Cooper's mission to Ghana. In January 1962 he went to investigate the imprisonment of Nkrumah's opponents. Five months later 152 detainees were released. The Amnesty membership began to feel that they had a machine that could fly. Built by the simple technique of letter upon letter, followed up by a personal visit to the country, it seemed to produce results.

The next mission was a visit by the Indian lawyer, Prem Kher, to the German Democratic Republic to investigate the case of Heinz Brandt, a trade unionist who had been spirited out of West Germany and was in jail in the East, awaiting trial. Kher procured an interview with the East German attorney-general, who assured him that Amnesty would be allowed to send an observer to Brandt's trial. It was an empty promise. The trial was held in secret and Brandt was sentenced to thirteen years and six months' hard labour. In 1963 Brandt became Amnesty's 'prisoner of the year' (an appellation used to produce added publicity but later abandoned because it was said to imply a competition). Two British clerics with contacts in East Germany, Paul Oestreicher and John Collins, visited the GDR to continue the pressure. The philosopher Bertrand Russell, probably the most powerful non-government voice then alive, also joined the campaign. He told the East Germans that unless Brandt was released, he would return the Ossretzky Medal which they had awarded him for his services to world peace. Brandt was released just two years after the Amnesty campaign began.

Altogether 1964 was a year that succeeded beyond expectation. Eire released thirty-seven prisoners on United Nations Human Rights Day. That summer Romania freed thousands of political prisoners. Greece, Egypt and Burma all took significant steps towards cutting down their prison population.

But 1964 also brought the fledgling organization its first internal controversy. This blew up around Nelson Mandela, held prisoner by the South Africans on the notorious Robben Island. He had been adopted as a prisoner of conscience in 1962 when he faced charges of trying to organize a strike of African workers and attempting to leave the country without a passport. He had been leading non-violent campaigns against the government's apartheid system for almost a decade. At various times he had been banned from holding meetings and had restrictions imposed on his movement.

In 1964 he was convicted on a sabotage charge and sentenced to life imprisonment. The British group who had adopted him decided that his turn to violent opposition to the existing government meant they could no longer support him as a prisoner of conscience, although they kept up their campaign for him to be released one day. This triggered off a far-reaching debate that was settled only when Amnesty decided to poll all its members. The overwhelming majority decided in favour of maintaining the basic Amnesty rule that Amnesty should not adopt as prisoners of conscience those who used or advocated violence. But many Amnesty members were unhappy at abandoning Mandela just as he was being incarcerated with little hope of ever coming out alive. In the end, a compromise was reached. Mandela would no longer be a prisoner of conscience, but Amnesty would make representations to the authorities if it thought the trial had been unfair, the prison conditions were severe or if torture was ever used. This kind of compromise, used many times later, remained a source of controversy, not least when employed at the time of the imprisonment of the Baader-Meinhof gang.

Amnesty has been through long debates on the issue of violence, constantly reaffirming that it will argue for the right of a fair trial and humane treatment whatever the alleged offence of the prisoner. On the other hand, it will not ask for the release of a prisoner if it feels he or she has been objectively convicted for activities involving the personal use or advocacy of violence, however just the cause. In an explanatory note outlining their position, Amnesty states that many observers have thought, wrongly, that Amnesty is opposed to violence in any circumstance: 'This is not so. Amnesty International's position is entirely impartial. Amnesty International would be applying a double standard if it insisted that the police and prison authorities abstain from any act of violence or brutality yet maintained that those on the other side should be allowed to commit such acts and yet be unpunished.' It is clear why Amnesty must at least have this policy. In an age when guerrilla activity is principally, if not always, a left-wing phenomenon, Amnesty needs to maintain the credibility, support and influence of the right and centre if its work is to succeed.

The next great divisive issue in Amnesty – and the one that was to trigger a series of events that nearly led to its destruction – was the 1966 report on army torture in the British colony of Aden. A state of emergency had been declared by the colonial administration after a hand-grenade was thrown at the British High Commissioner. Mass arrests were ordered and suspected terrorists were rounded up and detailed indefinitely without being charged.

Amnesty handed the job of investigating the situation to its Swedish section, which in turn selected as its investigator Dr Selahaddin Rastgeldi, a Swedish national of Kurdish extraction. (One of Amnesty's early rules was that members should not investigate cases in their own country.) His report was extremely incriminating, alleging torture and violence by British soldiers against Arab prisoners and concluding that the state of emergency violated the UN Declaration of Human Rights. He also said the British Foreign Office had prevented him from visiting the internment camps so he had been unable to check the allegations at first hand. The high commissioner refused to see Rastgeldi and claimed that there were no political prisoners in Aden.

There is conflicting evidence about what Amnesty's London office did with the report. Robert Swann, by then the general secretary, said that everything possible was done to force the Foreign Office to take action by threatening to release the Rastgeldi report. Benenson, however, claimed that the matter was deliberately being suppressed by Amnesty under pressure from the Foreign Office. In September 1966 he decided to act himself. After a visit to Aden to check Rastgeldi's story, he took the report and had it published in Sweden. The reaction in Britain was savage. A large section of the British press accused Rastgeldi of bias, claiming that he could not be trusted because of his Turkish/Kurdish origins.

Benenson's suspicions about Amnesty's collusion with the Foreign Office continued to fester in his mind. Why had no action been taken until he intervened personally? Had somebody in the organization been persuaded to suppress the Rastgeldi report? If so, at whose request? Through his own high-level contacts in the Labour Party, he was able to arrange meetings with the foreign secretary, George Brown, the attorney-general, Sir Elwyn Jones, and the Lord Chancellor, Lord Gardiner – the latter two former Amnesty colleagues. Their obvious embarrassment over the Aden issue deepened his suspicions that someone was working to keep the matter quiet. And top of his list of suspects was Robert Swann.

Swann, like Benenson, was an old Etonian and a Roman Catholic. Benenson had chosen him personally as somebody he could trust to carry on Amnesty's work while he devoted himself to his farming and to pioneering new ventures. Before joining Amnesty Swann had worked for the British Foreign Office in Bangkok, and he admitted to Benenson that his work had involved 'para-diplomatic' activities. He was adamant, however, that his links with the Foreign Office had not made him susceptible to pressure. Benenson was unconvinced. The atmosphere at Amnesty became supercharged. Benenson began to suspect that Swann and many of his colleagues were part of a British intelligence conspiracy to subvert Amnesty. To his way of thinking, the only way the organization could survive was by moving its headquarters from Britain to a neutral country such as Sweden or Switzerland. But he could not convince anybody else at Amnesty.

In the end, he decided to resign as Amnesty International's president. He went off to the United States to explore the possibility of founding a new organization. Later he went into a Trappist monastery in France to try to think things out. He continued to write to Swann but the correspondence only seemed to add to Benenson's suspicions. Then, after much thought, he decided to withdraw his resignation and to fight it out with Swann and 'those behind him'. He contacted Sean MacBride, whom he regarded as a friend who would support him. After some discussion, they agreed to appoint an impartial investigator and chose Peter Calvocoressi, then reader in international law at Sussex University, whose findings and recommendations they would accept. Swann was asked by MacBride to take an indefinite leave of absence.

Before the Calvocoressi report was halfway completed, another bombshell exploded. An American source disclosed that CIA money was going to a US organization of jurists which in turn contributed funds to the International Commission of Jurists, of which Sean MacBride was secretary. MacBride loudly disclaimed all knowledge of CIA funding, but Benenson became convinced that MacBride was tied up in a CIA network. His suspicions about a vast conspiracy ranged against Amnesty were intensified. The rift between Amnesty and Benenson deepened.

Shortly after this the atmosphere was poisoned further by revelations in the British press about Benenson's own ambiguous relationship with the British government. They were made by Polly Toynbee, then 19 years old, who had served as secretary to the great ex-West Indian cricketer Sir Learie Constantine on an Amnesty mission to the then British colonies of Nigeria and Rhodesia in 1966. In Nigeria, according to Miss Toynbee, 'We stayed in the Federal Colonial Hotel outside Lagos. We sat around doing nothing but drinking and entertaining the press. We must have spent an enormous amount but we never achieved anything. We never saw anyone important. We just got vague assurances that the prisoners were all right.' The mission then went to Rhodesia. Following the white minority's Unilateral Declaration of Independence from Britain the year before, there had been mass arrests of the African political élite. The Amnesty group, however, seemed unclear as to what they were supposed to be doing. There was also a 'seemingly endless supply of money. I could go to the bank and draw out two hundred pounds at a time. And there was no check on what I did with the money.' When Benenson went out to Salisbury to join the team, Toynbee asked him about the money and the rumours then floating around Salisbury that it was coming from the British government. According to Toynbee, Benenson admitted it.

Later, Toynbee was expelled from Salisbury, but before she left she was handed a bunch of letters which had been abandoned in a safe. The letters were from Benenson, written in London in 1966 to the Amnesty representative in Salisbury. They were written in a thin code, some typed, some in Benenson's handwriting. Some were signed Margaret and some Peter. They contained frequent references to 'Harry', which Polly Toynbee assumed was a code name for the British government. A few extracts:

12 January. The only news of any import comes from Harry: He's giving us the money we asked for.

20 January. Harry's present has arrived so all is well. Cunningham should reach you in about a week's time with part of the present.

1 February. According to my calculations you have £2,000 at Jack Grant and the better part of £1,000 from each of Bernard and Michael – total £4,000. You can if you need have another £1,000 on 15 February by the method to be explained.

2 February. Harry has developed a sudden enthusiasm for litigation. What with North Hull Harry wants a fair buzz of legal activity. Harry's financial problems apparently have been solved and he's in a generous mood.

Toynbee deduced that the last reference was to the Labour government's new-found political strength. (On 27 January Labour had won the crucial Hull by-election, raising their paper-thin majority from three to four.) Her revelations caused a scandal. A parliamentary question was asked in the House of Commons. Harold Wilson, the prime minister, decided to answer it himself. He admitted that there had been an approach to the government for help, 'and we thought it right to suggest possible donors who might be willing to help'.

Benenson did not deny that he had approached the government for money. In his view there was nothing wrong in taking British government money to help British subjects who were illegally imprisoned in Rhodesia by a rebel government. The money, he claimed, was for the prisoners and their families and was not a gift to Amnesty. However, before agreeing to the arrangement, the British government, according to Benenson, had insisted for political reasons that it should be done secretly. Benenson had agreed, but very reluctantly, and the fact that Amnesty denied all knowledge of the arrangement only served to confirm his suspicions about British intelligence's infiltration of the organization's leadership.

By the end of 1966 Amnesty was in a state of severe crisis and in March 1967 its five-man executive held an emergency meeting at Elsinore in Denmark to try to resolve it. Benenson refused to attend. Sean MacBride said that the organization's crisis had been brought about by 'a number of erratic actions' by Peter Benenson, whom he blamed for 'wild and wide-ranging charges and some unilateral initiatives'.

The executive confirmed Benenson's resignation. The post of president was abolished and the new post of director-general (later changed to secretary-general) was created. One of Amnesty's founder members, Eric Baker, was provisionally appointed. The row surrounding Benenson's resignation had caused a major split between Amnesty's London office and many of the foreign sections. The Swedish section in particular had been very disturbed about the possibility that London had been bowing to British government pressure, and threatened to withdraw from Amnesty altogether. It was some time before their confidence was completely restored.

Peter Benenson retired to his farm near Aylesbury. His relations with Amnesty were understandably strained for some time, and for a while he seemed more or less to abandon the organization he had founded and nurtured. But he was not out of the public eye for long.

In 1968 he founded the Coeliac Society, an international organization to help victims of this little-known digestive allergy, from which Benenson himself suffers. He never lost his interest in humanitarian issues and in the 1980s was involved in another movement, called 'Nevermore', which has the ambitious aim of abolishing all war. It concentrated mainly on the problems of refugees and was particularly concerned with the situation in the Horn of Africa.

Benenson's relations with Amnesty are now restored and the bitterness of the 1960s is long forgotten. But he still fervently believes that Amnesty should be based in a neutral country. The fact that the headquarters are in London, he once said, seriously inhibited the organization's ability to investigate the problems of Northern Ireland, which in Amnesty's early years was to be one of its biggest failures.

For Amnesty in 1967 the loss of Benenson was a bitter blow. He had been the heart and soul of the movement. An incredibly charismatic figure by all accounts, he could inspire other people with his enthusiasm and energy. In the early days of Amnesty he was able to accomplish a great deal through his personal contacts on his own initiative. He was answerable to nobody and missions and initiatives were often undertaken just on his say-so. There was little in the way of organization or administration – budgets were so small they were often worked out on the back of a cigarette packet in the pub. Everything hinged on Benenson's own personality and he inspired deep affection and loyalty in those who worked with him.

The loyalty he engendered was difficult to break. Even the people Benenson attacked for being involved with the British secret service were unwilling to criticize him. They were concerned about his state of health and felt powerless to help him. Many of them still look back on it all with pain. They resent what they saw as efforts by the press to exploit his vulnerability. Many of Benenson's friends and colleagues believe that he suffered terrible disappointment and personal disillusionment over the Labour government's handling of the Aden torture report. He expected better of a socialist government and especially of his friends in the Labour government.

Early 1967 was the nadir of Amnesty's fortunes. Its leadership had been divided, financial disaster loomed. It was simultaneously unpopular with the British Foreign Office and accused of being in the government's pocket. Morale was at rock-bottom. But Baker's level-headed industriousness did much to save Amnesty International from the early death widely predicted at the time. Between June 1967 and June 1968 the number of groups grew from 410 to 550; 293 of the 2,000 prisoners adopted were released. By the end of 1967 Amnesty was going from strength to strength.

In July 1968 Martin Ennals was appointed secretary-general of Amnesty International. He was to remain in the job for twelve years. A dogged, persistent, if not always effective, administrator was one part of him; the other was a man of strong political motivation that lent a certain cutting edge to Amnesty. He had won his initial reputation when he worked as general secretary of the Anti-Apartheid Movement. He was a man of left-wing sympathies, but one who had a broad perspective on life and by no means saw all virtue on one side of the political fence.

Ennals, as one intimate described him, was 'like a man building sandcastles, but without buckets and moulds. He just shovelled the sand together. Inevitably when people looked at the sandpie from one side they concluded it didn't look the same as from the other side.' He was essentially an inspirational figure rather than a nuts-and-bolts administrator. But his enormous warmth helped reduce the tensions that had built up in the earlier crises and he steadied the organization's nerves. He slept four hours a day. He could go anywhere he was needed at the drop of a hat and when he stepped down staff missed the man with the big heart.

Under Ennals's supervision, the organization grew and expanded. The mood of disillusionment in the West as the Vietnam war progressed helped it in its recruitment. The right-wing coup in Chile engineered by Augustino Pinochet in 1973, overthrowing a democratically elected government, also encouraged people to join. Amnesty became recognized in the public mind as the source of accurate information on human rights. Its capacities changed. Its purpose did not. It maintained a narrow focus on the prisoners of conscience, but it is a measure of Amnesty's achievement during

Ennals's secretary-generalship that human rights, instead of being generally regarded as a problem marginal to the real affairs of state, became the issue which determined governments' images in the eyes of the world. When in 1980 President Marcos of the Philippines abruptly cancelled the planned state visit of Chile's President Pinochet because of Chile's human right abuses, it was an indication that the world of the 1980s was very different from the one Amnesty had looked out on in 1961.

Not all the credit can go to Amnesty. The International Commission of Jurists, Freedom House (the New York-based human rights organization), the churches and the unions had all been active. But Amnesty symbolized the concern, provided much of the raw data on which other organizations based their efforts, and was a constant inspiration to groups of individuals around the world, in countries where persecution was an everyday occurrence, to set up their own human rights watchdogs.

Jimmy Carter's decision to make human rights the focus of his presidency was also a major milestone. Martin Ennals rightly foresaw that it would be impossible for the US government to sustain its commitment untainted. It was bound to become intertwined with other aspects of foreign policy and in so doing be devalued. Nevertheless, it did help to raise human rights to a new level of political potency. Certainly in Latin America, Washington's new concern emboldened church, labour and liberal groups to be more openly critical of their regimes. And it provided a yardstick against which the foreign policy of Western nations had to be judged, even when Carter began to turn his back on his earlier commitment. Amnesty – the atmosphere it created, the people it inspired – must take much of the credit for this. Certainly these were some of the factors that weighed with the committee which awarded the Nobel Peace Prize to Amnesty in 1977, for its contribution to 'securing the ground for freedom, for justice, and thereby also for peace in the world'.

Characteristically, Ennals did not go to Oslo to receive the prize himself. He already had another commitment – a conference in Stockholm to mobilize support for Amnesty's opposition to the death penalty. This was a cause close to Ennals's heart. He wanted Amnesty to replace its rather half-hearted concern with a fully fledged campaign. Instead, the International Executive Committee sent to Oslo a small delegation headed by the committee's chairman, Sweden's Thomas Hammarberg – the man who took over from Ennals as secretary-general in July 1980.

It was during Ennals's tenure that Amnesty became systematic about its method of work – in its missions and interventions. Not least, it had perfected the art of 'intervention by letter writing'. One example I came across, among many, illustrates how effectively Amnesty worked in those days. A trade union leader, seized in one of the big police swoops made in the Dominican Republic in 1975, was being held naked in an underground cell. Amnesty International learnt of the case and, after investigation, issued a world-wide appeal on his behalf. Letters were mailed addressed to him in prison and that Christmas members in many countries sent cards. The following January he was released by order of President Joaquin Balaguer.

The prisoner, Julio de Peña Valdez, later recalled the effect of the hundreds of letters and cards he received:

When the two hundred letters came the guards gave me back my clothes. Then the next two hundred letters came and the prison director came to see me. When the next pile of letters arrived, the director got in touch with his superior. The letters kept coming and coming: three thousand of them. The President was informed. The letters still kept arriving and the President called the prison and told them to let me go.

After I was released the President called me to his office for a man-to-man talk. He said: 'How is it that a trade union leader like you has so many friends all over the world?' He showed me an enormous box full of letters he had received and, when we parted, he gave them to me. I still have them.

In 1979 Amnesty International's regional liaison officer for Latin America met Julio de Peña in the Dominican Republic and showed him the case-sheet prepared by Amnesty International's research department after his arrest. De Peña read it carefully and slowly. There wasn't a single error in it, he said. He was astonished by how much personal information Amnesty had dug out about him.

Among those working for his release was a former refugee from

Nazi aggression, Hannah Grunwald, living in New York. She regularly phoned Balaguer to protest about the treatment of de Peña, who had now started to call her 'mia mama gringa' (my Yankee mother).

In 1999 61 countries were known to be holding prisoners of conscience. Extra-judicial executions were carried out in 38 countries. Political prisoners received unfair trials in 35 countries. People were arbitrarily arrested and detained, or in detention without charge or trial, in 51 countries. Armed opposition groups committed serious human rights abuses, such as deliberate and arbitrary killings of civilians, torture and hostage-taking, in 37 countries. In the last three years there were allegations of torture or ill-treatment by security forces in 150 countries; it was widespread in 70, even though 119 have ratified the treaty banning it. In 90 countries, the death penalty was in force, in many for politically related offences. (However, of this total, 23 countries have not carried out any executions in the last ten years.) Since Amnesty was created in 1961, it has dealt with the cases of 47,000 prisoners of conscience and other victims of human rights violation. More than 45,000 of these cases are now closed. Since 1973, Amnesty has issued 10,400 urgent action appeals.

The adoption group – now called 'Amnesty International groups' – is the central cog in the machinery Amnesty uses in its struggle on behalf of political prisoners. The adoption group might be based in a factory, church or a neighbourhood. A small group of people, often with not very much in common politically, but sharing a commitment to free speech, free thought and free association, write carefully worded letters to a prisoner, the jailer, the political authorities and anybody who might be able to help get their prisoner released. Amazingly there are instances, some well-documented like Julio de Peña's but most less so, where it seems to produce results.

Most of the letters go unanswered. Groups can work for years on behalf of prisoners and never know whether or not their work had achieved anything. Even if they are actually released, it is hard to know if the group was responsible for their freedom. Amnesty is always reluctant to claim credit in such circumstances. So keeping up morale is a major problem. In the end, the work depends on the sheer dedication of the group members. But it helps if new ways can be found of bringing pressure to bear, apart from the standard letter-writing rota. Publicity is a most powerful weapon, and local groups have devised interesting ways of attracting it.

One group in Islington, North London, had been working for more than two years on behalf of two political prisoners, one in the Soviet Union and one in Uruguay. The group noticed that both prisoners had a birthday in May. Why not have a joint birthday party? It seemed a good idea. They hired a local hall and invited the press, local politicians, trade union leaders, local businessmen and church leaders – anybody, in fact, who might be able to use their influence to help. The group provided food (including a birthday cake), drink and entertainment, all paid for out of group funds raised from membership. In return, the guests were asked to contribute to a birthday appeal on behalf of the prisoners and their families, and to take what other action they could to help get them released. Another of their ideas was a 'soup kitchen'. One day they provided people with a lunch of bread and soup in order to draw attention to the meagreness of a prisoner's diet.

But apart from what might be called 'publicity stunts', the Islington group tried to find more ways of bringing direct pressure on the Soviet and Uruguayan authorities. They discovered that their Russian prisoner had been a construction worker before his arrest, so they wrote to twenty-five construction companies asking them to appeal to the Soviets on his behalf. They did the same with the relevant trade unions in the belief that unions might get a more sympathetic hearing from the Russians. They had postcards and a short text printed in both English and Russian explaining who he was and why he had been adopted by Amnesty as a prisoner of conscience.

All these things take time and money and, most important of all, information about the prisoner. So each prisoner was allocated a case-worker in the local group whose job it was to find out as much as possible about his or her background – family, occupation, hobbies, interests, political causes and so on. Getting information from the Soviet Union was relatively easy, thanks to the chain of informants who are now expert at getting messages out. Consequently, the North

London group found they were devoting more time and energy to their Russian prisoner and less to the Uruguayan, about whom they knew little other than his name and where he was being held. At one time the level of interest was so low that they even considered abandoning him and asking the International Secretariat to allocate another case. But consciences were pricked and instead they appointed two new case-workers and redoubled their efforts on his behalf.

At the core of Amnesty is 'the mandate', a set of rules which determine the scope and limitations of Amnesty's action, and which, twenty years ago, when Amnesty was a smaller – and simpler – organization, was likened to an onion. The fundamental concern (the inner part of the onion) was to seek the immediate and unconditional release of prisoners of conscience. These were people detained any-where for their beliefs, colour, sex, ethnic origin, language or religious creed, provided they had not used or advocated violence. Second (the middle layers of the onion), Amnesty worked for fair and prompt trials for all political prisoners, and worked on behalf of such people detained without charge or trial. The third point (the all-embracing outer skin of the onion) was that it covered without reservation all prisoners, for whom Amnesty opposed the death penalty and torture or other cruel, inhuman or degrading treatment. All this still holds, but added to it is campaigning to end attacks on civilians in armed conflicts, the ending of impunity for human rights abusers, the ending of forcible exile, mass expulsions and the destruction of homes, and even (some would say this is making the Amnesty mandate too diffuse) the ending of abuse against women in the family.

No Amnesty group works for prisoners in its own country. Nor are Amnesty workers expected to provide information on their own country, and they have no responsibility for action taken by other groups or by the international headquarters about their own country. However, Amnesty groups are free to lobby their own governments to ratify and implement international human rights conventions and instruments.

Every prisoner of conscience whose case is taken up by Amnesty International becomes the object of a world campaign. The relevant government and prison officials are faced with persistent, continuous and informed appeals from a number of adoption groups urging a reconsideration of the case. Letters are dispatched to government ministers, embassies, leading newspapers and international organizations. Public meetings and vigils are arranged. Influential people are asked to add their names to petitions and protests. In emergencies, distinguished lawyers and jurists are sent to controversial trials or to plead for the life of a sentenced victim.

Individual Amnesty International members and adoption groups have a handbook which tells them what to do and lays down the rules of the organization. Amnesty International's monthly *Newsletter*, bi-monthly magazine and website keep them in touch with new developments and present to them the cases of three 'prisoners of the month' selected by researchers of the International Secretariat (more about this below). These are people who are in urgent need of help because they may be facing imminent execution, or they may be very ill or have been detained in bad conditions for a long time. Rapid action for prisoners and others who are in immediate danger from torture or execution is mobilized by the Urgent Action Network of around 85,000 volunteers in 85 countries. They are organized through e-mail, fax, courier and mail to send fast appeals on behalf of those at risk.

Originally, Amnesty International had a 'prisoner of the year' scheme which for a time proved fairly successful. Heinz Brandt of East Germany, who was 'prisoner of the year' in 1963, was released in 1964. In 1964 Julieta Gandra of Portugal, imprisoned since 1959 for 'plotting against the internal security of the state', was adopted as 'prisoner of the year'. Early in 1965 she, too, was released. However, the following year a teacher in Guinea, Madou Ray-Autra Traore, sentenced to five years for opposing the nationalization of education, was 'prisoner of the year'. His selection had hardly been publicized when news came that he had already been released. Amnesty International had to apologize for its activities on his behalf, and that year the scheme, already criticized by some members, was dropped.

Every two years around two hundred delegates from the national sections (and other bodies such as the UN and the Red Cross) attend the International Council, which is Amnesty's main, democratically elected governing body. It decides on long-term policy for the movement, discusses priorities for the coming year and reviews the activities of the national sections, International Secretariat and the International Executive Committee.

The nine-member International Executive Committee is elected by the International Council to implement policy. It meets usually four or five times a year. It gives general strategic guidance to the International Secretariat, and appoints its senior staff. Its chairpersons have been as varied as an Irishman (Sean MacBride), a German (Dirk Börner), a Swede (Thomas Hammarberg), a Chilean (José Zalaquett) and an American (Susan Walz). Currently the chairman is Mahmoud Ben Romdhane from Tunisia.

London HQ, although leaving much of the agitation work to the local groups, still makes many of the critical decisions. It is the researchers in London who examine who can be named as prisoners of conscience. HQ then passes on to the local groups the dossier containing information on the country and instructions for coordinated action, a case-sheet giving personal details of the prisoner, information about the arrest, trial and health, and news of the family.

Each prisoner-of-conscience dossier is compiled by, or under the supervision of, one of the researchers using information collected from press reports – not least from the local press, which, even if censored, may carry a line or two on an arrest – government statements, interviews with lawyers and refugees, and, often most important, news provided by recently released prisoners. The researchers build up links with local human rights organizations and exile groups. In certain parts of the world the church is a particularly valuable ally. Often, yesterday's adopted prisoner can be today's government minister, perhaps part of a government that is engaged in its own repression. Nigeria is one example. The problem then is keeping good relations while maintaining vigilance.

Amnesty reckons that approximately a third of a researcher's time is spent on investigating individual casework. The rest is spent studying legislative and political changes and preparing missions, reports, campaigns and policy proposals. The case of Norma A. gives an insight into how Amnesty works. (Although it is a case from over twenty years ago, the method has not changed.)

In October 1979 Amnesty's London office received a letter from an Argentinian refugee now living in Sweden. Juan V. wrote to Amnesty about the 'disappearance' of his brother. He also asked Amnesty to take up the case of Norma A., who, he claimed, was being held under PEN (*poder ejecutivo nacional*: national executive power), a notorious legal weapon widely used in Argentina whereby prisoners were held in preventive detention by presidential decree. With two sources of information now available, Amnesty decided to act. It wrote back to Juan V. requesting more information concerning Norma A., the circumstances of her arrest, where she was being held, and whether she was a member of any revolutionary group committed to violence.

In reply Juan V. provided extensive details about Norma. She had been arrested along with himself, his wife Marta and another man, Adolfo, in 1975, and charged with possession of subversive literature. Her only political connection was her membership of the Metal-workers Union. The lawyer appointed by the relatives of the accused was forced to leave the country after threats against his life. All four had been convicted and given sentences ranging from five to seven years. Norma was sentenced to five years, which, on appeal, was reduced to three years plus PEN. All the others had now been released but Norma was still being held in Villa Devoto jail. She had also been refused 'the right of option', which is enshrined in the constitution and entitles people detained under PEN to go into exile as an alternative to imprisonment. The other woman imprisoned with her, Marta, had been given permission to leave the country and was now living in Sweden. According to Juan V., Norma had visas for England, Sweden and France.

Amnesty then contacted the other two ex-prisoners, Adolfo and Marta, and they confirmed Juan's story. Amnesty also tried to find out if there was any reason why Norma was the only one of the original four who had not been released. Juan suggested that it might have something to do with her behaviour while in prison. He said that Norma had mixed a lot with members of guerrilla groups like the Montoneros and the PRT (Partido Revolucionario de los Trabajadores: Workers' Revolutionary Party) during prison recreation periods. The authorities held this against her. Amnesty then checked the story with sources on the ground in Argentina. Satisfied she could not be accused of belonging to a guerrilla group, the organization formally adopted Norma as a prisoner of conscience in October 1980. A French Amnesty group was asked to take up her case.

It is difficult to imagine just what emotions prisoners feel when they suddenly learn out of the blue that far away in London or Mexico City or Tokyo someone is actually aware of their existence and has written them a letter.

Friday, 9 June 1978 remains etched into the memory of 32-year-old Shahid Nadeem, a Pakistani television producer and trade unionist imprisoned four times for his union work and student political activities. It was a day of searing heat. One of his fellow prisoners died of heat-stroke. Eight others collapsed in the factory at the notorious Mianwali maximum security prison in the semi-desert region of the Punjab. It was also the day a letter arrived.

In 1978 Shahid Nadeem had been sentenced to one year's imprisonment and fifteen lashes. His crime: organizing a staff occupation of four television stations in Pakistan. The occupation was completely peaceful and followed a refusal by management to abide by a pay and conditions agreement. The security forces had moved in and more than a hundred arrests followed. Shahid Nadeem and thirty others were held in a cell measuring 10 by 15 feet. The next day they were tried in a military court. Within hours of sentence being passed, they were on their way to Lahore central prison. Two months later they were sent to Mianwali. There the prisoners worked in temperatures of up to 45°C. Shahid Nadeem's cell was next to an open toilet used by seventy prisoners, and the stench often made sleep impossible. Mianwali houses 1,200 inmates. There was no doctor.

Shahid Nadeem describes how at about 6 p.m. on 9 June 1978 a fellow prisoner arrived in his cell just before locking-up time with a piece of paper which he called 'your letter from the USA'. It was a copy he had made of a letter in the possession of the prison superintendent, who was studying it, suspecting it contained a secret coded message. Addressed to Shahid Nadeem, the letter said: 'You are not alone; don't lose heart. We pray for you. If there is anything you need, don't hesitate to ask.'

Nadeem later recalled that moment: 'Suddenly I felt as if the sweat drops all over my body were drops from a cool, comforting shower . . . The cell was no longer dark and suffocating.' Soon the whole prison knew about his letter from an Amnesty International adoption group member in San Antonio, Texas. 'My colleagues were overjoyed and their morale was suddenly high.' That evening the deputy-superintendent summoned him. 'He was so friendly and respectful I was shocked . . . He explained his dilemma as a God-fearing jailer who has to obey orders and follow the rules . . . The head warden also began to "behave himself". Taking their cue, the junior staff changed as well.' After a week, the original letter was handed over to Shahid Nadeem. He was later released, and often muses on how 'a woman in San Antonio had written some kind and comforting words which proved to be a bombshell for the prison authorities and significantly changed the prisoners' conditions for the better'.

Writing from prison in 1976 a martial law detainee in the Philippines sent this message to an Amnesty International group: 'I have just been adopted as a prisoner of conscience by your organization. Political prisoners in the Philippines have always regarded your organization as their beacon of hope and sentinel of human rights . . .' His words were echoed in dozens of letters that came out of camps and prisons in the Philippines during the long period of martial law imposed by President Ferdinand Marcos that ended only in early 1981.

Amnesty International sent a mission to the Philippines in 1975 and reported evidence of systematic torture. Case after case was taken up by the organization, and international appeals were made in an effort to halt the torture of prisoners. In early 1977 came a letter with more news. It read:

I was released from detention last December 14, 1976 – thanks to the efforts of your organization. Immediately after my release I was summoned to the office of under-secretary Carmelo Barbero where they showed me the folders of letters from Amnesty International pressing for the release of political prisoners ... I do hope your organization will continue to exert pressure ... There are still hundreds of political detainees. And the dictatorship continues to arrest and incarcerate political dissenters.

Critically important though they are, the adoption groups and their letter-writing and lobbying campaigns are not the only weapons in Amnesty's hands. The special mission is another important tool. Between April 1999 and March 2000 Amnesty sent 130 delegations to nearly 80 countries and territories, to countries as varied as Albania and Australia, and, more recently, as described in the Prologue above, to monitor a precarious situation in Nigeria.

Proposals for missions and suggested delegates are made by the Senior Management Team. Delegates are selected according to their specific experience, expertise, country of origin and gender. For example, the mission sent to India to collect evidence on what had happened during the emergency and to look at safeguards to prevent cruelty was led by James Fawcett, president of the European Commission of Human Rights. He was chosen because of his experience of high-level talks with officials of governments and supreme courts. In other cases, lawyers familiar with the legal traditions of a particular country have been chosen. Since the late 1970s missions have often included a medical expert. Mission members, apart from Amnesty's staff, are unpaid.

Missions are subject to a strict set of rules. For example, no mission is allowed to enter a country clandestinely. Often a decision is made not to make a statement to the press while the mission is in the country. (This avoids undue pressure for a statement on their findings.) A memorandum is then sent to the government with the findings and recommendations. In some cases, there will be follow-up exchanges with the government about the interpretation of the law, more detailed information on prisoners, and so on.

Not all missions publish the full results. Some are not sent for the purpose of enquiry but rather to present Amnesty's point of view, as in the case of an execution, or to witness a trial to make sure it conforms to international standards. Sometimes missions are refused entry into a country. In other cases, missions are harassed. For example, in July 1966 Nils Groth, a Danish lawyer sent to Guinea to enquire about prisoners of conscience, was arrested shortly after his arrival. He was detained without trial until September, when he was sentenced to ten years' hard labour for alleged espionage. Fortunately, he was released twenty-two hours after sentencing under a special amnesty declared by President Sékou Touré. In October 1970 in Iran, Hossein Rezai was arrested while accompanying a German lawyer sent by Amnesty International on a mission to investigate allegations of torture. The lawyer was expelled from the country but in October 1971 Mr Rezai was sentenced to ten years' imprisonment after a trial by a secret military court in Tehran.

More recently, in 1996 the secretary-general, Pierre Sané, was prevented by Thai riot police from delivering the organization's report on human rights violations in China to the Chinese embassy in Bangkok. In Togo in 1999 Sané was ordered to appear before a local judge on charges of contempt. Ameen Ayodele, an active member of the organization, was detained and tortured by Togolese security forces.

Often, traditional adoption and mission methods have proved insufficient or even harmful in certain situations, and Amnesty has had to develop new techniques to cope. In Guatemala, where there were 'no political prisoners, only political killings', the adoption system had to be virtually discarded. For many years applications to send a mission were ignored. The country was taken on in a more direct way with a public report sharply denouncing its practices. In some countries, such as Iran under the Shah, the Amnesty intervention on behalf of a prisoner was seen by the regime as proof of the prisoner's links with Western subversive organizations, and conditions sharply worsened as a result. In Malawi, Dr Hastings Banda announced that he would be happy to punish individually every prisoner named by Amnesty. In both cases, Amnesty switched attention from individual cases to the country's regime: special reports and press releases were issued in an effort to make sure the spotlight stayed on the general problem even though specific, personal lobbying efforts had to be quietened.

Amnesty groups are encouraged to develop their own new techniques. One group discovered the Soviet respect for telephone calls: having had no response to their letters, they made a call direct to the mental hospital where their prisoner was being held and had a remarkably frank conversation with the doctor in charge. It did not lead to a release, but at least the group was aware that it had registered its protest. Another group asked for a reverse-charge call to their prisoner in Greece and, although they couldn't speak to him, the director of the prison was in such confusion that he agreed to pay for the call. For the first time, the man on the spot became aware of international concern for the prisoners in his charge.

Often Amnesty gets feedback from governments, but only rarely do they acknowledge the force of Amnesty's criticisms. No government likes to admit that the release of a prisoner or the slow-down in executions or killings is due to pressure rather than clemency. But there are occasional stories, such as this one mentioned by Sean MacBride: unofficially and very much off the record, a high official of an East European country told MacBride that it was the cumulative effect, the infuriating load of Amnesty-inspired letters, which led his government to review the imprisonment of thousands of social democrats, priests and members of the old order who had been locked away for fourteen years. In 1965 the country released 12,000 political prisoners.

Less well known is the financial assistance that Amnesty sometimes gives. In the twelve months 1998/1999 the International Secretariat received donations for relief totalling £78,249. In the same period, drawing on relief funds already in hand, it sent £273,831 to prisoners and their families in Africa, the Americas, Asia, Europe and the Middle East. It also sends, whenever it can, medical supplies, books and funds for food and clothing. On occasion, too, it will pick up the legal bills. Relief often goes to the families of prisoners who are suffering hardship and deprivation because of the imprisonment of a close relative. Here are a few examples:

£600 to ex-prisoners of conscience in Ethiopia for general living needs;

£500 to enable a refugee to travel out of Jakarta, where he might be threatened with arrest and possible torture;

£386 to cover medical costs for a former political prisoner requiring surgery as a result of having been repeatedly beaten on the soles of the feet with an iron bar while in detention in Iran;

£2,000 to a rehabilitation programme for individual surviving victims of political terror under the regime of President Idi Amin of Uganda;

£1,000 for assisted emigration from Colombia to prevent an arrest;

£2,000 for assisted emigration from Xinjiang Uigur Autonomous Region of China.

Archana Guha was completely paralysed from the waist down as a result of torture during police interrogation in Calcutta, India. At the time of her arrest she was headmistress of a girls' school and, as far as Amnesty International is aware, was not involved in politics. She is believed to have been detained because the police suspected some of her relatives were involved in a violent left-wing political movement, the Naxalites. She was arrested at about 1.30 a.m. on 18 July 1974 and taken to Calcutta's then notorious Lal Bazar police station. Her hands and feet were tied to a pole placed behind her knees. The pole was placed across two chairs, so that she hung with her head down. She was hit on the soles of her feet by one inspector while another stubbed out burning cigarettes on her soles and elbows. The nails of her toes and fingers were also burned. Later that day she was again hung from a pole while drops of water were dripped on her forehead. The next day the interrogation continued. She was beaten on the head and forced to sign a paper she could not read. She was threatened with rape and beaten on the head with a rope. At this point she was unable to walk back to her cell. But she continued to be interrogated almost every day for ten days and was then transferred to prison as an 'under trial prisoner'. Her physical condition deteriorated rapidly; she often fell unconscious. She received no medical treatment. She could no longer walk. On the insistence of other women prisoners a specialist was eventually called in. But it was not until 22 December 1975, four months after transfer to prison, that Archana Guha, by then paralysed from the waist down, was taken to hospital for a minor operation on a gland.

She was returned to prison on a stretcher on 24 January 1976. On 9 February the prison authorities arranged for her transfer to Medical College, Calcutta, as a 'life-saving case'. She remained in hospital for nine months until she was released on parole. She could not walk. She was suffering from a lesion of the lower part of the spinal cord. After unsuccessful attempts to treat her in Calcutta lasting more than a year, her case came to the attention of an Amnesty International mission visiting India. The mission interviewed her and described her plight in its report.

Amnesty International's Danish Medical Group arranged for her to be taken to Copenhagen in January 1980 for intensive diagnosis and treatment. After two months of care she was able to rise from bed, steady herself and walk short distances without assistance. On 1 May 1980 she wrote from Calcutta: 'My friends and relatives are simply astonished to see me walk again! ... now I can walk and move! ... The secretary and colleagues of my school are waiting eagerly [for the day] when I'll be able to join the school. I have improved much in walking and climbing the staircase ... You have given me a new life – you have caused rebirth to me!'

A question often thrown at Amnesty is: how does it maintain its impartiality? How does it stop itself becoming an anti-establishment lobby? More than that, how does it make sure it doesn't become a left-wing lobby, since a social-conscience organization is bound to attract in its staff a disproportionate number of ideologically committed people? That it does remain impartial is evidenced by the abuse it has received equally from, say, the columns of *Izvestia*, the Soviet daily, and the South African regime of Piet Botha or today from the Malaysian government on the one hand and the Cuban on the other. Amnesty's brief reply to this constant refrain of abuse is to quote its own motto, the words of Voltaire: I may detest your ideas, but I am prepared to die for your right to express them. More precisely,

Amnesty International officials point to Article 2a of its statutes, which requires the organization 'at all times [to] maintain an overall balance between its activity in relation to countries adhering to the different world political ideologies and groupings'.

In practice, Amnesty has a method of work that goes a long way to protect it from partiality. During the Cold War years adoption groups had to work simultaneously for at least two prisoners of different ideological, political or religious persuasions. Groups are still not allowed to work for prisoners arrested by their own governments. The selection of a prisoner to be adopted is carefully controlled. Before researchers make a final decision, they must check their judgement with a researcher working on a different country. If any doubt then arises, the choice can be referred to the Borderline Committee, which is made up of three people from different countries, appointed by the International Executive Committee. Each month Amnesty researchers propose cases they consider suitable for inclusion in the world-wide appeals. These proposals go to an editorial board headed by the deputy secretary-general, which makes the selection.

The organization is careful not to get drawn into campaigns that support the beliefs of prisoners. It does not co-operate with exile groups in their lobbying or other activities. Whenever possible, major reports are sent to the government involved before they are published. Comments are invited. Amnesty insists it will always publicly correct its errors.

Fund-raising has to be carefully watched. Ever since the Rhodesia scandal in 1966 it has been a sensitive issue. Money will be accepted for use for a specific purpose, but cannot be limited to research on one particular country. Any donor who would want to give more than 5 per cent of Amnesty's income at any level of the movement must be vetted by the International Executive Committee. Amnesty takes great pride in the fact that it is independently funded, and receives no government's funds except those for relief work and educational programmes. Far the greater part of Amnesty's funding still comes from individual members and donors.

*

When in mid-July 1980 Thomas Hammarberg took over from Martin Ennals, he had a hard act to follow. Thirty-nine years old, Hammarberg was by background a journalist, a former foreign editor of the popular paper *Expressen* and a correspondent for Swedish Radio. Politically a social democrat, he was probably nearer to the centre of the political spectrum than Martin Ennals. A former chairman of Amnesty International, he had an intimate feel for the organization, a detailed and practical knowledge of the issues that concern it, and a well-developed political sense. Diffident in manner, his appointment suggested that, after Ennals's exuberance, Amnesty consciously wanted a low profile for its leadership. The issues it was now handling were difficult and sensitive. A man with an ego, even a 'presence', might complicate the already difficult job of making Amnesty's criticisms palatable.

Hammarberg's watchword was clarity. One of his lieutenants described him as like the guy who comes in with the ruler and measures all the angles on Ennals's old sandcastle and decides to rebuild the walls and make them solid and straight. He wanted those who spoke on behalf of Amnesty to have clarity, coherence and consistency. But he didn't tinker with the vision.

One story told about him recalls a visit to Hanoi in December 1979 to discuss the issue of political prisoners with the Vietnamese authorities. Just as official talks were about to begin, a messenger came in and whispered in the ear of the senior Vietnamese hosting the mission. A BBC news bulletin had just announced that Amnesty had accused Vietnam of holding more political prisoners than any other country. Amnesty's diplomacy looked as if it was skewered. The Vietnamese were irate. Hammarberg set to work to assure them that the BBC had got it wrong. It was Amnesty policy, he told them, never to make comparisons. The rough edges soothed by Hammarberg's gentle but purposeful arguments, tempers cooled and the Amnesty team was allowed to stay and continue its work. In June 1981, after exchanges of memoranda with the Vietnamese, Amnesty published a report calling for the abolition of re-education camps, officially said to hold some 20,000 people who had not been charged or tried.

Hammarberg presided over an organization that doubled its membership and level of financial support in his first two years. An ambitious target – half a million members world-wide and a budget of £4 million. But the big question he confronted was whether the organization would acquire twice the vigour, or whether it would become more careful, cautious and weighty, chewing over its decisions among more staff, losing its former straightforward effectiveness.

The great strength of the Amnesty he inherited was its lack of pretension or cultivated sophistication and its ability to react quickly to turbulent events. Hammarberg, with his cardigan and sandals, easy smile and soft-spoken manner, was determined that it would stay on its current course. But dealing with the Vietnamese was perhaps easier than confronting the cold logic of bureaucratic growth in which caution started to replace spontaneity and Amnesty faced the danger of itself becoming a prisoner, hemmed in by the inertia of size and the immobility of responsibility.

It is difficult to say at what point the bureaucratic standardization, and its inevitable corollary, the push to uniformity, began to intrude on the earlier way of doing business, which, spontaneous to a fault, sometimes veering to the undisciplined, was nevertheless tellingly effective. This development may well, indeed, have gained impetus during Hammarberg's tenure, when his efforts to reorganize and streamline were done with a Swedish eye for maximum output and effectiveness. (Not for nothing has the relatively small country of Sweden made such an impact on the world outside with its great multinationals as various as Ericsson, Volvo and Tetrapak.) Attention to detail combined with great efficiency, all done with maximum regard for avoiding conflict by talking things out, is at the heart of the Swedish model. Hammarberg's unpretentious style certainly had some of this.

Nevertheless, a year after Hammarberg took over, the organization still could give the impression of being run by the seat of its pants, as I well recall from a long conversation with Richard Reoch. At the time he was not only Amnesty's head of information, but an all-purpose general, not least because he could often be found in the office at all times of day and night. He told me what had happened the weekend before. At 11 o'clock on the morning of Saturday, 28 February 1981 the telephone rang at Amnesty's old office in Covent Garden. Reoch took the call, since Amnesty, beguilingly if perhaps deceptively amateurish, then had no duty officer for the weekend, not even an answering machine. The call was from Buenos Aires. The caller identified himself. Reoch recognized his name because his brother was one of Amnesty's adopted prisoners whose case had been featured in an appeal for the Abolition of Torture campaign.

As Reoch took notes, the caller told him the police had arrested Dr José Westerkamp, who had toured Europe to raise support for the campaign on behalf of his son Gustavo, an adopted prisoner of conscience. Also arrested were Boris Pasik, Carmen Lapace and Gabriela Iribarne, who had lived in Canada for the past fifteen years and was only in Argentina on holiday. 'We don't know where they are. My mother is now at the central police headquarters trying to find out.' He went on to tell how plain-clothes police had entered the offices of the Centre for Legal and Social Studies at 9.30 the evening before. They had presented an arrest warrant. Reoch told the caller that he would contact the Amnesty researcher on Argentina and phone him back.

The researcher was traced at an Amnesty meeting outside the secretariat building. By noon she had been briefed and was ringing Argentina for more details. She was told of new developments: the arrest of Emilio Mignone, a leading lawyer who often conducted the defence of political prisoners in Argentina, and of Augusto Conte MacDonell, the co-president of the Argentine Permanent Assembly for Human Rights. Two other lawyers working for El Centro de Estudios Legales y Sociales (CELS) had been arrested in their homes. Important files documenting abuses of human rights had been confiscated both from the CELS offices and the home of Mr Mignone. There was no news about which police station they were being held at.

These arrests were the culmination of a long period of police harassment and intimidation of members of CELS. They had been threatened, their homes placed under surveillance, and their post and telephone communications often intercepted. Most of those detained had sons or daughters who had either been abducted by security forces and 'disappeared' or had been severely tortured.

In the course of the afternoon Amnesty International received several calls from the USA and Canada, Europe and England from people active in human rights work, who were concerned about the situation in Argentina, and wanted more information from Amnesty. By chance, the former editor of *La Opinión* of Buenos Aires, Jacob Timmerman, was in London, and he visited the Amnesty offices to discuss the situation with the researcher. He made suggestions about people it would be useful to contact in the USA to help raise the alarm. The Amnesty International representative to the United Nations was also in London and she came in to discuss moves that could be made to influence the UN machinery.

It was important to alert the world to what was happening. A news release was drafted as soon as it was realized that so far the wire services had carried no information. Reoch consulted Amnesty's secretary-general on the basic outline of a statement, which was then issued to the news agencies AP, UPI, AFP and Reuters. The news release drew attention to the fact that Emilio Mignone had testified on behalf of CELS to the UN working group on disappearances. The group's report, published only the week before, analysed thousands of cases of Argentinians who had been abducted by security forces and never seen again. It included extracts from Emilio Mignone's testimony.

A film on two prisoners of conscience, one of whom was Gustavo Westerkamp, was due to be shown on British television the following evening, and included an interview with Dr José Westerkamp. Reoch phoned the BBC producers and arranged for a snap item on the arrests to be included at the end of the programme. The BBC also put him in touch with producers of a news programme being prepared for transmission in the morning. Contact was made with Amnesty International's Toronto groups, which alerted the Canadian media to the arrest of Gabriela Iribarne. The press officer in Toronto later told Amnesty that she had also spoken to Gabriela's father, who was living in Canada.

Meanwhile, on the advice of the researcher and the Amnesty representative at the UN, and with the agreement of the secretary-general, a telegram deploring the arrests was sent to the chairman of the UN Commission on Human Rights. A cable was also sent to General Videla, president of Argentina, urging that the reasons for the arrests be made clear and that the people be granted access to their families and lawyers.

The following day, Sunday, the press officer in Toronto told Amnesty International that Canada's major newspapers and networks had reported the events. The Amnesty International representative in Canada had also spoken by phone to the Canadian ambassador in Buenos Aires and, as a result, the Canadian government had asked for a representative to be allowed access to Gabriela Iribarne.

At about 8 o'clock on Sunday evening the news was phoned through that she and two others had been released. Reoch asked if the charge against the leading figures had been clarified, but apparently Gabriela had said, on her release, that she had been unable to see the others; however, police had told her they would be charged on Monday.

At 2 o'clock on Monday morning, the researcher received another call from Buenos Aires. She was informed that the Argentinian press had reported the case, stating that those arrested were being held incommunicado and would be charged under article 224 of the penal code for the possession of diagrams and plans of military establishments. (This carries a possible penalty of eight years' imprisonment.) The researcher surmised that the only plans of military establishments likely to be in the possession of the human rights activists would be diagrams of torture centres and secret detention camps drawn by former prisoners.

It seemed clear that those who remained under arrest would not be quickly released. Amnesty decided to issue an Urgent Action memo alerting its co-ordinators in a number of national sections to send telegrams to the Argentinian authorities urging that those detained be properly treated while in custody. By the middle of the week press coverage of the events was extensive. The Latin American correspondent of the *Guardian* wrote a major piece based on Amnesty information. A critical editorial appeared in the *Washington Post* and was reprinted in the *International Herald Tribune*. The *New York Times* carried a lengthy news item.

Exactly one week after the arrests, the phone rang again in the Amnesty researcher's office in London. The judge dealing with the case had called everyone into court for an announcement. At 11.45 that evening, a phone call from the American section of Amnesty brought the news that although the judge had said police investigations would be continued, he had issued an order for the prisoners' release, citing insufficient evidence. On 15 May 1981 a court in Buenos Aires cleared the defendants of all charges against them and ordered the return of nearly all confiscated documents. The judge ruled that the seized material had no legal value as evidence (it had not been taken in the presence of the defendants). Nevertheless, he ordered that certain papers should be sent to the military authorities because they contained accusations against members of the security forces.

For Amnesty, this was a typical piece of Urgent Action, which also highlighted two interesting facts: that relatives increasingly trusted Amnesty to take fast action and were careful to accumulate and pass on detailed information so that it could move into top gear; and that relatives and friends were prepared to take some personal risk in ringing directly Amnesty headquarters in London. And it also showed how the organization under Hammarberg kept intact that *esprit de corps* that Ennals had bequeathed.

Ian Martin, Hammarberg's successor, was of a different mould. Certainly less spontaneous. As head of the Asia research department he was known as a stickler for accuracy. No matter what country or issue, his meticulous handwritten notes were a common sight throughout his office. This didn't go down well with everyone. Some found the constant checking and redrafting of texts not only superfluous, but an unnecessary burden to already taxing jobs. The so-called 'approvals process' could have as many as seven different stages.

Needless to say, Ian Martin, who had gravitated to Amnesty from being secretary-general of the Fabian Society, a highbrow political education body affiliated to the British Labour Party, had his reasons.

Having worked close to government, although not in it, he knew how easily politicians could rubbish a non-governmental organization and how credibility was the greatest tool in Amnesty's cupboard. Amnesty, he well knew, had more than its fair share of enemies, in ministers, embassies and government-hired public relations firms, who lay in wait for the slightest error in an Amnesty letter or report that then could be used to undermine the organization's public persona.

In the five-and-a-half years that Ian Martin was secretary-general, he had to steer the organization through some of its most turbulent patches. For a start, the world landscape began to shift and by 1989 was in convulsion. The massive political changes throughout the Soviet Union and Eastern Europe were leading to the freedom of thousands of political prisoners and the demolition of the apparatus of state repression. Surprising as it seemed at the time, Amnesty knew its work was not ending in that part of the world. Indeed, it had to increase its vigilance as a single monolithic political system fractured into smaller, troubled fragments.

The changing political currents opened up new possibilities for the spread of Amnesty as a world-wide organization – often as former prisoners of conscience now sought to create groups in countries where that had previously been unthinkable. Part of Martin's lasting contribution to Amnesty was to welcome these activists into the Amnesty fold and to constantly urge that the organization broaden its global reach.

The new Amnesty needed to reach out to a new generation as well. Ian Martin was central to the planning of the pioneering rock tour led by Peter Gabriel, Bruce Springsteen, Sting, Tracy Chapman and Yousou N'dour. The Human Rights Now! Tour played twenty concerts in nineteen countries over a six-week period, reaching millions world-wide – distributing hundreds of thousands of copies of the Universal Declaration of Human Rights produced in dozens of languages. He was an unstinting traveller, leading twenty-five high-level Amnesty missions, to countries ranging from the USSR and Hungary, through Israel, Egypt and Syria to Cuba, Colombia and Peru.

To steer Amnesty's ship through these stormy waters, Martin

needed a strong leadership team inside the secretariat. He introduced a senior management group, comprising the heads of departments and two deputy secretaries-general. Below that, a broader management group included the heads of smaller units. Management training was identified as a pressing need, since people were normally hired for their political experience and specialist skills, rather than the increasingly complex skills needed to run a secretariat of some three hundred people recruited from nearly forty countries.

As secretary-general, he insisted on a review of the secretariat's recruitment policies to enable a far greater spectrum of nationalities to be brought into the workforce. At times the recruitment drive brought him into head-on conflict with the restrictive immigration policies of the UK, but there is no record of Amnesty having backed down. Perhaps the final tribute to the changes he introduced was that his own successor in 1992 was Pierre Sané from Senegal, the first secretary-general from outside Europe.[1]

The decision Sané took that carried the greatest political impact, both on the organization and on human rights as a whole, was to carry Amnesty into the forefront of the campaign for a United Nations High Commissioner for Human Rights. At the 1993 Vienna World Conference on Human Rights, Amnesty lobbied vigorously for this post, arguing that the international human rights structure needed to be strengthened – a high-level human rights advocate was needed within the UN bureaucracy itself. Sané knew too that the 170-nation conference needed to be able to show a result – voting for the High Commissioner would fit the bill. He was right. By the end of the 1990s Mary Robinson, the former Irish president, had transformed the position of High Commissioner into an outspoken figure carrying moral authority, a frequent sight on the world's TV screens and a force to be reckoned with inside the UN itself.

Pierre Sané was to be not only the organization's first Third World secretary-general but someone who, harking back to the more free-wheeling days of Martin Ennals, worried a lot of staff by openly

---

[1] Sané will be succeeded at the end of September 2001 by Irene Zubaida Khan, a Bangladeshi.

declaring he was going to shoot from the hip. One veteran staff member, recollecting Sané's first staff meeting, said that when he explained that in his view Amnesty International had a lot of political capital in the bank and could afford to take some risks and make mistakes, 'you could almost hear a gasp of air in the room'.

Soon after he took office the staff saw he meant exactly what he said. Angered by the genocide in Rwanda that the world had done little to head off – indeed the USA and Britain stalled a UN attempt to send in an intervention force – Sané took aim at the arms suppliers. Although Amnesty at that time did not have 100 per cent proof that the arms were coming in large part from dealers in Western countries in contravention of an official UN embargo imposed in 1994, Sané decided to wait no longer and spoke forcibly and in public about what Amnesty believed was going on, despite the reservations expressed by influential staff members. Only later did Amnesty marshal conclusive evidence that Sané had been right.

'Yes, we do have to work in a hurry,' he explained to me.

We do often have incomplete information and manipulating information is part of the conflict . . . But we always deal with reliable sources and do exhaustive cross-checking . . . If we want to check everything, we can be too late to be effective . . . If the weight of information converges in a certain direction then we may well decide to move. If we've dealt with reliable sources, and done some minimal cross-checking, the decision to go becomes a matter of judgement. If we have a situation like Rwanda and Burundi, and half a million lives are at risk and we still are not quite sure about this or that piece of information, I think I have a duty to put the organization into action . . . The world is different than it was ten and twenty years ago. There are more armed conflicts than there were. We are dealing with a situation where the speed of response can make all the difference . . . With Amnesty, as it was, we may be dealing with a guy in prison for ten years or more, working to get him out. But when we are dealing with arms being flown in to a raging civil war, time is not on our side. Speed becomes essential.

No wonder this puts the wind up those trained by Hammarberg and Ian Martin to measure every syllable. It does raise troubling questions. Is an unspoken reason for Amnesty's new speed the competition that now prevails in the human rights arena? Twenty years ago Amnesty almost had the field to itself. Now there are a plethora of human rights organizations, together with some offshoots of other non-governmental organizations which find that speaking out on human rights has become a necessary ancillary to their primary purpose – the Red Cross and Médecins Sans Frontières, for example. There is also the UN Human Rights Commission and its High Commissioner, which now has its own on-the-spot offices in troubled areas. Not least, there is the USA-based Human Rights Watch, that has carved out in a short time a very strong niche for itself, with a discipline that concentrates on evaluating country or area situations rather than concentrating on individual prisoners, as was Amnesty's original mandate.

The competition may be friendly. The organizations often work hand in hand, and with local human rights bodies, too. But they are competing for funds, volunteers, idealistic (if ill-paid) staff, press publicity and the ear of governments. To be seen as a careful laggard may not be the way to keep Amnesty as number one. One sees this in the corporate world in the recent setbacks of companies as varied as Marks and Spencer and Coca-Cola; upstarts and locally based companies can outmanoeuvre the old international brands.

It is a difficult predicament Amnesty faces. Credibility is everything and critics can point out a range of problems: press releases and reports issued with bad grammar and spelling, seemingly makeshift administration, unreturned phone calls, and the loss of face when Amnesty's allegations of Iraq's treatment of babies in incubators turned out to be without foundation.

When Sané is confronted with this sort of criticism he accepts it as the price. Yet speed is not always everything to him. He says he is not prepared to run Amnesty in the more authoritarian ways of most of his recent predecessors even if, on occasion, it slows down the decision-making. He believes in delegation; he doesn't believe in hierarchy. If there is a clash of wills or interpretation lower down the chain of command, he wants them to thrash the issue out between themselves rather than having recourse to him, the boss.

I want the strength of argument to prevail. In the long run, when people do what they have to out of conviction, they do it better ... I do have to mediate on occasion. Also, as secretary-general, I have one foot in the secretariat and one foot in the membership movement. The membership is often asking 'Why can't this be done? Or why can't the secretariat give a straight answer?' With Kosovo and Chechnya, for example, I had the movement asking 'Why can't we get into the field quicker? Why can't we issue authoritative reports faster?' So I'm engaged in conflict resolution inside Amnesty. I tell my secretariat that often their response is not good enough. On the other hand, I have to explain to our membership sections around the world the constraints the secretariat operate under. Our researchers can't quickly move into a war zone like Rwanda or Chechnya like a journalist. Our people don't have the protection of the more neutral journalist; we'll be seen often as very much on one side, as the enemy. That is life-threatening.

Amnesty is in some ways constrained by its mandate too, Sané argues.

We can't call for intervention, or the use of force. All we can do is to try and shame the actors, convince them that their own purpose would be better fulfilled by an adherence to international law. Of course, when a report of some atrocity first comes in one's first reaction is you want to kill those people. But our self-discipline is to get on top of those emotions. We want to bring to bear a civilized response. We believe in the law – and not the death penalty for personal punishment, or the force of arms in a larger situation. We become very uneasy, as in Kosovo, when the main Western countries say they are waging war in the name of human rights. We activists are very uneasy about this.

Not since Ennals has Amnesty had such an open secretary-general. No debate seems to be off-limits to him and he doesn't have the bureaucrat's natural fear of washing the organization's dirty linen in public.

When the stress gets too much he takes himself off to a spa in St Malo in France and thinks the unthinkable. He goes alone without his family and, while being rubbed down in a hot mud bath, he tries to work through one major problem. 'What was it this year?' I asked.[1] 'Kosovo raised a lot of questions. What alternative did we have to the bombing, if we want to avoid ethnic cleansing? In Rwanda half a million people were slaughtered whilst the international community stood by. If the UN had gone in might they have engineered a stalemate with less people killed?'

Much of the day-to-day, humdrum work of Amnesty continues under Sané's stewardship. Amnesty has initiated a number of broad educational initiatives, of which the 'personal pledge' to support the Universal Declaration of Human Rights is the most noteworthy. Thirteen million people from 124 countries signed up and the pledges were handed over at a ceremony attended by the UN Secretary-General Kofi Annan in the Palais de Chaillot in Paris, the building where the UN had adopted the Declaration exactly fifty years before.

The weight of the combined pledges was such that they could not be safely deposited on the floor of the stage. Pierre Sané made a simple speech: 'The pledges, signed by so many people from all walks of life in so many countries, show not only powerful global support for the Universal Declaration, but a demand to governments that they live up to the promise they made when adopting it – a world without cruelty and injustice.' Kofi Annan's response in accepting the pledges was similarly pointed: 'This is a day when the people have spoken, and have spoken as one. This is a day when they have put our conscience on notice.'

The organizational flair that made possible the assembly of this vast number of names was remarkable. In Ireland, a third of the total population signed; in Morocco, a million people signed; and in Tanzania, a country with appalling roads and a minimalist phone system, 600,000 pledges were made.

The campaign had begun with the Burmese opposition leader, Daw Aung San Suu Kyi, who lives under permanent house arrest, making the first signature. This was followed by the UN High Commissioner for Human Rights, Mary Robinson, and a spread of politicians, some of whom, doubtless, meant it more than others – Yasser

---

[1] This interview was conducted in late 1999.

Arafat, Tony Blair, Rafael Caldera, Jacques Chirac, Bill Clinton, Kim Dae Jung, Václav Havel, Yoweri Museveni, Lech Wałęsa, Ezer Weizmann and Abderrahmane al-Youssoufi. Human Rights activists also signed. So did the Mothers of Plaza de Mayo from Argentina, Danielle Mitterrand and Graça Machel. There were religious leaders such as the Dalai Lama and Archbishop Desmond Tutu and a number of popular entertainers and film stars, U2, Annie Lennox, Mick Jagger, Courtney Love, Nour Sharif, Harrison Ford and Julia Roberts. Not least, there were the national football teams of South Africa, France and the Netherlands and the great boxer and anti-Vietnam war hero, Muhammed Ali.

The Body Shop was one of several commercial companies that joined the campaign. Customers at Body Shop stores in thirty-four countries were invited to 'Make Your Mark', a thumbprint in favour of human rights. Altogether, three million of them did so. In the Netherlands, the television company AURO collected another three million signatures. MTV, the popular music channel, collected signatures from entertainers working in its many studios around the world. In Qatar, the satellite television station Al-Jazira promoted the campaign throughout the Middle East.

For Amnesty, this was a new way of campaigning. But it made sure it fused it with its tested way of seeking the protection of individual human rights defenders. Twenty-eight appeals were circulated. It had an impact. Many of them found the conditions of their confinement were improved and two were released – Dr Beko Ransome-Kuti in Nigeria and Akhtam Nu'aysa in Syria.

Both the campaign in support of the Universal Declaration and its next campaign, launched in 1998, 'USA: Rights for All', were firmly within the traditions of protest of Amnesty International. However, there were many – and some within the movement – who saw the second campaign as nothing more than Euro and Third World 'America-bashing', an age-old pastime in new guise. But Sané believed that it was appropriate to give special attention to the world's one remaining superpower, that has the influence to set much of the world's agenda. Moreover, it is a country that had long seen itself as the champion of the rights of freedom of the individual. Yet the USA, more than any other Western country, has 'failed to deliver the promise of rights for all'. Across the country people have been injured and killed by police using excessive force or deliberately brutal treatment. In many prisons inmates have been ill-treated, even tortured. Asylum-seekers are detained indefinitely in conditions that can be inhuman and degrading. Since 1990 more than five hundred people have been executed, some for crimes committed when they were less than 18 years old (see Chapter 9).

Sané also launched at the beginning of 1998 at the World Economic Forum in Davos, Switzerland, which brings together high fliers in business and politics, a campaign directed at business: 'Human Rights Principles for Companies'. These principles, drawing on the precepts of international law, summarize companies' responsibilities for human rights. Amnesty is pushing the business sector to respect human rights both in their own operations and when talking to governments. Amnesty now regularly gets itself invited to business conferences, where it discusses the need for companies to develop their own codes of conduct. And special Amnesty International business groups have been launched in Australia, Denmark, France, Italy, Switzerland, Belgium and the UK.

For the long run, Amnesty's most significant 'diversification' is the energy it is now putting into children's education. It is campaigning hard for the incorporation of human rights in all educational curricula. In late 1998 Amnesty produced a manual for teaching human rights in Africa. It was called *Siniko*, which in the African languages of Bambara, Mandingo and Dioula means 'things that we want for a future generation'. This was followed up by a training workshop in Dakar, Senegal, inviting delegates from the Côte d'Ivoire, Togo and Senegal, itself the homeland of Pierre Sané. In Morocco, Amnesty's local chapter has staged a national human rights forum for children and young people. It was attended not just by hundreds of children, but by youth workers and prominent figures in civil society. At the same time Amnesty Morocco organized a three-day workshop for thirty teacher-trainers. In neighbouring Tunisia, where the local branch set out on a similar venture, the authorities refused to allow an educational manual on human rights to be printed. In

Asia, similar moves are afoot. In Taiwan there have been a number of human rights education conferences. They have produced human rights teaching plans and materials. In Thailand, local Amnesty has organized a network to train teachers.

The Irish section of Amnesty has published *The Rights Stuff*, an educational resource manual. The local branch in Ukraine has developed and implemented an extensive programme of teacher training run by educators based in three different cities. They too have published a manual, for primary schools. In the Czech Republic and Poland there are now similar efforts. Amnesty has also brought together human rights education co-ordinators from all over eastern Europe, in part so that they could formulate a joint regional strategy.

In South America, the local group in Guyana organized a three-day music workshop, sponsored by the Ministry of Education, to develop musical themes that would convey a human rights message. Amnesty human rights educators now exist all over Latin America and they are designing a continent-wide strategy. In Peru they are training human rights education 'multipliers' who will then pass on to others the knowledge and skills they gain during training. In Mexico, the local group has published a manual. In Argentina where, not very long ago, some of the worst abuses of the twentieth century occurred, the local branch has published a book of children's stories with human rights themes. There is also an award to encourage children to write and draw their own. More than two thousand teachers have now been trained in the teaching of human rights.

All this is a long way from the early letters, newspaper articles and back-of-cigarette-packet-planned visits of thirty and forty years ago. It is, indeed, a rather different, much broader-fronted Amnesty than only a decade ago. Under Pierre Sané, the organization has not only mushroomed in size, but has spread its roots in a dozen different directions. Perhaps it could spread even faster if it had less bureaucracy and less control and direction from the top. Or perhaps it would, over time, just fizzle out as its more activist staff fired off in a thousand directions. Getting that balance right is Pierre Sané's constant pre-occupation. The organization is certainly more effective than it was, but perhaps not quite so much fun to work for. What began as one man's idiosyncrasy became a movement and now is an industry. Even the free-wheeling Pierre Sané with a gun at his hip cannot change that.

5

Northern Ireland – Britain's Dirty War

During the hearing at Bow Street Magistrates' Court in London on whether General Pinochet could be extradited to Spain to stand trial, his lawyer argued in his defence that 'there's torture everywhere, including in Britain and Northern Ireland'.

Indeed, it is true that only the degree is different. If in Chile it was inflicted on a large scale, with quite bestial methods meant to sexually degrade and physically near-destroy the detainee, in Northern Ireland in the early 1970s it was done, albeit to far fewer people, but still to great effect. If electrodes were replaced by high-pitched noise and the bucket of faeces to drown in was replaced by bright lights and sleep deprivation, the results were not dissimilar: unbearable distress and pain, and the urge to admit to anything to end the suffering.

Amnesty, not for the first time, was compelled to campaign in the country which had given it birth. For all Britain's long tradition of free speech and liberal democracy, which has inspired peoples all over the world, and given birth or nurture to many pioneering movements – against colonialism, against apartheid, against the death penalty and, not least, against the infringement of human rights with the founding of Amnesty International – the government had been able, as late as the 1970s and 1980s, to convince itself that, faced with domestic insurrection, although of limited numerical and geographical proportions, torture was a necessary counter-weapon.

The use of torture had been exposed in 1971 by the crusading journalism of the *Sunday Times*. But it was not until eighteen months later that Prime Minister Edward Heath decided that the reports, amplified in Amnesty's campaigning but, until that moment, fervently denied, were essentially correct, and he gave the order banning the use of five techniques of interrogation – hooding, subjecting to high-pitched noise, forcing to stand for long periods against a wall, and deprivation of sleep and diet. They were banned, although not without much disquiet within the army, the local Northern Ireland police force, the Royal Ulster Constabulary and, indeed, within the prime minister's own Conservative party.

Yet, nearly thirty years on, Amnesty was still publishing reports alleging the use of 'torture and cruel and inhuman or degrading treatment and punishment'. It made the charge in a briefing written in November 1998 for the UN's Committee against Torture, which monitors the Convention Against Torture and Other Cruel, Inhuman or Degrading Treatment or Punishment, which Britain, among others, had duly ratified. In the report Amnesty described and detailed deaths in custody, regimes of detention or imprisonment that were unnecessarily cruel, and cases of torture and ill-treatment by the police. If these allegations were no longer part of a systematic pattern of torture, as in the past, nevertheless, argued Amnesty, there were enough beatings and ill-treatment for police and army behaviour to come under the scrutiny of the UN Committee Against Torture.

Perhaps Amnesty was overstating it. An improper beating is not in the same class as the studied methods of torture chambers. Still, for a liberal democracy that believed it was leading the world in abiding by high judicial standards, it was a very serious charge. It allowed despots everywhere to argue, as Pinochet's lawyer did, that Britain upheld two standards, one for itself and one for others abroad. It also made Amnesty itself appear suspect in the eyes of some. Why did the organization not simply concentrate on abuses in its own backyard, rather than campaigning around the world?

The truth is Amnesty's work over thirty years in Northern Ireland has been both rigorous and sustained and carried out as a lonely effort without a great degree of support from Britain's own media, which, with noticeable and occasional exceptions, has not pursued the matter with the day-to-day diligence that Amnesty itself has demonstrated. The task of upholding the highest standards of human rights observance, moreover, won only modest support from the British judiciary and from the British parliament. Neither Labour nor Conservative governments come out of the history of the last thirty years with anything but a muddled record. Although governments of both parties tried, in the end successfully in 1998, to bring the antagonists to the peace table, in the course of the effort to stop the fighting much of Britain's proud heritage of fair play and the rule of law was trampled on.

Historians who trace the origins of the Northern Ireland conflict look back to the Middle Ages and the British drive for hegemony and control over all of Ireland. Its present-day division between Catholics and Protestants in Ulster, the northern province, is rooted in the late sixteenth and early seventeenth centuries when, following the successful crushing of Irish rebellions, British settlers, made up of English and Scottish nobles and war veterans, settled on the confiscated land that was called 'The Plantation of Ulster'. Since then the Catholic community in Ulster has lived as a discriminated-against minority within a Protestant majority.

When the Anglo-Irish war of 1919 was negotiated to conclusion in 1920, the compromise was to divide Ireland. The south gained independence. The Protestants of the northern six provinces, Ulster, remained as part of Britain, but with their own parliament. The Protestants, with a majority at that time of about six to four, ruled Ulster more or less as they wished, their numerical dominance strengthened by administrative advantages such as proportional representation and lopsided electoral districts. The segregation, if by no means absolute, was severe, infecting all aspects of daily life, schooling, housing, employment and job opportunities.

In the 1960s economic decline led to an increasing delegitimization of the political system. It was matched by the rising political consciousness of the young Catholics who, inspired by the effectiveness of the Civil Rights movement in the USA and student rebellions on the European continent, began their own Northern Ireland Civil Rights Association in 1968.

Perhaps inevitably, given Ireland's charged and violent history, a peaceful non-violent movement was infiltrated by militants more sympathetic to the old-style Irish Republican Army, the IRA. From the autumn of 1968 on, marches which hitherto had been largely peaceful began to disintegrate into violent clashes in part provoked by the Protestant-dominated police, the B-Specials. The IRA, effectively dormant since the end of the Second World War, reconstituted itself. In 1969 there was the first death. And in that year the IRA built up its strength by armed robberies and bombings. In response, militant Protestant Unionists founded the Ulster Defence Association, the UDA. In 1971 it planted a bomb in a Belfast pub and fifteen people were killed.

Unwisely, the British Labour government decided to send in the army, initially to protect the Catholic population. Ill-trained for urban conflict in its own land, it was too easily provoked, often overstepped the mark, and itself became a major provocative element.

The violence continued for almost another thirty years. In mid-1997 a cease-fire by the IRA changed the negotiating climate. Patient diplomatic work over the years by Prime Minister John Major, a Catholic leader, John Hulme, a Protestant leader, David Trimble, Gerry Adams of Sinn Fein, the political wing of the IRA, and, not least, the former majority leader of the US Senate, George Mitchell, the personal envoy of President Bill Clinton, who patiently and brilliantly chaired the critical negotiating sessions, had finally borne fruit. It took more tortuous months of negotiation, under the authority of a new British Labour administration led by Prime Minister Tony Blair, before a peace deal was finally agreed in April 1998. There was to be the formation of a joint executive in a newly devolved parliament for Ulster. It was thirty years and five months since the conflict's first death. Altogether 3,200 people had died, most of them civilians.

Internment without trial was introduced in Northern Ireland on 9 August 1971. That day, 342 arrests were made, and large numbers of arrests continued for several days. By the end of the week, the first reports of brutality on the part of the British army found their way into Irish newspapers. By mid-October, they had reached the British press, were taken up by the *Sunday Times*, and forced the government into action. On 31 August 1971 the home secretary appointed a three-man committee inquiry, chaired by Sir Edmund Compton, to investigate allegations of brutality. Amnesty, however, considered the inquiry hampered from the start by procedures which effectively, if not intentionally, prevented the complainants from testifying before the committee.

The committee did conclude that certain techniques, such as hooding, loud noise and sleep deprivation, had been employed by the security forces in an attempt to extract information from detainees. However, while the critics accused the security forces of physical brutality and torture, the committee's conclusions spoke only of 'physical ill-treatment'. It did not make a finding of brutality because 'We consider that brutality is an inhuman or savage form of cruelty, and that cruelty implies a disposition to inflict suffering, coupled with indifference to, or pleasure in, the victim's pain.' Amnesty, in a comment on the report, noted: 'According to this definition, the regretted use of electric shock to obtain information would be neither cruel nor brutal.'

About two weeks before the Compton Report was published in early November, Amnesty International set up an International Commission of Inquiry into allegations of torture in Northern Ireland. Unlike the official government inquiry, Amnesty heard evidence given by and on behalf of internees, ex-detainees and ex-internees. However, the UK authorities refused to co-operate and grant facilities to the commission. Members of the security forces were not permitted to testify.

Amnesty's findings concluded that 'it is a form of torture to force a man to stand at the wall in the posture described for many hours in succession, in some cases for days on end, progressively exhausted and driven literally out of his mind by being subjected to continuing noise, and being deprived of food, sleep and even of light.' The report presented medical and psychiatric evidence of the long-term damaging physical and mental after-effects suffered by the victims.

On 16 November, the day on which Compton handed in his findings, another government inquiry was launched – the Parker Commission – with the specific purpose of investigating the interrogation techniques. Although the majority report justified the methods used (provided there were safeguards against excessive use), Lord Gardiner produced a minority report. He refuted his colleagues' conclusions and leant strongly towards the Amnesty position. He described the interrogation methods in Ulster as 'secret, illegal, not morally justifiable and alien to the traditions of what I believe to be the greatest democracy in the world'.

Lord Gardiner's words were heeded. The Conservative government announced that the five techniques – hooding, subjecting to high-pitched noise, forcing to stand for long periods against a wall, and deprivation of sleep and diet – would no longer be used. In June 1972 the Palace Barracks, where these methods had been used, was closed down, interrogation decentralized and new regulations brought into force.

Nevertheless, the government of Ireland decided to bring a case against the UK before the European Commission on Human Rights. The investigation was exhaustive and dragged on for four years. Only in 1976 did the Commission in Strasbourg reach a verdict: guilty of 'torture, inhuman and degrading treatment'. Moreover, it found that this had constituted an administrative practice, condoned by the authorities. Two years later, after an appeal by the UK, the verdict was modified. The 'torture' count was dropped. Amnesty reacted to the Strasbourg court's modification with a sharp press release announcing that it would continue to denounce as 'torture' the use by any government anywhere of the interrogation practices used by the UK in 1971.

From 1972 onwards, when Amnesty published its path-breaking 'Report of an Enquiry into Allegations of Ill Treatment in Northern Ireland', the organization has maintained a fairly continuous drumbeat of revelations and recommendations. In a report published as recently as 1994, Amnesty went further than it had ever done before and accused the British government of complicity in political killings of IRA activists:

A series of killings by the security forces in 1982 gave rise to serious allegations of an official policy of planned killings of suspected members of armed opposition groups. Subsequent killings in the next decade increased suspicions that such a policy existed. Amnesty International remains unconvinced by government statements that the policy does or did not exist because such statements are not substantiated by evidence of an official will to investigate fully and impartially each incident, to make the facts publicly known, to bring the perpetrators to justice or to bring legislation concerning such matters into line with international standards.

Amnesty, in fact, was more than convinced that there was also active collusion in such political killings between the security forces and the armed paramilitary groups of the Protestant loyalist cause.

As a result of subsequent public protest, in May 1984 John Stalker, a senior British police officer, was appointed by the chief constable of the Royal Ulster Constabulary to investigate the cover-ups. Stalker was later to allege that he was obstructed from carrying out a full investigation. Before it was completed he was removed from duty in suspicious circumstances. The inquiry was completed in April 1987 by Colin Sampson, a British chief constable. The findings of neither have been published. But in January 1988 the attorney-general announced that the inquiry revealed evidence that Royal Ulster Constabulary officers had attempted or conspired to pervert the course of justice. However, because of 'national security' and 'public interest' considerations, no officer was prosecuted. (Disciplinary hearings led to eighteen officers being reprimanded and one cautioned.) John Stalker was later to state that he had uncovered new evidence of unlawful killings by the police. The inquiry had also reportedly recommended that charges be brought against MI5 (intelligence) officers for the deliberate destruction of a surveillance tape-recording of one of the killings. Amnesty International made it clear that the failure to bring prosecutions 'resulted in a concealment of evidence of possible unlawful actions of state officials. Furthermore, the failure to bring prosecutions for the destruction of the tape suggests that the government condoned the deliberate destruction of evidence in a potential murder case.' There were many subsequent such killings, when arrest would have been possible. Each time, the justification given by security personnel was identical: either that the person appeared to reach for a gun or was shot in self-defence or that a car drove through a road-block. In the killing of three unarmed people in Gibraltar in 1988, the soldiers testified at an inquest that the suspects appeared to be about to trigger a hidden remote control detonator. However, no such device was found on their bodies. When Amnesty called for an inquiry, Prime Minister Margaret Thatcher accused the organization of being 'IRA apologists'. So intense was the criticism of Amnesty by both the government and sections of the media that many British members resigned. Amnesty stuck to its guns and, finally, in 1995, the European Court of Human Rights declared that the killings by the British army were unlawful.

An earlier outcry from 1982 had led to the main responsibility for covert operations being returned to the army. In almost all the disputed incidents of killings since then the protagonists have been the army, not the police. Between 1976 and 1992, Amnesty believes, soldiers from the army's élite regiment, the Special Air Services (SAS), killed thirty-seven reported members of the IRA. There were no reports of SAS actions against loyalist paramilitaries. The unanswered questions, as Amnesty constantly reiterated, were whether the army, usually having received a tip about an impending IRA military action, could not, at least in some cases, have arrested rather than killed the paramilitaries. Were attempts to surrender disregarded? Indeed, were opportunities to surrender on offer, or was it simply a policy of 'shoot to kill'?

In a report, Amnesty recalled the events that led to the 1987 ambush of eight IRA men who were engaged in bombing a police station in the village of Loughgall. As they opened fire, they were shot by well-positioned SAS troops using machine guns. According to journalist Mark Urban, a senior army officer who played a key role in the operations said to him: 'Loughgall was a plum – it was an exceptionally heavy team of good operators. The terrorists played into our hands and everything went our way. Was it a decision to kill these people? I don't think it would have been phrased like that. Somebody would have said, "How far do we go to remove this group of terrorists?" And the answer would have been, "As far as necessary."'

Amnesty also reported the occasion in February 1985 when three IRA men were killed by the SAS while returning weapons to a cache after an aborted attack on police officers. At the inquest it was stated that an army patrol had encountered the armed men in a field and had only opened fire after the three men had pointed guns at them. Yet a pathologist testified that one of them had been hit by at least twenty-eight bullets, most of them fired as he lay on the ground. Moreover, all three had a single gunshot wound to the head, suggesting they'd been cold-bloodedly 'finished off'. 'The discrepancy between the testimony of the soldiers and that of the police suggested', concluded Amnesty, 'that the security forces had known of the IRA attack in advance, and supported the allegations that the SAS ambush was planned from the start to kill the suspects, regardless of the immediate threat or absence of a threat posed by them.'

Amnesty believes the British government had evaded its responsibility by 'hiding behind an array of legal procedures and secret enquiries which serve to cloud the issues'. For Amnesty the issues at stake are grave: 'Whether there was a policy at any official level to kill government opponents rather than to detain them; whether legislation acts as an effective deterrent to unlawful killings; whether disputed incidents are thoroughly and impartially investigated; and whether perpetrators of unlawful killings are brought to justice.'

Amnesty's approach to examining disputed killings has had three elements.

First, it has monitored investigative procedures to assess whether all the facts have been made known. Its conclusion is that in the main they have been ineffective. In some cases evidence has shown that police investigations have been deliberately superficial in order to protect the army and the RUC. When the Stalker/Sampson report was finally completed the RUC agreed that all further killings by the RUC would be investigated by an outside police force. But this has not happened. Any killings by the British army are also investigated only by the RUC.

In July 1991 Amnesty requested information on procedures for interviewing soldiers involved in killings. The government did not deign to reply. Since court proceedings involving security force personnel are rare, one of the main mechanisms for investigating suspicious deaths has been the coroner's inquest. Yet the deeply flawed inquests, the rules of which are more restrictive in Northern Ireland than they are on the mainland, obstructed the victims' families from obtaining the full facts. There was, more often than not, a refusal of security personnel to testify. There was the non-disclosure in advance of forensic and witness statements. Not least, there was a lack of legal aid. Inquests were often delayed inordinately, up to eleven years in one case. And the government has often issued Public Interest Immunity Certificates, which block the disclosure of crucial information concerning the planning of operations.

In January 1994 an inquest examined the circumstances of the killing of Seamus McElwaine, an IRA member. He had been shot dead eight years earlier by SAS soldiers as he was walking across a field to inspect a bomb. He was armed. According to Amnesty,

SAS soldiers did not testify to the inquest, only the commander of the SAS unit testified, speaking from behind a screen. Before the inquest opened the government issued a further Public Interest Immunity Certificate preventing disclosure of some details relating to the army's undercover operation . . . The jury decided that McElwaine had been wounded in an initial burst of gunfire, and that while incapacitated and in the custody of soldiers he had been questioned, after which he had been shot dead. The Coroner at the inquest, on hearing evidence by the surviving IRA member, said, 'If what you say is correct, that would have to be cold-blooded murder.'

Amnesty told the government that its investigative procedures in Northern Ireland do not meet the minimum standards as laid out in January 1988 by the United Nations Special Rapporteur on Summary or Arbitrary Executions. They also contravene the UN's principles on the Effective Prevention and Investigation of Extra-Legal, Arbitrary and Summary Executions, adopted by the UN Economic and Social Council in May 1989.

Second, Amnesty has monitored government action on the ground in Northern Ireland, in an attempt to establish the degree of collusion between the security forces and armed paramilitaries.

In August 1989, reported Amnesty, an Ulster Defence Association/ Ulster Freedom Fighters (UDA/UFF) spokesman justified the killing of a Catholic, Loughlin Maginn, by saying that he was an IRA member, and that this information was based on police files. There was a public outcry which led to the chief constable of the RUC appointing a senior British police officer, John Stevens, to investigate security leaks. By the end of 1989 he had compiled lists containing over 250 names of suspects on police files that had been leaked to the media or taken from copies pasted on Belfast street walls.

As a result of the Stevens inquiry, fifty-nine people were charged or reported to the Director of Public Prosecutions. The overwhelming majority, thirty-two of those arrested, were members of loyalist organizations. Amnesty regarded the inquiry as inadequate. By limiting itself to leaks of documents, the inquiry failed to look at evidence of collusion between members of the security forces and loyalist armed groups.

Amnesty also homed in on the case of double agent Brian Nelson, one of the UDA leaders arrested as a result of the inquiry. Shortly before his trial, the prosecution explained it was dropping fifteen charges, including two of murder. According to Amnesty, in the subsequent trial only 'fragments of the truth bearing on allegations of collusion emerged', even though the court proceedings confirmed that he was an agent of the army's Military Intelligence Service. 'It was clear', charged Amnesty, 'that the army and the RUC were aware of the flow of their own intelligence reports to the UDA, and their use in targeting suspects for killing.'

Since the Nelson trial Amnesty has monitored a number of other cases which have led it to conclude that the collusion it was alleging was an on-going business:

When killings by loyalists take place it has sometimes been claimed that just before the killing there was a heavy security presence in the immediate area, but that this was then removed, thus leading to the allegation that loyalist gunmen were assumed to have unfettered access to and from the scene of the crime . . . The ease with which loyalist gunmen raid homes in stringently monitored and controlled Catholic neighbourhoods and then leave without hindrance, has contributed to the lack of confidence in the RUC to provide full protection for the Catholic community.

Amnesty's call for a further and more extensive public inquiry has not been heeded, despite its rigorous compilation of further evidence and case studies.

Third, Amnesty compared British legislation with international standards and found it wanting: 'The laws and regulations in Northern Ireland which govern the use of lethal force by security forces are inadequate to prevent and deter unlawful killings.'

Article 2(2) of the European Convention on Human Rights speaks of 'absolute necessity' and 'strict necessity' to justify the deprivation of life. In contrast, the Criminal Law Act (Northern Ireland) of 1967 states that 'such force as is reasonable in the circumstances' may be used to prevent crime. Amnesty, however, believes that the concept of 'reasonable' use of force 'is too flexible both to improve standards of behaviour in the security forces and to deter excessive force'.

In 1991 Amnesty sought clarification from the government on what steps it had taken to bring international standards to the attention of official bodies in Northern Ireland. It also asked whether the government was considering formulating appropriate legislation and policy directives in order to implement UN Basic Principles on the use of Force and Firearms by law enforcement officials. Once again, there was no reply.

In November 1998 Amnesty published its briefing to the UN's Committee Against Torture on the occasion of the Committee's examination of the United Kingdom's third periodic report on the measures taken to implement the provisions of the UN Convention against Torture and Other Cruel, Inhuman or Degrading Treatment or Punishment.

The briefing was as dry as the above paragraph, but its contents were dynamite: 'Amnesty International is concerned about cases of political killings and inquest procedures which have impeded the discovering of the full circumstances in such killings.'

Amnesty singled out the case of an IRA member, Diarmuid O'Neill, who was shot dead by police in London in September 1966.

Initial statements about why he was killed proved false, since he was unarmed. Questions were raised about why he was shot after CS gas had been sprayed into his room. During the trial of people who were arrested when O'Neill was killed it emerged that there had been a tape-recording of the police raid on the house. The tape-recording contradicted oral evidence given by the police officers involved and raised serious questions about the circumstances in which Diarmuid O'Neill was killed instead of being arrested.

Amnesty also picked up once again the critical question of the inquest procedure, charging that the inquests still were not examining 'the full circumstances of deaths'.

The inquest, held in June 1996, into the killing of Patrick Shanaghan, a Catholic, by loyalist paramilitaries in 1991, exposed the inadequacies of the procedure. It was beyond the scope of the inquest to examine the police investigation of the incident and the RUC Chief Constable was successful in blocking evidence concerning allegations that while Patrick Shanaghan was held at Castlereagh interrogation centre his life was threatened by police interviewers who said his name would be leaked to loyalist paramilitaries.

Amnesty drew attention to the fact that cases of alleged intimidation and ill-treatment by the security forces had declined since the peace process began in 1994. Nevertheless, it 'continued to receive reports of ill treatment' and it singled out the case of David Adams to highlight the abuse that still occurred 'in the absence of essential safeguards for suspects detained under emergency legislation in Northern Ireland'. Amnesty campaigned hard on Adams's torture and ill-treatment in detention, issuing a special report and highlighting his injuries: fractured ribs, a punctured lung and an eye injury. In addition, his leg was broken by police who took running jumps at it.

In February 1998 the High Court in Belfast awarded David Adams £30,000 compensation for the assault he suffered in the hands of the police during his arrest in February 1994 and in the Scenes of Crime room at Castlereagh holding centre.

The Adams case was not alone. In 1996 there had been twenty-six formal complaints of assault lodged against interrogating officers. Although these were down from eighty the previous year, Amnesty was particularly concerned about the reports it continued to receive that detectives made comments during their interrogations, including death threats, about the suspects' lawyers. One lawyer was criminal defence and civil rights specialist Patrick Finucane. He was killed in February 1989 by the loyalist armed group, the UDA/UFF, who said he was a member of the IRA.

In April 1998, after years of campaigning by Amnesty and other NGOs, the UN Special Rapporteur on the Independence of Judges and Lawyers urged the British government to initiate a judicial inquiry into the allegations. The recommendation was ignored. Amnesty is still campaigning for an inquiry, convinced there is 'suspicion of an official cover-up'.

Amnesty believes that it contributed to the amelioration of some practices in Northern Ireland. During the 1980s the reports of systematic torture ceased. Its campaign for the introduction of audio- and video-recordings of interrogations bore fruit in the late 1990s. It also won reform of situations where access to a detainee had been heavily circumscribed. Northern Ireland was the only part of the UK where those detained on suspicion of terrorist activities were not allowed to have a lawyer present during interrogation.

In 1990 and 1991 Amnesty took up the cases of those assaulted during interrogation and lobbied the UN's Committee Against Torture to investigate. In 1991 the UN produced a report highly critical of the government and there was subsequently a marked decrease in the number of allegations of assault in custody.

Finally, after years of campaigning, the new Labour government made two important decisions. In February 1999, it set up a Human Rights Commission for Northern Ireland. Its chairman is an Amnesty International member, Professor Brice Dickson, and its first task is to draft a Bill of Rights for Northern Ireland. And it announced it was re-opening 'a full scale judicial inquiry' into 'Bloody Sunday', an event in 1972 when, it was alleged, the army opened fire on unarmed demonstrators, killing thirteen. The army was subsequently absolved of blame after an enquiry chaired by Lord Widgery, a former Lord Chief Justice.

Yet for all the progress made – the final peace settlement itself and the step-by-step ameliorations as just described –Amnesty cannot be said to have profoundly altered, or slowed, the direction of the conflict. For thirty years the 'troubles' had their own dynamic that seemed all but impervious to either reason or diplomacy. Whether it was criticizing the British government or the paramilitaries (including often the IRA), Amnesty's words fell most of the time on deaf ears. The protagonists were locked in conflict and could not bring themselves to the point, until very late in the day, when they could be at the same starting line. Amnesty had more success in foreign parts than it did in its own backyard.

'Many questions remain unanswered, especially in relation to the role played by military and police intelligence,' says Amnesty researcher Halya Gowan, responsible for the Northern Ireland desk. 'We need an independent mechanism to be established to deal with thirty years of state violations, if we are ever to arrive at the truth.' Her checklist is not particularly long, but it goes straight to the point:

- Investigation of the allegations of collusion between the Protestant paramilitaries and the security forces.
- A quick implementation of the recommendations of the official government-appointed commission chaired by Chris Patten, the former governor of Hong Kong, into the need for reform of the Royal Ulster Constabulary.
- The establishment of an independent inquiry into the covert operations of military intelligence and MI5. A civilian body to oversee intelligence and covert operations should be established.
- The formation of special units to investigate possible criminal offences by police officers.
- Make the chief constable of the RUC accountable to an independent body charged with reviewing operations which are deemed to involve national security.
- The creation of a civilian body which could step in and immediately review an investigation if the victim or the victim's family believe that a police investigation was not carried out thoroughly and impartially.

- The disbanding of those units within the RUC which are associated with patterns of human rights violations, in particular the Special Branch and its undercover armed units. The units should be reconstituted with new personnel and new leadership in order to ensure that they operate in an accountable and impartial manner.
- All emergency and anti-terrorist legislation needs to be brought to a swift end. Anything that remains on the statute book must not violate international standards on human rights.
- From now on lawyers should be able to attend all interrogations of those detained.
- Prisons must be radically reformed so that their conditions are neither cruel nor degrading.
- The Human Rights Act, introduced in 1999, should be amended so that its writ extends, not just to minimum standards, but to include the best practice as called for in international conventions on human rights, which often go beyond the requirements of the European Convention on Human Rights.
- An overhaul of the inquest system.
- A change of legislation on the use of lethal force.

The thirty-year war in Northern Ireland not only took an appalling and unnecessary toll on its people, it revealed with stark clarity how even the most liberal-minded democracy can succumb to the temptation to permit the security forces a free hand to take short cuts that would not normally be tolerated.

Of course, the torture and brutality meted out by the British army and the Royal Ulster Constabulary cannot be compared with that inflicted by their counterparts in, say, Chile or Guatemala. Nevertheless, by the self-imposed standards of a long-standing, mature state, governed by the legislation of freely elected parliamentarians and enjoying an independent judiciary, it has been a serious falling-short.

Human rights standards are not meant for periods of harmony in society, but for situations of conflict and stress in the body politic. In this light, successive British governments ignored the gospel they regularly preached to the world outside.

Perhaps the greatest tragedy of Northern Ireland was the lack of evidence that the British government, most of the country's media or even its intellectual class felt they learnt anything from the experience. Northern Ireland, although an integral part of the United Kingdom, was always off the political map for most Britishers. It was governed and watched as a world apart. It could have been Malta or Malaya, a colonial conflict in a faraway place, about which most of the British knew little and cared even less.

Yet this was not how the outside world perceived it. It asked more than once: how could the country that gave birth to Amnesty International become itself a state that bent the rules, subverted the law and undermined the world-wide raising of standards it was always intent on promoting?

If Britain couldn't behave better, why should anyone else?

6

Amnesty's Black Mark –
the Baader-Meinhoff Gang

Passions are not supposed to be engaged inside Amnesty International. There is a method and a purpose that transcends the passage of ideologies and movements that is meant to raise Amnesty personnel to the status of angels, unsoiled by the struggle, torment and conflicts beneath. Of course the reality is a poor shadow of the image. Amnesty is full of men and women with intense convictions, emotions and political beliefs.

It is in fact remarkable that Amnesty most of the time is so credibly impartial, does cast its net so wide, is independent of the big powers and maintains an internal discipline that gives it credibility in the four corners of the world. But there are events, usually close to home, that make Amnesty's life difficult, that tax its strengths and tempt its virtue. The Baader-Meinhof gang was one of these. The West German branch of Amnesty International took up the cause. And it proceeded to cajole and push London HQ to get involved in a case about which some members felt very dubious.

The guerrilla group, the Baader-Meinhof gang, which functioned in West Germany (as it was then) during most of the 1970s, was an outgrowth of the student turbulence of the 1960s. It called itself the Red Army Faction but the world knew it by its two leading lights, Ulrike Meinhof and Andreas Baader. Ulrike Meinhof, the daughter of two art historians, had been a gifted journalist and an ebullient star of Germany's radical-chic circles before she joined the guerrilla group. Andreas Baader, the son of a historian, was the original driving spirit of the organization and he was said by one critic to have 'infuriated all those who ventured close to him with a Promethean mission of fire and immolation'.

Their purpose was to overthrow the bourgeois state. They developed their maximum strength at a time when much of German society seemed inward-looking, with many of the older generation over-beholden to their Nazi past, concerned only with its own comforts and protection, and instinctively hostile to social and political reforms that would diminish its security and cosseted well-being. (Even more strait-laced protesters – such as Germany's present foreign minister, Joschka Fischer – were angry enough to throw cobblestones at the police, such was the temper of the times.) For most of their active lives, the leaders of the Red Army Faction were in prison, organizing from their cells, via a network of lawyers, friendly guards, friends and family, a means of escape. The great headline-hitting dramas – the escape to South Yemen, the shoot-out in the library of the university, the murder of Schleyer (head of the West German industrialists' federation), and the final audacious act of hijacking a Lufthansa airliner to Somalia – were all efforts at escape or obtaining ransom for release. Nevertheless, such was their ruthlessness, their organizational powers, their determination, that they seemed on occasion to rock the very stability of the state. Even when isolated from the outside world in whitewashed cells, lit twenty-four hours a day, they managed to communicate and organize. They seemed possessed of a laser-like purpose that could cut through prison walls and reach their targets unimpeded.

The Baader-Meinhof liaison began while Andreas Baader was serving a sentence for politically motivated arson. He had been allowed to continue his sociological research and received permission to visit the Sociological Institute in West Berlin. On one of his visits in May 1970, Ulrike Meinhof led a raid to release him. The library was stormed with pistols and tear gas, and an attendant was critically wounded. Baader and Meinhof fled to Jordan and started their training in guerrilla warfare with the Popular Front for the Liberation of Palestine. On 9 August they slipped back into West Germany.

The next two years were punctuated by bank raids, shootings and bombings. Within Germany, there was a great groundswell of support for them, which reached beyond traditional hard left circles into the liberal intelligentsia. 'Safe-houses' were easily available. The police found it difficult to trace them, but in the end they cornered them. On 1 June 1972, after a fierce gun battle in Frankfurt, Andreas Baader and two companions were arrested. A week later, Gudrun Esslin, Baader's mistress, was arrested while shopping in an elegant Hamburg store, her revolver visible. A week after that, a disillusioned leftist, whose house was considered 'safe' enough to give Ulrike Meinhof a refuge, phoned the police.

Three years were to pass before the five hard-core members of the gang were brought to trial for murder, attempted murder, robbery and forming a criminal association. A special, fortified courthouse was built in which to try them. Initially they were kept in solitary confinement, which was usual for prisoners accused of violent, politically motivated crimes. Although they were allowed visits by lawyers, priests, family and, on occasion, representatives of Amnesty, their lawyers launched a protest campaign against what they called 'isolation as torture'. They said that they were being subjected to 'sensory deprivation' in silent cells, painted all in white, with the lights burning through day and night. In fact, only Ulrike Meinhof, who in November 1974 was sentenced to eight years in prison for freeing Baader, suffered a lengthy period of solitary confinement.

Either because of the campaign or because of rethinking by the prison authorities, their conditions did improve. The gang members were allowed to share a cell. They could have more exercise, watch colour television and play table tennis. Their cells were lined with over 2,000 books. Unlike common-law prisoners, men and women could mix freely. As Paul Oestreicher, then chairman of British Amnesty, observed after a visit, it looked more like a student hostel than a prison.

The months of detection were punctuated by hunger strikes and protests. They were still not satisfied with their conditions. The campaign to ameliorate them became more intense after one of the gang, Holger Meins, died during a hunger strike. Outside, members of the gang shot dead the president of the West Berlin Supreme Court. They said it was revenge for the death of Meins.

German public opinion was polarized between those who thought it was time for the government to crack down with all means at their disposal and those, including people of the stature of Heinrich Böll, for whom the state was becoming an ugly monster that allowed for no flexibility or tolerance. Members of the German Amnesty group could not help being infected by the atmosphere. Although national sections are not supposed to take up issues in their own country, the German Amnesty members became deeply involved, pressing London to investigate the charges of torture and other human rights abuses. After a long period of investigation, Martin Ennals, Amnesty's secretary-general, wrote letters in November 1974 to individual ministers of justice in each of the *Länder* where Baader-Meinhof prisoners had been detained – they were by now scattered around Germany in a number of prisons.

During one of the hunger strikes, a private mission of mediation was undertaken by Paul Oestreicher. In a public statement issued in December and confirmed by the International Executive Committee, Oestreicher said: 'In the opinion of Amnesty International at the present time, the allegation of so-called torture by isolation is not justified. As such, the organization cannot intervene. That Amnesty International is ready and willing to help find a solution in the present crisis is demonstrated by my presence in Germany.' In February 1975, there was a new crisis. The prison authorities had smelt it coming, but no one seemed to work out what form it would take. The gang had called off their hunger strike, and were assiduously using gymnastic equipment to build up their strength.

Baader issued one of his secret cell circulars – it was sent to Ulrike Meinhof and Gudrun Esslin and communicated via one of the gang's many secret channels. It read:

To g/u. [Gudrun/Ulrike, probably.]

I no longer bothered about it: I had n radio + have the sequence + analyzed the reporting that will still have to be done in the newspapers in the next few days: sequence of decisions, Fundamental decisions (important!) n diagram of the times they need be able decide: to become grand Crisis staff (state ministers, presidents, minister of interior, minister of justice, buback [Buback, chief federal public prosecutor]) air flight times etc. hanna [Hanna-Elise Krabbe] is to do it. That is very important + must go quickly. I will pass on the stuff from Wednesday.

On 24 April the import of this murky message became all too clear: six outside members of the gang captured West Germany's embassy in Stockholm, demanding the release of those imprisoned. They must be flown out of the country, they insisted. If there was any delay, the twelve hostages they had taken would be shot dead one by one.

When the police entered the building, the terrorists shot and killed the military attaché. When the deadline passed, they shot the economics attaché. Then the Swedish government decided enough was enough. It had reached the same conclusion as the West German government – there could be no more blackmail. Countess Marion Donhoff, the publisher of *Die Zeit*, summed it up when she recalled the old Frederickian maxim: 'Better that a man die than justice disappear.' The police stormed the embassy. One terrorist died and the other five were captured.

Nearly three years after the original June arrest, the trial of the gang began in May 1975 in the most secure penitentiary courtroom ever devised.

The government, meanwhile, in an attempt to outwit the Red Army Faction's lawyers, who seemed in many ways to be part and parcel of the gang, passed laws restricting their rights. Within days of the opening of the trial, all the lawyers defending Baader were excluded from the case on suspicion of participating in or abetting the crimes of which their clients were accused.[1] Although Amnesty did not challenge the German government directly on this, they drew attention to it in their regular published reports. They also kept up their pressure to ameliorate the near-solitary confinement that many of the Red Army Faction prisoners experienced. In the spring of 1977 there was a modest shift in government policy. The prisoners were

[1] One of their lawyers, Otto Schily, later came to prominence as the German minister of the interior, responsible for law and order, in the Social Democratic–Green government of Gerhard Schröder.

given permission to use larger rooms and to associate with groups of up to ten fellow prisoners. This was in addition to the other concessions granted three years before.

Members of the gang, meanwhile, despite high-pressure courtroom tactics, were becoming increasingly demoralized. The chances of rescue after the Stockholm fiasco were low. Gang members in prison began to quarrel among themselves. Ulrike Meinhof's will was the first to crack. On 15 May 1976 she was found hanged in her cell. The others, however, maintained their morale, discipline and daring for another year. In April 1977, after 103 weeks of trial, Baader, Esslin and Jan-Carl Raspe were found guilty of four murders and thirty-nine attempted murders. They were each sentenced to life imprisonment plus fifteen years for offences including bombings, using firearms and founding a criminal organization.

Despite the vigilance of the prison authorities, the imprisoned gang members continued to pass orders to the outside world. On 31 July 1977 Jurgen Ponto, the head of the Dresden Bank, was shot down in his home. The prison authorities reacted by attempting to end the agreement allowing the prisoners to meet in larger groups. The prisoners began a combined hunger and thirst strike.

On 12 August Martin Ennals sent letters to the German authorities requesting information on the transfer of Red Army Faction prisoners to single cells. The next day, Amnesty expressed concern about the lives of thirty hunger strikers. A week later, two leading members of the West German section of Amnesty, with the consent of the International Executive Committee (though breaking the Amnesty mandate on the non-involvement of national sections in the affairs of their own country), visited the prisoners and officials involved. On the same day, Amnesty International requested its membership to send appeals to the West German authorities. On 26 August an Amnesty delegation was sent to West Germany.

While attention was focused on the hunger strike, the gang struck again. On 5 September 1977 industrialist Hans-Martin Schleyer was kidnapped. His chauffeur and three-man security guard were machine-gunned to death. The price for Schleyer's freedom was the release of the prisoners and travel to the country of their choice. The government this time was in no doubt it could not give in. Schleyer was later found in the boot of an abandoned car, murdered.

Amnesty was now being increasingly criticized. In the eyes of some, Amnesty had come dangerously close to being seen as a friend of a ruthless band of terrorists who were still totally engaged in their effort. They were not prisoners cut off from their political friends, isolated and badly treated. They seemed able still to call the shots and direct the campaign for their release. Did not Amnesty, by pressing for a looser prison regime, give them more opportunities to organize their deadly work? It was one thing for Amnesty to work for the amelioration of the lives of passive prisoners, but to work on behalf of such activists was almost to be a part – or at least a tool – of their cause.

Amnesty's reply was to insist that their job was to stop human rights violations. Prison was meant to rehabilitate prisoners, not to 'break them'. It should be possible to build a high-security prison that was liberal within the walls, even while entry and exit was carefully controlled. Besides, Amnesty said, there seemed to be no correlation between the degree of isolation of the prisoners and the number of violent events organized by the gang outside. Even during the most severe isolation the gang seemed to have ways of communicating between its members and the world outside.

On 13 October a Lufthansa airliner with sixty-eight passengers and crew was hijacked by members of the gang. It was flown to Somalia and the bargaining began. It was a long-drawn-out process, carefully orchestrated by the Bonn government, which, with the connivance of the Somali government, was secretly flying an élite group of commandos into Somalia. On 18 October they stormed the plane in a lightning surprise attack. The passengers were freed. Hours later, Andreas Baader and his friend Jan-Carl Raspe were found shot in their cells. Gudrun Esslin was found hanged, and a fourth prisoner, Irmgard Muller, attempted to cut her throat, but survived. Amnesty was invited to the autopsy but decided not to go, because of the lack of warning time given. Nevertheless, the local German authorities claimed they had been in attendance.

The prisoners, since the Schleyer kidnapping, had all been in solitary confinement. But, as a search of their cells revealed after their death, it had not stopped them setting up a communications network. The police discovered batteries, cables and electrical plug combinations. The terrorists made contact with each other through the prison radio system, even though the lines connecting their cells were cut. In a cell which had once been occupied by Baader, and in the cell in which Raspe died, police found a hollow space in the wall that could have been used for hiding the gun used in the suicides. It is possible they even masterminded the hijacking, although observers who have tried to study how they kept their chain of command so effective so long have concluded that a number of their lawyers were senior figures in the gang.

In May 1980, Amnesty issued the results of their long-awaited enquiry into the use of isolation for prisoners held in connection with politically motivated crimes in West Germany. Amnesty said that more than a hundred Red Army Faction prisoners had been subjected to the isolation treatment at some time. The memorandum quoted findings of the European Commission for Human Rights, the Council of Europe and medical research to emphasize that isolation can gravely damage health. Symptoms, it said, included psychosomatic disturbances, low blood pressure and circulation problems, including dizziness and headaches, disorders of the stomach and intestines, sleep disturbance, difficulty in concentrating and speaking, hallucinatory symptoms in extreme cases, and emotional disturbances, including depression and ultimately suicidal tendencies.

Amnesty argued that security and humane treatment were not contradictory goals, and asked the German government to seek alternatives to solitary confinement and 'small-group isolation'. 'In institutions where a higher standard of security is needed, this reasonably high standard against the outside world generally allows a more liberal regime inside the institution.'

The German authorities rejected the Amnesty conclusions. They invited Amnesty to inspect their prisons and said that Amnesty had overlooked the fact that members of the Red Army Faction had refused to accept more contact with non-political prisoners. They had demanded to be put into groups of at least fifteen politically motivated prisoners. They even attacked other prisoners. To the extent that the gang were isolated, it was by their own choice or when they abused the opportunities for contact.

Amnesty disagreed with this assessment, countering that not all the Baader-Meinhof gang had rejected contact with non-political prisoners and criticizing the distribution of the remaining Baader-Meinhof prisoners around numerous jails, making it difficult for them to associate even in small groups.

Amnesty stresses that it is part of its mandate to raise its banner against 'torture, or other cruel, inhuman and degrading treatment or punishment'. No one following the case of the Baader-Meinhof gang could be unaware of Amnesty's commitment to stick to its own standards. But they came dangerously near to being used by a group that had no sympathy for the values Amnesty stood for and which sought to overthrow the kind of West European democracy that allowed Amnesty to flourish. Nevertheless, it seems in retrospect they were right to intervene and insist on a decent prison regime. Only if the German authorities could prove that isolation broke the political and military chain of command of the Baader-Meinhof gang would they have had a duty to rethink their role.

Looking back, the Baader-Meinhof effort was not the organization's finest hour. Against the better judgement of some of its members, Amnesty allowed the German national group to push it in deeper than the case properly deserved. The Baader-Meinhof gang's imprisonment, measured against Amnesty's terms of reference and other interests, was a marginal affair. But in terms of energy, emotion and time it became much more than that.

7

Amnesty's Success Stories

Amnesty staff would not be in their jobs if they did not possess above-average resilience. The wear and tear of constant failure – as it often seems – of dealing with intransigent authorities, the bereaved and the seriously distressed on a daily basis is not a way most of us would choose to earn our daily bread. It is, indeed, surprising that the turnover in staff is about normal for an organization of this size. People do come and go, yet often to jobs in other organizations that have a human rights brief. Ask a staff member what keeps them going and they certainly don't say elections in Guatemala or the death of Bokassa. They say: 'Look, it's because I had this letter from so and so's wife,' or 'Did you hear what so and so said last week when he came into the office to thank us?'

On its website, Amnesty now runs a section called 'Amnesty works', which gives the good news.[1] It's not only useful for the staff who most of the time are deep inside their own burrows and don't hear much about what their colleagues are up to; it's good for the membership at large. Half an hour a week spent on the Amnesty website is an antidote to depression.

A recent case from Burundi, a country seized with continuing violence over the last decade and a half, is a web story worth repeating:

Torture and ill treatment are systematic in Burundi, particularly in the early stages of detention in police and military custody. The vast majority of torture allegations are not investigated and many 'confessions' made under

[1] See: www.amnesty.org and look for 'good news'.

torture are accepted as evidence by the courts – sometimes as the only evidence in the case.

In October 1998, however, signs that a new attitude might be developing towards such 'confessions' occurred when a court ruled that evidence against Jean Minani, which had been extracted under torture, was inadmissible in court. He was subsequently acquitted of all charges.

Jean Minani, a peasant farmer, was accused of involvement in the murder of Lieutenant-Colonel Lucien Sakubu, a former major of Bujumbura. He was arrested in March 1995, when Lieutenant-Colonel Sakubu's body was found in a suburb of the capital. Around eighty people from the area were rounded up by police and taken to the Gendarmerie's Special Investigation Unit (BSR) for interrogation. All but twelve were subsequently released.

Jean Minani and others who remained in detention were severely beaten. When Amnesty International representatives met and interviewed Jean Minani, shortly after his arrest in March 1995, he displayed visible scars and open wounds from torture. He told Amnesty that he had confessed to killing Lieutenant-Colonel Sakubu because he had been tortured during questioning, but denied that he had committed the murder. The Commander of the BSR admitted to Amnesty that they had been authorized to use 'more or less violent means' to procure the suspects' statements. In August 1995 Jean Minani appeared before the attorney-general and repeated his allegations of torture, denying once again that he had been involved in the killing of Lieutenant-Colonel Sakubu.

When Amnesty delegates met and interviewed Jean Minani for a second time in May 1998, shortly after his first court appearance, he was being detained in Mpimba Central Prison, Bujumbura, and had been held without trial for more than three years. Photographs of his injuries resulting from torture, taken by Amnesty representatives during their first visit in 1995, were subsequently submitted as evidence of torture during his trial. Amnesty delegates also met and discussed the case with Jean Minani's lawyer.

There were only two pieces of evidence that were brought against Jean Minani – the confession that he had made under torture at the BSR and the statement of a witness for the prosecution, also made in 1995, which implicated Jean Minani in Lieutenant-Colonel Sakubu's murder.

On several occasions Amnesty expressed concern that Jean Minani could be convicted solely on the basis of a statement extracted under torture. Of the twelve who were beaten in detention, Jean Minani was the only one who confessed under torture to involvement in the murder. He was the only one whose case was submitted to the criminal chamber of the Court of Appeal and, therefore, the only one charged with a capital offence. Amnesty called for the charges against him to be fully investigated and, if found to be substantiated, for a full and fair trial to be held in accordance with international standards and without recourse to the death penalty. In October 1998 Jean Minani was finally acquitted of all the charges against him, with the court accepting the defence lawyer's argument that statements made under torture or duress could not be admitted as evidence. In the trial, the prosecution witness also retracted her 1995 statement against Jean Minani, claiming she had been threatened by the authorities and forced to co-operate.

Before Amnesty International was created, who, outside his village, would have heard of a peasant farmer, Jean Minani?

Amnesty's weekly case-load is made up of hundreds of cases like this: keeping up the spirits of a Mexican army officer imprisoned after publicly accusing his superiors of sadistic behaviour; encouraging local groups to write letters to a prisoner in South Korea who had been incarcerated for forty-three years before his release; or pursuing into court the off-duty policeman in Brazil who opened fire on a group of over fifty street children sleeping rough in Rio de Janeiro, killing five.

Yet, while sometimes in individual situations there is a discernible link between Amnesty's efforts and the outcome, often enough with a situation-at-large, as in Nigeria and Guatemala, it is not easy always to discern cause and effect. There are exceptions, however, when events make clear that it was the intervention of Amnesty that significantly changed government policy. Sri Lanka, Morocco, Colombia and the United Kingdom each have a story to tell that throws the work of Amnesty into hopeful relief.

Sri Lanka is a country that has been torn apart by a civil war, now in its eighteenth year. Michael Ondaatje, the Sri Lankan writer, in his latest novel *Anil's Ghost* refers to it as a 'Hundred Years War with modern weaponry'. Despite being a country with less social inequality than any other Asian developing country and with a high level of literacy and education, its future has become hostage to a vicious war between a guerrilla group, the Liberation Tigers of Tamil Eelam (LTTE), claiming to represent the minority Tamil community of the north-east, fighting for an independent state, and the army of the central government. Both the army and the guerrillas have committed atrocities and, over the years, Amnesty has roundly criticized the infractions of both sides. Somewhat to its surprise, Amnesty has found that it has been able to win reform of the army's practices and, to some extent, those of the Tigers. The war still goes on but, at least on the government's side, without so many of the excesses that were common before the Amnesty-instigated reforms.

For many years, torture has been prevalent in Sri Lanka, the tool of both the Liberation Tigers and government troops. In addition, police officers regularly torture criminal suspects and people taken into custody for such matters as land disputes or other private issues. There is also a long-term pattern of 'disappearances'. Many of the thousands of such cases concern detainees alleged to have died under torture in police and army custody, whose bodies were subsequently disposed of in secret. The arrest and torture of children by security forces is not common, but several chilling reports have emerged of young Tamil children being tortured in custody on suspicion of being LTTE members or as a means of forcing family members to hand themselves over.

Amnesty succeeded in pushing the central government to prosecute members of the security forces and to launch an investigation, involving exhumation of bodies, to get at the truth behind allegations of widespread disappearances and army torture in Jaffna in 1996. In Amnesty's opinion, Sri Lanka has turned an important corner and prosecutions can now be more regularly expected.

In a landmark judgement in July 1998, the Colombo High Court sentenced to death five members of the security forces, having found them guilty of rape, 'disappearance' and murder. Two years before the soldiers had raped a teenage girl, Krishanthy Kumarasamy, then killed her, her brother, mother and neighbour. One of the accused said in court: 'There are 300 to 400 bodies on this land [where

Krishanthy's body was discovered]. Almost every evening dead bodies were brought there and the soldiers asked to bury them.' A year later Amnesty persuaded the government to begin exhumations in the Chemmani area of Jaffna, where the soldier said the bodies were buried. Human rights organizations were invited to observe the exhumation.

Amnesty's Ingrid Massagé was present. One of the most important aspects of this case, she said, was 'that other than the US in Vietnam, the government of Sri Lanka is one of the rare governments to have ordered an investigation of mass graves suspected of being the work of its forces during its own term of office'. Another aspect, she added, is that 'when action was finally taken against the perpetrators of rape and murder, the level of disappearance in the Jaffna area dropped. Before, it had increased dramatically. So the trial, followed by the exhumation, did send a very important signal that this sort of thing won't be tolerated. Last year we recorded fourteen cases of disappearances in Sri Lanka and none of them were reported in Jaffna.'

Amnesty's Rory Mungoven, director of its Asia Pacific programme, makes the additional observation: 'Besides the prosecutions conveying a message to the army that they are not necessarily going to escape responsibility for this kind of abuse, there are also the effects of a number of directives issued by the president of Sri Lanka. These directives on basic safeguards for people once they are taken into custody have been fairly rigorously enforced in Jaffna from mid-1997 onwards.'

Before 1996, the tendency in Sri Lanka, Mungoven continues, was not to regard 'disappearance' as a problem.

Then, in 1996, you had this outbreak in Jaffna. We produced our report. We were rejected. We were told we were lying. But now that they've gone through the trial followed by the exhumation, there is a very important psychological shift going on in the government. They now recognize, despite a public commitment to human rights, that without action it is not enough. But still there is a long way to go. It remains to be seen whether those alleged to be responsible for the torture and killing of the bodies exhumed will ultimately be brought to trial.

Mungoven also points out Amnesty's success in Sri Lanka is because of its build-up of a

very solid body of painstaking research over many years. Ingrid's experience, alone, stretches back over ten years. We have proved in Sri Lanka that we are not buffeted around by political groups and that we are very cautious with our use of information. The other thing is that, unlike some other organizations, we do tackle abuses on both sides. We tackle abuses by the opposition and we use the whole framework of international humanitarian law to hold them accountable for their actions as well. I feel we can honestly say we have had a salutary effect of the overall human rights situation.

King Hassan of Morocco, who died in July 1999 after a forty-year rule, seemingly bequeathed his son, King Mohammed VI, a weak hand. A weak hand, that is, if you judge power by autocratic reach. A little over three years ago the autocrat surprised everyone and voluntarily handed over a good slice of power to a former Amnesty-adopted political prisoner, once sentenced to death, the Socialist parliamentarian, Abderrahmane Youssoufi. Most royal functionaries were sidelined, apart from the king's powerful but much reviled minister of the interior, Driss Basri. Democracy finally had a chance to flap its wings, even to alter the direction of government policy towards the poor, who have been largely by-passed by Morocco's volatile, but steadily progressing, economic growth.

Yet close observers were not so surprised by this decision. There had been strong indications from the early 1960s on that the king did not want to be remembered as a tyrant, whose cruelty would be talked about for generations to come. In the early 1990s, under pressure in particular from Amnesty and local political parties and human rights groups, the king began to allow the release of most political prisoners, relax censorship and rein in the security forces. The Morocco of the late 1990s, when the king finally died, bore little resemblance to the Morocco of most of King Hassan's forty years of iron rule.

In a short period of time his new prime minister, Youssoufi, managed to carve out a distinct identity. Funding for health, education and housing rose. The turgid bureaucracy was reformed. Most important, a minister for justice was appointed who once had headed the country's largest human rights organization. Within a few months of taking power the new king, continuing his father's reforms, allowed the return from exile of Abraham Serfaty, leader of a communist organization, the Ilál-Amam, which had been accused in the 1970s of trying to overthrow the monarchy. The king also allowed the return to Morocco of the family of Mehdi Ben Barka, a radical leader of the 1960s, who was murdered by Moroccan security agents after being kidnapped in Paris.

Then, to everyone's relief, the king decided to sack Driss Basri, finally turning the page on Morocco's dark past. Now, claim his spokesmen, he is paving the way for Morocco, where the king still effectively has a final say in all government decision-making, to build the foundations of a true democracy in the Arab world. The king then released from house arrest Sheikh Abdesalam Yassine, leader of one of the more militant Islamic groups. It remains unclear, however, how much official tolerance will be extended to Islamic radicals, although those who choose a parliamentary path are given a wide degree of latitude.

An important start to dealing with the past was King Mohammed's decision to establish a commission to offer compensation to victims of arbitrary arrest and the families of those who 'disappeared'. One former political prisoner, incarcerated for many years in the notorious prison of Tazmamert that clings to the edge of a mountain in eastern Morocco, observed: 'It's all over now with the death of Hassan. The new king wants to change Morocco – and lift taboos.'

Despite a widespread new mood of optimism, more sober opinion points to three issues that suggest the king is moving rather more slowly than the rhetoric and his gestures suggest. Demonstrators are still being brutally repressed; the press is still censored; and the king remains an autocratic ruler. There remains the vexed issue of the Western Sahara, once a separate Spanish colony, but since 1975 a country at war, either hot or, since the UN-engineered cease-fire brokered in 1991, cold. Many of the local people, the Saharawis, led by Polisario, a political movement, want independence. But Rabat believes this phosphate-rich chunk of the Sahara is an integral and important part of Morocco.

In 1998 the UN reached agreement with Morocco and Polisario for a settlement, and a referendum has been repeatedly promised to decide the question. But once again, in the face of Moroccan and Polisario disagreements on who is eligible to vote, the UN has decided to postpone it. The Western Sahara question is not only a drain on the country's scarce economic resources, it has been the source of many of the country's human rights abuses. A final settlement would allow the king to devote his political energies to making the new democracy at home work more effectively.

Amnesty had its first real success in Morocco in 1991. Then, more than three hundred prisoners were released after being held in secret detention for up to nineteen years in appalling conditions. It was the climax of a long, detailed and energetic campaign by Amnesty, but it also capitalized on the mood of euphoria in high Moroccan government circles, following the defeat of Saddam Hussein in the Gulf War.

The greatest number of 'disappeared' were people of Western Saharan origin. A full accounting still cannot be made. The best estimate, says Amnesty, was over a thousand. Although there was this significant large release in 1991, very few were prepared to speak about others still detained; they simply feared arrest if they opened their mouths. They knew their movements were restricted and every communication monitored.

'"Disappearance", as used in Morocco,' wrote the Amnesty researcher responsible for the country,

is used not just to eliminate from the scene people against whom the state has no sustainable legal charges, but it is meant to create an atmosphere of fear which spreads through the country. For the family of the victim, 'disappearance' may be a greater punishment than execution: death ends the matter, grief heals, life resumes. Since the authorities never admit to holding a 'disappeared' prisoner, the family do not know what has happened and whether their relative is alive or dead.

Many of the 'disappeared' were incarcerated at Tazmamert, where, over a seventeen-year period, about half the inmates died. Semi-starvation in extremely harsh conditions appeared to be part of the punishment. A letter smuggled out of Tazmamert in 1989 described the experience as being 'buried, without even the rights enjoyed by beasts, totally isolated from each other and from the outside world'.

In 1981 Group 214 of Amnesty's Dutch section began working on the case of Abdi Mayara, one of the Saharawi 'disappeared'. The group wrote over four hundred letters to King Hassan, the minister of Saharan affairs, prisons, hospitals, human rights organizations, local authorities, headmasters, mayors and the Moroccan ambassador to Holland. A year later, two identical replies were received from the Ministry of Justice: 'The person cannot be found on any prisoner list . . . searches made by the ministry have yielded no result.'

Over the next twelve years Dutch and many other groups wrote thousands of letters and postcards about Abdi Mayara and many other 'disappeared', eliciting only minimal responses. Between 1981 and 1991 Group 64 of Amnesty's German section sent over a thousand letters and postcards on behalf of just one prisoner, Heiba ould Omar ould Mayara, a cousin of Abdi. Nine prisons returned the letters, marked 'unknown'.

In July 1991, when the first handwritten list of the forty-eight Saharawis who had died was received, it appeared that Abdi had died many years before in 1977 at Agdz prison. But, to everyone's surprise, Abdi was released in June 1991, fifteen years after his disappearance. (This first handwritten list was given by Moulay Ahmed al-Leili, who had washed the bodies of each one and recorded each name. On his release he recited the names from memory, they were recorded and then he died, saying his work was done – presumably the mistake was his.)

Besides Amnesty, solidarity groups of Moroccan or Saharawi exiles living in Western Europe also kept up pressure. So did the UN Working Group on Disappearances. In one case, that of the three Bourequat brothers, the government of Morocco replied to the UN: 'The ministry of justice and the prisons have been searched, but no record of criminal charges or any other judicial procedures regarding the brothers has been found. In the government's view, they should be sought outside the country.' On 30 December 1991 the three brothers were at last released from over ten years in appalling conditions in Tazmamert. They had 'disappeared' for a total of eighteen years.

As an Amnesty report observes, 'It is difficult to believe that people could still be alive in a secret cell after "disappearing" for fifteen years or more.' Part of the difficulty was the shortage of information. To be sure that a 'disappearance' has been perpetrated, the victim needs to have been seen to have been arrested by the security forces – preferably by more than one witness – and the government must have been asked to account for the arrest and to have denied holding the person. A clamp-down on information from the Western Sahara made it almost impossible to get this sort of information. The climate of fear was such that it meant that even a family might not ask after its 'disappeared' members.

In one case Amnesty had been writing letters for eight years on behalf of one supposed prisoner, unaware that he had been released. The Moroccan government used this to argue that Amnesty's information across the board was suspect and that all the others on their list of 'disappeared' had probably also come out of detention and were living happily elsewhere, perhaps under different names. The government suggested that the fluidity of the Saharawi name structure had confused Amnesty, or that, part of a nomadic culture, they had travelled to Mauritania, to the south, or to the Polisario camps around Tindouf in Algeria.

But, from time to time, Amnesty did get a break, a chink of light, that enabled it to peer into the horror on the far side of the prison walls. In the summer of 1990 a former prison guard at Agdz and Qual'at M'gouna prisons, troubled by his conscience, described the situation to Christine Serfaty (wife of Abraham Serfaty, the prominent Moroccan dissident), who passed it on to Amnesty. On another occasion, the family of one Saharawi 'disappeared' started to receive smuggled letters. Amnesty, of course, kept the confidence to itself but it did enable it to pinpoint the secret centre in Laayoune and to ascertain that most of those who had been detained there were still alive.

The Moroccan authorities played their hand carefully. Coupled with official denials, there were off-the-record messages from those close to the government that there could be releases as long as there was no publicity. Western governments were also persuaded to keep quiet. The US State Department was told, when it pursued the case of a prisoner married to an American, that as long as it kept the situation to itself the man would be allowed to correspond with his wife.

But the atmosphere did begin to change within Morocco in King Hassan's later years. From 1988 on, the local human rights movement became more active and vocal. The press, too, became more outspoken and some political prisoners (but not the 'disappeared') were allowed to reply to letters from Amnesty groups. Their observations on prison conditions were even published in the local press. A few courageous Moroccan papers occasionally mentioned the cases of the 'disappeared'. The foreign press, although in general giving more coverage than the local press, was not always as courageous. In December 1989, when King Hassan was interviewed by French journalists for the television channel Antennae 2, the interviewers caved in to a warning beforehand not to mention the Oufkir family. (The whole family, including six small children, had been incarcerated since 1972. Their father, a former minister of the interior, General Mohamed Oufkir, who had turned against the king, died in mysterious circumstances.)

Amnesty points to December 1990 as the moment when the dam appeared to break. One trigger was a batch of letters smuggled out of Tazmamert which reached some prisoners' families and which urged them to speak out, otherwise it might be too late. The families sent a petition to the ministers of the interior and justice, and copies were delivered to political parties and newspapers. At the same time another letter, with a vivid description of Tazmamert, was sent anonymously to a number of human rights organizations, including Amnesty. It was first published by a Moroccan human rights association in Paris and provided the first information that the Bourequat brothers were alive. The heightened awareness of the Moroccan situation in the international arena appeared to strengthen the readiness of families, as well as local journalists and human rights activists, to speak more openly.

That month the leader of an opposition party raised the issue of Tazmamert in parliament. Newspapers inclined to the socialist cause reported his question. In February 1991 the Oufkir family was released and by May and June the debate widened and the plight of other prisoners began to be openly discussed.

Amnesty had helped fire the debate. It had sent a delegation to meet with King Hassan in February 1990 and then issued a long report. Other factors were the publication in Paris in September 1990 of the book, *Notre Ami le Roi* (Our Friend the King). The book provoked a good deal of publicity and, to dampen discussion, the Moroccan government tried to buy up the whole edition. But enough copies were circulating to keep the fire bright, and many were smuggled into Morocco. Such was the debate in France that the French government, hitherto a staunch supporter of King Hassan, felt obliged to put some pressure on the human rights front.

There was also, in November 1990, the occasion of the consideration of Morocco's periodic report on its implementation of the International Covenant on Civil and Political Rights. Numerous human rights groups, including the Moroccan Organization for Human Rights, submitted memoranda. Added to that, the constant daily pressure from Amnesty groups, including those based in other Arab countries, kept the authorities on the defensive. Much of Amnesty's information was used in speeches and statements at the European parliament. It was, as Amnesty has observed, 'an example of the interweaving of internal and external pressures for change'.

Three hundred Saharawi 'disappeared' were released. Tazmamert was emptied and three long-term prisoners in Kenitra central prison were released. President Mitterrand of France publicly thanked Morocco; but there was no remonstrance about past injustice.

Today most political prisoners have been released, more Moroccan families are prepared to speak out about the 'disappeared' and more information on those that remain unreleased has been gathered. But the silence still continues. Reports of torture and ill treatment, particularly of Saharawis, are still received by Amnesty every month.

The new king, like his father before him, appears unable to grasp the nettle of the Western Sahara.

After Kosovo, why not next Colombia, land of the drug barons and forty years of near continuous civil war? The rest of the world may drop its jaw at the idea of North Atlantic Treaty Organisation (NATO) troops being sent to pacify leftist guerrilla groups, army-backed, fascist paramilitaries and the world's most ruthless drug barons. But in Bogotá, Colombia's capital, it is being touted by some as a necessary solution. And if not NATO, at least the US army.

Don't drop your jaw too far. For no less than the former US commander-in-chief, Bill Clinton, said in 1999 that vital American interests were at stake in Colombia. It is 'very much in our national security interests to do what we can'. When a US president uses these code words it essentially means that the backbone of the US military, intelligence and national security bodies has decided that, if necessary, the United States is prepared to go to any length, even war, to deal with the problem. Although Clinton's statement was sparked off by the relatively trivial loss of a US military reconnaissance plane flying over Colombia, it came after a long period of slow-burning, mounting frustration at the inability of successive Colombian governments to get to grips with the irregular armies that threaten to destabilize the government, and with the country's narcotics dealers who for decades have been the principal suppliers of hard drugs on to the American market.

In August 2000 Mr Clinton made a one-day visit to Colombia to formally announce a $1.3 billion aid package, most of it to supply sixty military helicopters and train a new army anti-narcotics brigade, for use not only against the drug traffickers but also against the guerrillas who provide them with armed protection. Before Mr Clinton's visit the US House of Representatives stripped the aid legislation of safeguards designed to improve military professionalism, and Mr Clinton waived one of the remaining human rights provisions so that the military aid could start flowing immediately.

If US intervention were likely to be even-handed, perhaps there could be an argument for it. After all, Colombia is often exhibit A for those who say 'look what happens when the outside world doesn't intervene: the local fires just burn brighter and fiercer'. But 'even-handed' does not appear in the current lexicon of the Pentagon's thinking on Colombia. Almost perversely, the Clinton administration seems to be ignoring what Amnesty International Human Rights Watch describes as 'the root of these abuses . . . the Colombian army's consistent and pervasive failure to ensure human rights standards and distinguish civilians from combatants'.

Terrible violence is being inflicted both upon each other and on innocent civilians by all four sides in the armed struggle. But by no stretch of the independent reporting available, whether it be done by Human Rights Watch, Amnesty International or the very few outside journalists who have dared to risk their lives studying the situation close up, can it be said that the left-wing guerrillas are the most responsible. The clear consensus is that the army is in league with the right-wing paramilitaries, who, in turn, are in league with the drug mafia. It is they who consistently set the pace in assassinations, organizing death-squads, inflicting torture and practising widespread intimidation. The army has not only failed to move against the rightist paramilitaries in any significant way, it has tolerated their activity, even providing some of them with intelligence and logistical support. On occasion, it has even co-ordinated joint manœuvres with them.

In a report issued in 1999, the Bogotá office of the UN High Commission for Human Rights observed that 'witnesses frequently state that massacres were perpetuated by members of the armed forces passing themselves off as paramilitaries'. It is true that both the preceding government of Ernesto Samper and the present one of Andres Pastrana have moved to suspend or close down particular units, such as the army's notorious Twentieth Brigade. Yet officers are rarely, if ever, prosecuted, and some have even been promoted. Occasionally there is a dismissal.

The Clinton administration's attempts to be even-handed have been inconsistent. It allows the State Department to issue human rights reports that are highly critical of the Colombian establishment, even, in its 1999 report, accusing the government of 'tacit acquiescence' in abuses. In May 1999 the United States revoked the visa of one particularly corrupt and cruel general. Nevertheless, the main direction of the Clinton administration was clear – increasing levels of aid for the Colombian military, fewer strings attached to how it is used, and the deployment of CIA and Pentagon operatives to work with Colombian security force units even though they have not been given a clean bill of health on human rights abuses. Last year, General Charles Wilhelm, head of US Southern Command, told a committee of the US Congress that criticism of military abuses was 'unfair'.

Now, with the pace being set by a new Republican administration, Washington is giving more and more aid to the Colombian military, supposedly for combating the drug menace, but in practice aimed disproportionately at the left-wing guerrillas. Already Colombia is the third largest recipient of US aid after Israel and Egypt.

Washington's sense of frustration is understandable. The left-wing guerrillas have not responded well to the significant steps taken towards them by President Pastrana. But then nobody in their right mind expected the betrayals, bad memories and fears of forty years of war to be quickly set on one side by handshakes and face-to-face meetings. But if the United States, angry at the slow pace of events in Colombia, allows itself to be drawn in, it will be quite counterproductive. It will simply give substance to all the Marxist twaddle that has been talked for decades across Latin America by left-wing intellectuals and guerrillas about who really pulls the strings. And it will embolden the Colombian army and its paramilitary allies to even worse excesses.

The path to peace and respect for human rights in Colombia lies where it has long been – in honest and humane government within the country and serious moves by the world's largest drug-consuming nation to pull the rug out from under the illegal drug industry by amending its outdated and outmoded laws on prohibition.

Amnesty, for its part, has decided to concentrate much of its effort on the narrow but unavoidable task of keeping human rights defenders in Colombia alive. Amnesty's HQ in London now has two members of staff permanently assigned to the task (although human rights workers at risk in other Latin American countries are also part of their mandate).

'Defending human rights in Colombia is a dangerous profession,' says Susan Osnos of Human Rights Watch. Since the beginning of 1997 more than twenty-five Colombian human rights defenders have been assassinated. Yet it continues to attract unusually dedicated people. Last year assassins gunned down the president of a human rights committee in his office in Medellin, the drug traffickers' home town. He was the fourth president to be killed since 1987. But still someone has taken his place.

'Pledges to protect human rights defenders are common, even routine, in some countries of the region,' says Amnesty. 'Nevertheless, in reality, promises often remain empty and unfulfilled.' Local Amnesty sections, combining with local human rights NGOs, have engaged in several high profile actions to support besieged human rights defenders.

The Americas Defenders' Network, using electronic mail, enables the Human Rights Defenders' Programme to act more swiftly and efficiently. It organizes press coverage and special appeals from high profile personalities and arranges meetings with diplomatic representatives. Last year more than ten such actions, involving more than forty human rights defenders, were initiated by the network. When in January 1999 four Colombian human rights workers were kidnapped, such pressure helped to bring their release within a couple of weeks. On occasion, rights defenders have little choice but to leave the country. In 1999 ten Colombian workers and their families were given Amnesty internships to continue their human rights work in less dangerous countries, in Spain, Costa Rica, Uruguay and Argentina.

There is little sign of any easing of the danger. If anything, it is likely to worsen. In March 1999 the national paramilitary organization, the United Self-Defence Forces of Colombia (AUC), formerly Autodefensas, declared human rights activists *un objetivo militar* – a military target.

In May 1999, Señora Piedad Córdoba, president of the Colombian

Senate's Human Rights Commission, was abducted in Medellín by a group of fifteen armed men. The next day Carlos Castaño, the leader of the AUC, issued a statement claiming responsibility. Piedad Córdoba, a mother of four children, is renowned for her bravery. Only the day before her abduction, she took part in a Forum for Peace in the war-torn Magdalena Medio region, where she called for civilians to be respected and not drawn into the conflict. Recently she had campaigned for legislative proposals to criminalize 'disappearances' and reform of the Military Code so that army personnel accused of human rights violations would cease to be given impunity. The Americas Defenders' Network campaigned vigorously for her release. To no small surprise, she was released, on 4 June.

Less fortunate were three American indigenous activists who had been campaigning for the rights of Colombian Indians. Their bound and blindfolded bodies were found in March dumped over the Venezuelan border. Their car had been intercepted by two gunmen from the left-wing guerrilla group, the Colombian Revolutionary Armed Forces (FARC). The FARC leadership, embarrassed by the publicity given to the case, said the soldiers had acted without the authorization of the national command, and that the soldiers would be disciplined and perhaps executed. Amnesty, in turn, true to form, condemned the possible summary trial and use of the death penalty.

Amnesty believes that it has marshalled enough evidence to prove to the Colombian government that many killings of activists could have been prevented if the authorities had taken action to investigate the complaints they had received of threats, intimidation and harassment. Two startling cases illustrate this point:

Dr Josué Giraldo Cardona was president of the Meta Civic Human Rights Committee. He was being threatened at regular intervals and had filed several statements with the police. The Inter-American Court of Human Rights had intervened and asked the Colombian government to take special measures to guarantee his safety. But the authorities, which had taken virtually no action when three former committee presidents had been killed, did not investigate his complaints. A short while later, in October 1996, he, too, was gunned down.

Similarly, when a renowned Colombian human rights lawyer, Dr José Umaña Mendoza, lodged complaints about the constant threats he was receiving, the authorities took no action. In April 1998 two men and a woman called at his office, announced that they were journalists wishing to interview him, and then fired several gunshots at his head. Amnesty, in collusion with other human rights groups, has ratcheted up the pressure on the Colombian government. Recently the authorities have begun supplying security equipment for the offices and homes of those under threat. Last year the government established a Special Integral Protection Programme, chaired by the vice-president. Amnesty also lobbied successfully for the General Assembly of the Organisation of American States to pass a resolution in June, last year:

(1) To recognize and support the work carried out by human rights defenders.
(2) To urge member states to persist in their efforts to provide human rights defenders with the necessary guarantees and facilities to continue freely carrying out their work.

Very slowly, the Colombian government has begun to realize that its failure to head off the threats made against human rights workers has led to a growing international groundswell of critical opinion.

This may seem a small 'success' for Amnesty. But it is an important one. If the intimidation and violence promised by AUC boss Carlos Castaño – 'The recent abductions mark the beginning of a regrettable, but inevitable stage in the conflict' – were allowed to grow unchecked, very soon Colombia would be effectively bereft of human rights workers. If that were to happen, the likely escalation in the civil war, seemingly implicit in the decision by the Clinton administration to sharply increase military aid and direct US involvement, would go largely unmonitored from inside the country.

A 'blind' human rights movement might serve the Colombia military well. It might give a freer hand to their collusion with paramilitary groups. It might give the US more freedom of action. But it would be a serious setback, almost immeasurably so, for the cause of human rights in Latin America, a continent that had only recently and belatedly appeared to have largely escaped its dark and miserable age of massive human rights abuses.

South Korea has not only moved from rags to riches in a single generation, increasing the average household income tenfold, it has, over the last decade, taken political leaps towards liberty and democracy of a magnitude that has left onlookers almost breathless.

In a daring move in 1995, the authorities decided to arrest two of its former presidents and throw them in jail while they awaited trial for their part in the 1979 coup and the massacre of civilians that followed it. Well reported as all this was, no one, to my knowledge, has posed the question: Do we have Amnesty and former US president Jimmy Carter to thank for much of this?

There is evidence, which I gathered and wrote about in the days after the assassination of President Park Chung Hee in October 1979, that pointed to Carter's critical influence in helping to give courage and guidance to those in South Korea who wanted to move their country out of the iron grip of military dictatorship. Much of it was anecdotal, but it filled pages of my reporter's notebook. But there was also some harder evidence. We now know for certain what was suspected at the time, that Kim Jae Kyu, head of the Korean Central Intelligence Agency, shot President Park at a banquet after a violent argument with Park over his decision to use troops to put down a nationwide student demonstration planned for three days later.

Why did Kim feel so strongly that President Park was set on a dead-end course? Because his intelligence service told him exactly what I found in interviews – how deep-rooted and widespread was the sense of unease in the country, and how young people, in particular, had been fired up, first by Amnesty and then by Carter's human rights crusade. Kim also knew, being by all accounts a man with highly sensitive antennae, the dangers of too fierce an oppression that would fly in the face of South Korea's American patron. He knew from observing events in Iran that repression that was not supported by Washington could not be sustained. Better not to begin a clampdown if they were to be forced by the United States to ease up at the wrong time.

But if Carter helped the cause of liberty with his anti-repression stance, he also passed up an opportunity to push post-Park South Korea towards its obvious destiny – democracy. The Americans held back, contenting themselves, as the US ambassador said at the time, with 'pushing for a broadening of the base of the government'. This was a dangerous and unhelpful place for US policy to be. A majority of the South Korean political establishment, including the army, wanted change. (We now know that fifty-one of the top Korean generals met a month after the assassination to consider their stand on allowing a more liberal expression of political views. Forty-nine voted in favour, two against.) They were divided, however, on how fast and how far to go. They looked towards the United States to help them crystallize their options, but a reticent Washington tipped their scales towards caution, one of a string of failures by Carter to follow through on his first and better instincts. Carter missed a historic opportunity.

The political situation in South Korea at that moment was unusually stable. The opposition was in a conciliatory mood. The economic foundations were already deep and secure and, unlike Iran, whose trauma after the overthrow of the Shah was still unsettling Washington, the country did not have the harsh economic, social and religious divides that in Iran were so explosive a mixture.

So with Washington back-pedalling, in effect, General Chun Doo Hwan, one of the two generals to vote no, saw his chance. On the night of 12 December 1979, he led a *coup d'état* against the top ranks of the military, deposing about forty of the generals who had voted yes. He went on to declare a nationwide state of emergency, banned all political activity, closed the universities and then, when the students rebelled in Kwangju city in May 1980, allowed the army to massacre more than two hundred of them. Six months later the newly elected US president, Ronald Reagan, hosted a banquet for him in the White House. Clearly Chun had read the short-term political tea-leaves in Washington as well as anyone inside the beltway.

The massacre in Kwangju, however, was never forgotten and, in due course, even Chun felt compelled, under the sustained pressure of the democratization movement that Kwangju triggered, to loosen up. In time liberalization produced elections and elections finally brought the old-time dissident, Kim Young Sam, to power. History caught up with Chun and in November 1995 he was arrested and later sentenced to a long prison term. Kim Young Sam, in turn, was succeeded by Kim Dae Jung, also an ex-political prisoner. He took office in February 1998. Expectations in the human rights community, both at home and abroad, were high. Kim had thanked Amnesty personally for saving his life. And in his long struggle to change South Korea from dictatorship to democracy he had endured every hardship, long years in prison, attempted murder and the persecution of his family.

Yes, despite an obvious willingness to better the human rights situation at home, progress, though incremental, has been often painfully slow. On a number of occasions Amnesty has had no choice but to criticize the new government's practices publicly. Even with a sympathetic president in office, human rights are not necessarily the first consideration of those in power. The political manœuvring necessary for Kim to hang on to office and to ensure that his supporters triumph in the election for the National Assembly and that he himself wins re-election with a stronger mandate has led to a strategy of two steps forward and one step back. It is clear that without Amnesty's continued pressure, and its emulation by thriving home-grown human rights groups, there would not have been the progress there has been.

Two years into his five-year term Kim became locked in an ugly fight for his political life. His position was under attack, not just from conservatives for his policy of engagement with North Korea, but from liberals, who charged that he had taken an increasingly vindictive approach to critics and perceived political enemies. The government was particularly faulted for a clumsy attempt to arrest a lawmaker, Chung Hyung Keun, on charges that he defamed the president. Many Koreans were grumbling that Kim had adopted much of the imperial style of his authoritarian predecessors.

Although Kim himself was detained for many years under the National Security Law, his administration has also had recourse to it. In 1998 Lee Sang-Kwan was arrested for publishing books about the lives of long-term political prisoners. A young student, Ha Young-joon, was arrested for posting a socialist text on a computer bulletin-board. A 78-year-old minister, Kang Heenam, was arrested for organizing a rally on behalf of Pomminyon, a group alleged to be pro-North Korea.

Fifteen trade union and political activists were sentenced to long prison terms for establishing and joining the 'Youngnam Committee' with alleged links to North Korea. Amnesty believes the charges are unfounded and that the arrests were carried out principally because of their opposition to government policies and as a means of curtailing anti-government protests. On 1 December 1998 hundreds of demonstrators were arrested for protesting to mark the fiftieth anniversary of the National Security Law. Despite the regression, Amnesty does believe that Kim is more on its side than against. He has met Pierre Sané and keeps an open door for Amnesty representations. He has promised yet again to revise the National Security Law's 'poisonous clauses', as he told Pierre Sané, and he has set up a national human rights commission, albeit with less independence than Amnesty lobbied for. His government has also introduced laws to outlaw discrimination in the workplace and to enable teachers to join trade unions. No death sentences have been imposed or carried out since 1998 and mass arrests have now ceased. Within South Korea, there has been a mushrooming of non-governmental organizations that were simply not allowed to exist a few years ago; many of them are working on some aspect of human rights.

When Kim took office, South Korea had some of the longest-serving political prisoners in the world. In two successive amnesties 150 of those were released. Yet a good number – 190 – remained, many because they refused to sign 'a law-abiding pledge', a condition for release not asked of ordinary criminals.

The president and his minister of justice both told Amnesty delegations that the severe economic crisis with which Kim was confronted when he took office, together with the strength of the political opposition, severely reduced their room for manœuvre. They do have an agenda for more human rights reform, they argued, but building a political consensus behind it is slow, uphill work. Hundreds of draft bills were delayed while the National Assembly became embroiled in party political disputes. Amnesty's riposte in these private meetings has been 'that human rights protection is particularly important in a time of crisis and that stronger legal and institutional human rights protection would actually help South Korea to overcome its current economic and political problems'. Pierre Sané has pointed out to President Kim that the organization's world-wide experience has taught it that basic human rights, in particular freedom of expression and association, are essential prerequisites to economic recovery and long-term development.

The elections for the National Assembly held in April 2000 marked the moment when it would become apparent if Mr Kim could deliver on his commitments. He made it clear what he believed the stakes were: 'Only with a mandate', he said, 'can we promote our agenda on a new human rights law, a new anti-corruption law, a new national security law and legislation to further democratize this country. We must win those elections.' He did win, by a modest margin. Most observers said the margin was not large enough to give him the room to manœuvre he needed. But then, in June, came the triumph of his summit with the North's reclusive dictator, Kim Jong Il. At a stroke, it seemed, tensions were sharply reduced. In mid-August both the North and the South marked the fifty-fifth anniversary of liberation from Japanese colonial rule by celebrating their recent reconciliation, including a tearful reunion of families divided by the Cold War's last frontier. To mark the occasion, Kim Dae Jung announced that he was releasing or reducing the sentences for 110 political prisoners, most of whom had been convicted of espionage or other activities linked to North Korea.

The British section of Amnesty International, one of the three largest and most active of Amnesty's ninety-five branches, has seen a dramatic growth in recent years – in membership, in income and in press attention.

In shouldering much of Amnesty International's effort to bring Pinochet to trial in Spain, it raised its profile even further. In 1998, with the publication of its first annual human rights audit of British foreign and asylum policy, it laid down an important and influential marker both for the government and also for itself – an annual appraisal of just how much effect Amnesty was having on government policies. It also made clear just how much Amnesty had broadened its brief from those now almost distant days in the 1960s when it campaigned only for the release of prisoners of conscience.

Clearly, the debate in Britain about human rights and government policy has been ratcheted up. Both in the print and broadcast media there has been, over the last two years, an unprecedented level of reporting and commentary on human rights questions, much of it seeking to highlight governmental inaction and to measure it against the new left-of-centre government's stated or implied intention. Different aspects of the government's record have also been analysed in several major reports by parliamentary select committees. It is fair to say, as an Amnesty report puts it, that the foreign policy of the government of Tony Blair 'is now more routinely judged by ethical standards than probably that of any of its predecessors'.

Amnesty has seized on the statement of the foreign secretary, Robin Cook, that he wished to include an 'ethical dimension' in foreign policy – to enlarge the argument that promoting human rights, rather than being an 'add-on' to long-established policy, is in the immediate British national interest. 'World peace and stability are in our interests,' says the British section, 'and are more likely to be threatened by countries in which human rights abuses are widespread and in which power is concentrated in the hands of repressive governments. Both economic and human development flourish in stable societies.'

Britain, a member of the European Union, a leading member of NATO and the Commonwealth, with its permanent seat on the UN Security Council, and with a more or less guaranteed membership of the UN Commission of Human Rights, has a position of influence that can make a noticeable impact far and wide. Thus, when the prime minister led the Cabinet in a personal demonstration of goodwill towards Amnesty International, by signing the organization's personal pledge to uphold the values and rights of the Universal Declaration of Human Rights, it produced a resonance in diplomatic and political circles that reached well beyond the confines of the British Isles.

The government has expanded the staff within its bureaucracy dedicated to human rights. It has further entrenched human rights criteria in overseas funding programmes by the Foreign and Commonwealth Office (FCO) and the Department for International Development. It has also increased the training of FCO staff on human rights and brought in a former Amnesty staff member to advise the FCO at its senior levels on the issues of the day. At home, the government initiated a programme of training and instruction for courts, magistrates and officials to prepare for the implementation in October 2000 of the Human Rights Act of 1998, which made the rights obtained in the European Convention on Human Rights directly enforceable in the United Kingdom.

There is one area of foreign policy where the present British government has taken a much more proactive stance than its predecessors, and that is the death penalty. It is actively using its diplomatic representation to promote its world-wide abolition. Initially, the credibility of its new activism was weakened by Britain's own retention of the death penalty for a handful of exceptional war-time offences under the Armed Forces Act, together with statutes permitting it for treason and piracy. However, the last execution under military law was in 1942 and to all intents and purposes Britain has been an abolitionist state since 1965. Still, the decision by parliament in 1998 to abolish the death penalty for every offence both closed the chapter and gave the British campaign for its abolition in other countries a sharper edge.

Britain's present government has also made progress in both enlarging and meeting a number of relatively new international standards. In nearly all cases the initiative had been taken by its Conservative predecessor, but the Blair government, encouraged by Amnesty and many other human rights-orientated lobbies, in a short time ran up an impressive list of achievements.

Most important, it was the only permanent member of the UN Security Council to take an active and positive role in preparing the statutes of the International Criminal Court – in marked contrast to its ally, the USA. The new court will make permanent the work pioneered by the Nuremberg and Tokyo war crimes courts that followed the Second World War, and the more recent international war crimes court established by the UN for ex-Yugoslavia, Rwanda and Sierra Leone. It will be possible to prosecute human rights abusers anywhere in the world by a central court.

Unfortunately, thanks to mainly American and Chinese opposition, the court's powers, although a welcome departure from the void that preceded it, will be circumscribed. For example, it will have to win the permission of the suspect's own country or the state where the crime occurred before it can exercise jurisdiction. The Security Council, moreover, has the right to delay an investigation or prosecution.

The government, having conducted in 1999 a review of the British position in regard to ratification of international human rights instruments, decided to move and ratify Convention 111 of the International Labour Organisation on discrimination in employment; and also announced that it intended to ratify the seventh protocol to the European Convention on Human Rights, which includes such issues as the equality of rights and responsibilities between spouses and a number of fair trial rights including the right to appeal and the right to compensation for miscarriages of justice.

The government also helped push for a new Convention for the Elimination of the Worst Forms of Child Labour, which was agreed to by the International Labour Organisation in June 1999. However, the government attempted successfully to weaken the proposals in the convention on the issue of child soldiers, arguably the most hazardous form of child labour of all. The Coalition to Stop the Use of Child Soldiers, of which Amnesty is a part, lobbied hard. Yet, despite support for an outright ban by countries as diverse as Spain, Uruguay and Canada, together with all the African governments, Britain joined the USA and the Netherlands to limit the ban to forced recruitment. In other words, when recruitment is voluntary, even if the children are under age, it will still be permitted.

Amnesty has long been a campaigner for more open government and noted with satisfaction the British government's introduction at the end of 2000 of a Freedom of Information Act, albeit one not as far-reaching as Amnesty would have liked.

Amnesty has long noted that many human rights abuses are accompanied by deliberate and systematic attempts to suppress information. Over many years Amnesty has observed this, not just in Northern Ireland but in mainland Britain too. Successive British governments have failed to investigate, independently and fully, serious allegations of human rights abuses by law enforcement officials and security forces personnel, to make public the results of internal investigations and to bring perpetrators of abuse to justice. The many cases of court damages to plaintiffs and the large number of out-of-court settlements have highlighted the issue of ill-treatment, without properly dealing with it. Amnesty campaigns have drawn attention to the paucity of prosecutions or disciplinary sanctions against law enforcement officials allegedly involved in assaults or ill-treatment, as well as in disputed killings.

The indications are that there have been a significant number of deaths in police and prison custody, a disproportionate number of which were of people from ethnic minorities. Successive governments have resisted pressure to establish an independent inquiry into these deaths. However, in response to continual pressure, the government launched in May 2000 a consultation on how to make investigations into police misconduct independent and impartial.

Amnesty's initial welcome of the government's decision to introduce a Freedom of Information Act was tempered by the self-imposed limits on full openness the government had insisted upon. The draft bill, for example, specified twenty-one categories of information to be exempted from the general right of access. National security is also given exceedingly wide exemptions. So broad were the exemptions that Amnesty told the government that information relating to the investigation of deaths in police custody would still be heavily circumscribed. Likewise, information made available on prison conditions and the treatment of prisoners would be insufficient if Amnesty is to know what exactly is going on. Moreover, on such questions as arms exports, which led to a major scandal during the previous administration, the government would retain the power to obfuscate and prevaricate by withholding clarity of information.

If Amnesty has had cause to praise the government for delivery on some of its promises, there are other issues where it has found itself on a collision course – in particular the question of the sale of arms used for repression and torture.

For many years Amnesty has argued that the government must exert firmer control over arms exports to prevent British arms from getting into malevolent hands. It is a necessary part of any strategy of conflict prevention. And it is of cardinal importance in promoting human rights in relations with foreign states. How can Britain, if it continues to sell arms that can be used for repression, honestly and credibly continue to raise human rights concerns? Amnesty has told the prime minister that in its opinion the Department of Trade and Industry, which has overseeing responsibility for arms sales, is out of step with the guidelines the government has set for itself. 'It is not meeting its responsibility to promote trade in a manner which is not harmful to human rights. It resists transparency in the control of strategic arms exports. It continues to provide information which the department itself acknowledges to be unreliable.'

The government began well. In July 1997 the foreign secretary, Robin Cook, announced that it 'will not permit the sale of arms to regimes that might use them for internal repression'. Shortly after, it introduced a formal ban on the export of equipment used for torture and other cruel, inhuman or degrading punishment. Under its presidency of the European Union, the government pressed for the introduction of an EU code of conduct on arms sales. This was agreed in June 1998. The government published in 1999 its first ever annual report on strategic export controls, which stands out as one of the most detailed of any European country. Amnesty welcomed it as an important first step towards transparency in the export control system, even while criticizing the government for unacceptably dated information and some serious omissions which make it difficult for Amnesty and other organizations to criticize a government's practice against stated policy until it is too late to have any relevance.

The government, observes Amnesty, has still to address such abuses of the system as the shady practice of end-user certificates, whereby one country (acceptable) is listed as the supposed recipient, while in fact the arms shipment is then transferred to another (unacceptable) destination. The government, in practice, has actually refused very few export licences and Amnesty has documented evidence that British equipment is still being used by countries to inflict human rights abuses. Amnesty's own research revealed that British armoured personnel carriers and water cannons were used to quash demonstrators, sometimes killing them, in Indonesia during 1996 and 1997. As late as 1999 British-made Hawk fighter jets were seen over East Timor. Although in the end the British government, along with the USA and the rest of Europe, welcomed the fall of dictator Suharto and the transition to democracy, in the early days of the protest movement their natural instincts leaned in favour of the status quo.

For decades British export controls on arms sales have been extraordinarily loose. Up until 1999 the reporting categories were so broadly based that it was impossible to ascertain whether a particular transaction was for, say, electro-shock weapons or riot shields. In December 1997 Amnesty raised with the government the issue of human rights violations by Kenyan security forces which, its research showed, had been using British-manufactured tear gas. On one occasion, paramilitary police stormed Nairobi's cathedral, attacking with tear gas and truncheons pro-reform advocators sheltered within.

The government, in defending itself from quizzical MPs, has often enough fallen back on the subterfuge of answering with information it acknowledges is unreliable (due to loose coding of types of weapons in its computer records). 'The Department of Trade and Industry's conduct could be described as a farce were it not for the serious danger involved in exporting military equipment which might be used to commit serious violations of human rights,' observed Amnesty in its 1999 audit.

Another loophole has been licensing agreements, whereby a British company allows another country to manufacture its products. The government permits such agreements without the need either to register them or to enter them in its export controls report. In Turkey, for example, a country which has long been an important concern of Amnesty's, Land Rovers with machine-gun mounts have been transferred from Britain under such schemes. They have been used at home in the savage repression of the Kurds. One Turkish partner company has exported rifles made under licence to Indonesia for police use, and also to Cyprus and Jordan, both notorious tran-shipment centres. Moreover, the government itself has noted in its Strategic Export Controls annual report of March 1999 that 'where they [small arms] are too readily available, they can accumulate in dangerous numbers. They can destabilise whole regions and create a culture of violence.'

Again, when Amnesty raised the matter with the minister respon-sible at the Department for Trade and Industry, it received a reply that indicated that the ministry itself was confused as to its responsi-bility. Yet, despite the evidence marshalled by Amnesty and the four-year time lapse since the publication of the official Scott Report recommending that there should be a new legislative framework for strategic export controls, the promised legislation was slow in being tabled. Despite pressure from Cabinet colleagues, Mr Blair decided not to legislate until he had won a second mandate. However, the government did announce an overhaul in the Export Credit Guaran-tee Department, which, it now admits, devotes too high a proportion of its financial resources to underwriting arms sales.

The Department of Trade and Industry has also developed some plans to introduce a register of brokers. But Amnesty still feels it does not go far enough. In February 2000 it wrote a letter to the *Guardian* arguing that 'to prevent arms getting into the hands of wanton killers, each individual deal made by brokers in any country, embargoes or not, should require a licence'.

At the beginning of the year 2000 Amnesty went back to the government, armed with an opinion poll that it had commissioned from Gallup that showed that 87 per cent of those polled thought 'the government should introduce tighter controls on UK arms sales as soon as possible', and 77 per cent thought 'the government had not done enough to stop the sale of arms to governments which have abused human rights since they came to power'. Amnesty argued yet again that Britain had a totally inadequate monitoring of the way UK arms exports are used overseas; and 'there is no provision to end arms export deals if human rights deteriorate in the purchasing country'. Amnesty's batteries, in fact, had just been recharged by Tony Blair's decision in January 2000 to override the foreign secretary, Robin Cook, who wanted to disapprove the sale to Zimbabwe of spare parts for British Hawk fighter jets. Yet there was evidence aplenty that the planes and other military equipment were being used in a wasteful and counter-productive war in neighbouring Congo, one which the British government had vociferously criticized. Zimbabwe seemed to be a repeat of the situation a year previously when, despite assurances from the Indonesian government, British jets were used to intimidate East Timor. In that case, Cook, who had earlier argued that contracts for new aircraft could not be broken, decided on a four-month suspension of Britain's arms exports to Indonesia, following intense pressure from Amnesty. Finally, as the situation deteriorated in Zimbabwe, with an often violent campaign to expropriate the land of white farmers, Blair agreed to stop the sale of spare parts. Yet later in the year the heavy hand of the prime minister was evident again. He overruled both Robin Cook and Stephen Byers, trade and industry secretary, who had fought for legislation to be introduced in the November 2000 session of parliament to strengthen regulation of the arms trade.

Amnesty International, in a significant broadening of its mandate from its concern with political prisoners and free political expression, has widened its remit in a number of ways. Perhaps its campaigning on behalf of persecuted homosexuals has been the most controversial. But its work to oppose the growing restrictiveness of asylum policy, particularly in Western countries, is the one that has had the most success. The issue was by no means bereft of long-time campaigners, but the addition of Amnesty's political muscle has helped draw more attention to it and, it appears, has produced results.

In Britain, reports Amnesty, the new government's 'treatment of refugees has been confusing'. In a few respects, refugee protection has been strengthened and made more transparent. But at the same time it is both illiberal and authoritarian. Government practices are also riddled with poor management and inefficiency. One example, highlighted by British Amnesty, is how the government, while justifying its military intervention over the crisis in Kosovo with the argument that it was doing so to head off the forced removal of the Albanian part of the population, actually at the same time made remaining in Britain much more difficult for those Albanian refugees who made it to the country.

Although Amnesty welcomed some of the changes in practice proposed by the government with its 1999 Immigration and Asylum bill, such as the provision to allow the European Convention on Human Rights to be argued in appeals, it was deeply disquieted by many other aspects of the bill. It has criticized a range of issues, from the provisions for detention and bail, to asylum appeals procedures, the inflexibility of pre-entry controls and the extended powers of individual immigration officers.

As Amnesty International has widened its brief, Western governments such as Britain's, which have long practised free speech and due process and thus escaped the searchlight of Amnesty's earlier years, have now become a larger target for its critical darts.

The Kosovo crisis is again a good illustration. Amnesty International was one of the few organizations to be concerned about Kosovo, at a time when hardly any British politicians, or even Foreign Office officials, could find it quickly on the map. For over a decade before the war Amnesty had been campaigning against the escalating abuse of ethnic Albanians in Kosovo. It also spoke out against the atrocities committed by the Kosovo Liberation Army led by ethnic Albanians. When the war broke out, Amnesty made it clear that it did not take sides in wars, nor did it take any position on the use of force to resolve international disputes. But it was concerned to ensure the protection of civilians and other non-combatants and the observance of the Geneva Conventions and other sources of international law.

British Amnesty worked hard to bring the interests of Amnesty International before the government, parliament and the press. Amnesty International wrote repeatedly to NATO to express concern that specific incidents in the bombing campaign had been unlawful attacks. It lobbied NATO Secretary-General, Javier Solana, on the importance of NATO forces adhering to the fundamental rules of humanitarian law. It asked for – but did not receive – the relevant details of the rules of engagement, to assess if they complied with international humanitarian law.

The lobbying, the writing and the press releases put British Amnesty at the centre of a strong debate in Britain about the pros and cons of how the war was fought. In the country where Amnesty was born, it finally shed, once and for all, its image of being an organization that only campaigned for the release of prisoners of conscience. Human rights, in its most broad sense, is now the organization's true interest.

Nevertheless, the unhappy truth about the work of Amnesty International is that for every success that can be pointed to – in this chapter in Sri Lanka, Morocco, Colombia and the United Kingdom – there are a dozen cases of failure. And even 'success', as in Colombia, can take place against a larger backdrop of failure. For all that, the overall direction and momentum of the world-wide human rights movement is forward. This will be examined in more detail in the final chapter.

8

China – from Better to Worse?

On the Peking Road in Canton an enormous poster was stuck up one night in mid-November 1974. The poster stretched for a hundred yards of wall. It was a plea, written at incredible length, with 20,000 Chinese characters, for the 'rights of the people'. It attacked the 'suppression' and 'miscarriages of justice' since the Cultural Revolution began in 1966. And it demanded a proper socialist legal system which would be applied to everyone.

The authorities described it as reactionary. They traced the authors, who had signed the poster with a pseudonym, and they were brought before a 'criticism meeting'. Two of the three men arraigned, having admitted their 'guilt', were sent to work under surveillance in the countryside in the province of Guangdong. The third author was a young man named Li Zhengtian, from a 'good' family background, who, as a young graduate, had participated actively in the Cultural Revolution, although he had been caught out in one of its many twists and turns and in 1968 was sentenced to three years' imprisonment. Bravely, he had put his address at the local arts college on the bottom of the poster. He refused to admit 'guilt' and strenuously argued that the message contained in the poster was right. His case dragged on, but in the spring of 1975 he was sent to work 'under the supervision of the masses' in a mine in Guangdong.

The matter did not end there. In June 1977 a traveller to Canton claimed to have seen a court notice announcing that Li Zhengtian had been sentenced to life imprisonment. Later, there were reports that Li Zhengtian had died in detention. Amnesty, however, continued to treat him as a prisoner of conscience and the authorities in

Peking and in Yunnan and Guangdong were regularly bombarded with letters and cards. In early 1979 he and the two others, alive and reasonably well, were released.

Communist China, at the last count, has experienced four cycles of opening and repression. There was the post-death-of-Mao liberalization of 1977–9, the intellectual thaw of 1985–6, the democracy movement of 1989 and, most recently, the 'Beijing Spring' of 1997–8. All have ended on a bitter note, with widespread disillusionment.

When Amnesty International published its blockbuster report, 'Political Imprisonment in the People's Republic of China', in November 1978, Thomas Hammarberg, the then chairman, made a simple but revealing observation: 'Official government statements and Chinese laws confirm the patterns of political imprisonment described by former prisoners. We are not dealing with a situation where the government says one thing and the prisoners say another.'

The report was one of the most detailed and thorough ever produced by Amnesty, creating enormous press interest. It revealed what only a few China specialists had been aware of – that China's great revolution, and later economic and political success, where nearly everyone was fed and absolute poverty had been abolished, had been bought for a great price – the near abolition of personal freedoms and the creation of a repressive machine that was often arbitrary and on occasion quite savage. Whereas the Soviet Union had long been charged by a wide spectrum of critics with being brutal and uncaring in its treatment of dissidents, China had for decades lived with the indulgence, even the favour, of many Western liberals who saw the economic and social progress but ignored the abolition of civil liberties.

The tide of opinion was changed by the Chinese themselves. The death of Mao Zedong in September 1976 allowed the shutters to be opened on the interiors of Chinese life. Amnesty was one of the first outside organizations to look inside. As Hammarberg said, they found the government confirming all they had discovered themselves. The period of daylight was all too brief. Within three years the shutters were closed again, not by any means as tightly as they were under Mao, but enough to make Amnesty's job of prisoner adoption increasingly demanding and exercising.

The Amnesty 1978 survey examined the evolution of Chinese law, the judicial process and penal policy. It was as detailed as a traditional Chinese landscape. The faces on the figures crossing the bridge to torture, imprisonment and, often enough, execution were vivid and real. The inscrutable mask had been dropped for a moment. More of the real China was there to see.

The writing of the Amnesty report was a painstaking affair. Information in China is not easy to come by. The size and diversity of the country, the complexity of the issues, the restriction of movement and the lack of access to information all made the investigation excruciatingly difficult. Nevertheless, there were government documents that were useful although they gave information only on official principles, practices and institutions, and little on individual prisoners and their treatment. The human picture was filled in by ex-prisoners, friends, acquaintances and refugees.

The report reprinted part of an article published in the Chinese *People's Daily* in July 1978 arguing for a 'criminal code', a 'civil code' and a set of 'rules of legal procedure' on the basis on which the 'masses of the people' could 'institute legal proceedings under the law so as to protect their legitimate interests'.

The truth is that, in China, politics and law are intimately entwined, both then and now. The Chinese constitution defined certain groups of people as 'class enemies'. They were deprived of their civil and political rights merely because of their 'class origin' or political background. As the report said, 'political considerations have always been taken into account in the treatment of offenders and this trend has been marked since the Cultural Revolution'. Visitors who had the chance to talk to Chinese judges confirmed this. 'Law', said the Amnesty report, 'is mainly used to enforce official policy,' and is phrased so as to make regulations 'applicable to any opponents of those in power, depending on the current policy line'.

The 'class enemies' concept is a far-reaching one. Mao in his writings, which profoundly influenced state legal policy, argued that classes still existed after the revolution and that the class struggle must continue through the period of socialist construction. Class enemies were broken up into sub-groups, some not well defined. Besides 'landlords' and 'rich peasants', there were 'counter-revolutionaries', 'rightists' and just 'bad elements'. Mao went so far as to declare that the concept of 'the people' varies in different periods of history. 'This argument', said the Amnesty International report, 'puts into broader perspective the policy of repression of political dissent,' as it implied that anyone can in fact become the 'object of the dictatorship' – in other words be deprived of freedom – 'depending on the political necessities of the period'.

Until new laws were adopted in January 1980, there was no habeas corpus in China. Before that a suspected political offender could spend years in a dark cell before being brought to trial. Usually, the aim of the authorities was to 'persuade' a detainee to confess his misdeeds in writing. It was common practice to ask detainees to write lengthy reports on their past thinking, relations and activities. The accused could not refuse to write such reports because this was officially considered as a lack of co-operation with the government and was treated as an offence in itself.

Torture and coercion to extract confessions were, according to the law, prohibited. In practice, the pressures were formidable. 'In some cases', observed the Amnesty report, 'it is reported that non-stop interrogation is used to "crack" a case.' In addition:

Tellingly named 'struggle meetings' can be organized to bring pressure on the accused to confess. These meetings can go on for hours, even days, and may become so tense that insults, threats, various forms of humiliating procedures and even blows are used by the people in the audience to undermine and weaken the prisoner's will.

It is a peculiarly Chinese invention, combining intimidation, humiliation and sheer exhaustion. Briefly described, it is an intellectual gang-beating of one man by many, sometimes even thousands, in which the victim has no defence, even the truth ... After three or four days the victim begins inventing sins he has never committed, hoping that an admission monstrous enough might win him a reprieve. After a week of struggling he is prepared to go to any lengths.

The Chinese legal system hinged on these confessions. When the confession was made and the dossier prepared, the police authorities then forwarded the material to a judge for trial. The trial was a formality. Trial is a misnomer. In many cases, it was merely a meeting to announce the sentence.

The Amnesty report, although sent to the Chinese government six months ahead of publication, received no comment or corrections. Officially, it has not been answered, nor were Amnesty's enquiries about individual prisoners. Nevertheless, it was known that extracts from the report were published in Chinese unofficial journals, which would have reached a restricted circle – young activists, intellectuals and some party officials.

The report came out while Vice-Premier Deng Xiaoping, the most influential personage in the ruling class, was pushing China into a period of political liberalization. Only a few months after the publication of the Amnesty report, there were large-scale releases and rehabilitations. Several million people had their reputations and jobs restored. The 'Democracy and Human Rights Movement' began and wall-posters flourished. Unofficial publications appeared and were even tolerated. In the spring of 1978 a new constitution had been enacted. And in the autumn the minister of public security said there was an urgent need to revise existing laws and to draft a criminal law, a civil law and a code of criminal procedure. In the *People's Daily*, he was quoted as saying that letters from people in various parts of the country had revealed that cadres 'have violated laws, wantonly abused their powers, and bullied and oppressed the masses and encroached upon people's rights'. The press carried many similar acknowledgements about past miscarriages of justice and the problems involved in redressing them.

Seven new laws, revising the criminal statutes, were submitted for approval at the Fifth National People's Congress in the summer of 1979. According to the director of the Commission for Legislative Affairs, the new laws stipulated the protection of a citizen's rights against infringement by 'any person or organization'. To extort confessions by torture, to gather a crowd 'to beat, smash and loot' and to detain illegally and prosecute on false charges were to be strictly forbidden. Nevertheless, the liberalization legislation seemed ambiguous. 'Counter-revolutionaries', defined sweepingly as anyone who 'attempts to overthrow the political power of the dictatorship of the proletariat and the socialist system', were still to be prosecuted. Besides this, a number of the more restrictive old laws were left standing.

It soon became clear that the political atmosphere which would allow liberalization to develop and strengthen was wanting. In late March 1979 the government took steps to ban posters and books 'opposed to socialism and to the leadership of the party'. Several human rights activists were arrested, including Wei Jingsheng, the 29-year-old author of perhaps the best-written and most outspoken of the wall-posters, 'Democracy the Fifth Modernization'. At his trial Wei Jingsheng was convicted of passing on 'military secrets' to a foreigner and of conducting 'counter-revolutionary propaganda and agitation'. He was sentenced to fifteen years' imprisonment.

Soon after his arrest, Amnesty adopted him as a 'prisoner of conscience'. His detention and trial were carefully watched and recorded by Amnesty's research department. The hearing, which lasted only a few hours, was not open to foreigners nor to the general public, but reports on it by the official press and an unofficial and illegally circulated transcript of the trial revealed that procedures had changed little if at all since Amnesty published its report. No defence witness was called, and the alleged 'secret' nature of the information was not considered. In fact, it seems that the information given by Wei Jingsheng to a Western journalist, concerning the China–Vietnam border conflict, was not particularly secret and was circulating widely among Chinese citizens.

A month later, three young men were arrested at 'democracy wall' while distributing the unofficial transcript of the trial. At the end of the year the authorities closed 'democracy wall' as part of the official campaign to 'restore law and order' and to put an end to unofficial publishing and discourage potential dissenters. In a major speech in Peking in January 1980, Deng Xiaoping stated that the central committee of the Communist Party was preparing to submit a motion to the National People's Congress that would delete from the constitution provisions legalizing wall-posters. He went on to say:

Factional elements still exist ... There are also so-called democrats and dissidents who openly oppose the socialist system and the CCP leadership, such as Wei Jingsheng and his ilk ... Although they sometimes say that they support Chairman Mao and the CCP, they actually want to oppose the CCP leadership and socialism ...

They are quite capable of banding together under certain conditions and forming a sabotage force capable of causing a great deal of turmoil and damage ...

It is the unswerving principle of our Party to persevere in developing democracy and the legal system. However ... they must be carried out step by step and in a controlled way. Otherwise, they may only encourage turmoil and impede the four modernizations, democracy and the legal system ... It is absolutely impermissible to publicize any freedom of speech, publication, assembly or to form associations which involve counter-revolutionaries. It is absolutely impermissible for any persons to contact these people behind the Party's back ... Where does the paper come from? These people do not have printing presses. Are there any Party members in the printing works who print these things? Some of the people who support these activities are Party members and quite a few of them are even cadres. We must tell these Party members clearly that their standpoint is very erroneous and dangerous and if they do not correct it immediately and completely they will be liable for Party disciplinary punishment.

If Mao's China was long protected by western liberals from censure, it was to find, perhaps to its own surprise, that from the time of Richard Nixon onwards a new wave of dispensation came from the right of the political spectrum. Nixon, while campaigning for the presidency, had written a sensational article in the magazine *Foreign Affairs*, anticipating a more conciliatory US policy towards China. Soon after Nixon's election the USA moved to recognize communist China, which it had refused to do for twenty-two years, and ejected Taiwan from the Chinese seat at the UN.

Nixon had decided to capitalize on the Sino-Soviet rift and enlist China as a strategic counterweight to Soviet power. His historic visit to Beijing launched a campaign to persuade the American and Western European electorates that China was the good communist power and the Soviet Union the bad one. 'The Chinese were courteous, industrious, family orientated, modest to the point of being shy. They had the most wonderful ancient and cultural tradition. They were wizards at ping-pong; they loved giant pandas. In less than a year public opinion completely turned around. Everyone loved the so-recently hated and feared China,' wrote, bitingly but perceptively, the Russian author Vladimir Pozner.

Later, during the presidency of Jimmy Carter, the Soviet invasion of Afghanistan spurred further co-operation with China. Carter, who had vowed he wouldn't 'ass-kiss' the Chinese and who championed human rights as a centrepiece of his foreign policy, paid no heed to the jailing of the Democracy Wall activists in 1979. Carter was intent on concluding the formal normalization of relations with China. Just like Nixon, who was either oblivious of or indifferent to the turmoil of the Cultural Revolution when he first met Mao, Carter looked the other way when the great Chinese dissident Wei Jingsheng was sentenced to fifteen years' imprisonment. The Carter State Department spokesmen said no more than that the US was 'surprised and disappointed at the severity of the sentence'. (Yet at more or less the same time Carter was lambasting Moscow for sending Soviet dissident Anatol Sharansky to prison.)

Ronald Reagan, Carter's successor, was very much part of the Nixon tradition of *realpolitik*, although with more than a dash of rightist romanticism thrown in. He spoke dreamily during his visit to China in 1984 of 'so-called communist China'. George Bush, who took over from him, had represented, as ambassador, Nixon's policy in Beijing. It was on Bush's watch that America's great strategic friend and pro-capitalist reformer, Deng Xiaoping, sent in the tanks and murdered in Tiananmen Square two thousand or more protesting students, armed with nothing more than their bicycles. But Bush, determined to keep the relationship on an even keel, whatever the cost, dispatched with unseemly haste his National Security Advisor, Brent Scowcroft, to reassure Beijing of Washington's solid, enduring relationship. China, however, had lost for all time what it could not win back – the fawning attention of the American and European press and the warm feelings of Western public opinion.

Bill Clinton, campaigning to unseat Bush, charged that Bush was soft on China and promised, if elected, that the age of conciliation would be over. But once in power it did not take long for Clinton to fall into line with the Nixon legacy, even though the main geopolitical reason for it – to balance the Soviet Union – was no longer relevant. The policy was to engage China, go for a long-term policy, tell the American public and the world that, in the words of Samuel Berger, Clinton's National Security Advisor, 'through engagement you can get a lot of serious things done and maybe even advance the process of change in China'.

Thus the American voice on human rights was muted once more – and the Europeans followed suit, convincing themselves that to take a 'lonely' stand criticizing Beijing's record on human rights would mean the loss of business contracts and influences, which would simply go to America.

Nothing could have been more revealing than the West's performance in 1997 when a vote came up at the UN Human Rights Commission in Geneva to condemn China's record. Denmark had tabled the motion in the spring. The Chinese lobbyists went into overdrive. Denmark was told by Beijing that its criticism would be 'a rock that smashed down on the Danish government's head'. Several Danish contracts were cancelled, and as Chris Patten, the present EU commissioner responsible for foreign affairs, wrote later: 'And what did anyone do? Nothing. What in particular did members of the European Union do? They looked the other way.'

In 1998 Europe went one step further or, as Human Rights Watch described it, 'a major step backwards'. Rewarding China for its behaviour the previous year, the European foreign ministers threw in the towel. They announced that 'in view of the first encouraging results of the European Union–Chinese human rights dialogue they would neither table nor co-sponsor the Geneva resolution in 1998'. The president of the European Union's Foreign Affairs Council, the British foreign secretary, Robin Cook, cited Wei Jingsheng's release as an example of the results of the dialogue, a proposition roundly denounced by Wei himself. In conversation with me, Wei Jingsheng observed: 'When Beijing's relations with the West improve, conditions get worse for the dissidents inside China's jails.' It was with an almost audible sigh of relief that Washington joined Europe in dropping its sponsorship of the resolution. A senior Clinton administration figure was quoted in the *New York Times* as saying: 'It is being done as a calculation. It is being done because we believe it is the way to make progress in the future.'

It is true, and should be stated before any further analysis of China's human rights practices, that compared with twenty years ago, when Amnesty published its great critique, the human rights situation is improved and the average Chinese citizen has much more liberty than ever under communist rule, both political and economic. The very fact that there is a great deal of economic and cultural liberty – to find one's own job, to make money independently, to wear the clothes one wants, to listen to Western classical or pop music, to make friends with foreigners and to travel, is a turnaround of immense proportions. Moreover, there is a thriving underground press that is more or less tolerated, and in the villages local elections are now held on a regular basis. Even in the National People's Congress the voting is no longer on every issue a foregone formality. (Li Peng, the former hard-line prime minister, only secured 88 per cent of the vote in his bid to win appointment as head of the Congress. This compares with the 99 per cent vote for Zhu Ronghi to be the new prime minister.) Citizens are allowed – and tens of thousands do – to bring lawsuits against the government. To this extent, the human rights lobby is now holding China to a higher standard than two decades ago. In addition, China is not an open-and-shut situation. Prime Minister Zhu Ronghi himself admitted on his visit to the USA in 1999 that China's treatment of dissenters remains inhuman and indecent.[1] Also remarkable were the interviews given to CNN and several liberal Hong Kong papers by Bao Tong, a former chief of staff to former president Zhao Ziyang, on the occasion of the tenth anniversary of the killings in Tiananmen Square.

Mr Bao spent seven years in prison after the crackdown, which

[1] 'Does China Matter?', by Gerald Segal, in *Foreign Affairs*, 78/5 (1999), p. 34.

also led to the toppling of Mr Zhao, after Deng Xiaoping had overruled him on the use of force. Mr Zhao, said Mr Bao, wanted negotiations with the students 'based on democratic principles and the use of law'. He went on to say: 'I continue to believe that most of the senior leaders did not want to see a crackdown and a halt to political reform. However, many of those high officials, prominent academics and company leaders who supported the students and recoiled at the thought of sending in troops later lost their jobs and now live in quiet retirement.'

'What the public didn't know', continued Bao, 'was that Zhao's policy had obtained support of a majority at both the Politburo meetings of 8 May and 10 May. [The Tiananmen Square massacre was on 4 June.] But Deng tragically overruled Zhao.'

If such divisions went right to the top of the Communist Party twelve years ago, one can be sure that they exist in today's China too. China is being tugged towards democracy and human rights by powerful forces within as well as without. It is also now very obvious that the Chinese people themselves care very much about open politics and civil liberties – this is not just Western concoction or imposition. Where has there been more political struggle? Where have there been more dramatic eruptions of outrage about civil liberties?

Does outside pressure add to or distract from this? Wei Jingsheng, who was, until his release at the end of 1997, Amnesty's longest-serving political prisoner in China, is very clear about that. His own treatment and conditions in prison, he says, bore a direct relationship to the amount of fuss made about him. The louder the noise, the better he was treated. Yet even Wei's release had a double edge, or rather a quid pro quo. The Americans in 1997 hatched a deal with Beijing: if he and fellow dissident Wang Dan were released, President Jiang Zemin would be entertained at the White House. The Americans – and their European allies – would also withhold their support for the annual resolution at the UN Human Rights Commission condemning China. Quiet diplomacy had been shown to get results, said the powers-that-be in the USA and Western Europe.

Thus, America's latter-day turnaround on the UN's annual vote on China's abuse of human rights is of great significance. In early

2000 Washington announced that it would itself introduce a resolution at the UN Human Rights Commission to condemn China for what it said was a deteriorating human rights situation. Trade, the sale of technology, exchanges of experts, and other foreign relations will be treated on their own merits, said Washington. Human rights, apparently, is now going to be treated on its own. The two will no longer be mixed, which has meant that for the best part of thirty years the West has diluted, often beyond taste, its efforts on behalf of China's dissidents. As Wei Jingsheng has shrewdly observed: 'The Chinese government's concept of human rights has not moved towards the universal standard of human rights. On the contrary, the human rights values of Western politicians have moved closer to those of communist China . . .'

For most of this time Amnesty has been on its own, a lone voice, digging out, piecing together and then, when a case was clear, megaphoning the latest case of abuse, false imprisonment or execution to the world outside. In recent years it has been joined by Human Rights Watch, a plethora of local human rights bodies based in Hong Kong and, uncertainly, by human rights groups inside mainland China itself.

Typical of the rat-a-tat of pressure Amnesty International keeps on the authorities was the letter written by Pierre Sané to Jiang Zemin on the fiftieth anniversary of the foundation of the People's Republic of China on 1 October 1999. 'At this juncture we believe that the Chinese leadership must decide whether China in the next fifty years will be ruled by law and justice and respect its citizens' human rights, or whether it will remain known as a country where serious human rights violations occur on a daily basis and state officials routinely ignore the law and abuse their power.'

'At one point', Sané wrote, 'Amnesty thought things were going for the better.' He pointed out that 'China in 1997 and 1998 had signed (but not ratified) two important human rights treaties[1] and

---

[1] The International Covenant on Civil and Political Rights and the International Covenant on Social, Economic and Civil Rights. In January 2001, Beijing announced it would soon ratify the second, weaker, treaty.

had made numerous revisions in recent years to legislation which governed the rights of criminal suspects.' (Sané could have added that earlier that year an official Chinese study of 4.56 million criminal cases reported 12,000 wrongful court judgements and nearly 1,500 cases involving illegal custody, forced confessions, retaliation or frame-up. This followed a similar study by the Supreme People's Procurator a year before in which for the first time China published statistics on the number of people who have been tortured to death by the police – 126 during interrogations in 1995 and 115 in 1994.) But recently, continued Sané, Amnesty had observed 'a major leap backwards with the most serious wide-ranging crackdown on peaceful dissent carried out by the authorities since 1989 [the time of Tiananmen Square] . . . The authorities arrested three key dissidents who had attempted to form and register an alternative political party, the China Democratic Party (CDP). They were put on trial within a month with a speed rarely seen in recent years and sentenced to harsh prison terms for subversion after unfair trial proceedings.' Since this trial, continued Sané, the pace of arrests has picked up among 'a broad range of people', including those who have raised a new (for China) range of issues, such as labour rights, the environment and corruption.

Sané singled out the crackdown on Falun Gong, a spiritual movement that the government has banned. 'Thousands of its followers were arbitrarily detained and put under pressure to renounce their beliefs and denounce the group . . . Some were reportedly tortured or ill-treated . . . While torture is prohibited by Chinese law,'[1] continued Sané, 'few of the perpetrators are punished. Many police, prison and labour camp officials show utter contempt for the human rights of detainees and for the law, knowing full well they are unlikely to be punished.'

Sané then pointed out how in 1997 the Chinese government had won international plaudits when the overly political 'counter-revolutionary crimes' were removed from the Criminal Law but now,

when challenged, officials explain that the change from counter-revolutionary to national security crimes in the law was in name only.

[1] China has signed and ratified the International Convention Against Torture.

The UN Working Group on Arbitrary Detention, which visited China in December 1998, has determined that the new crimes against national security, instead of bringing Chinese law more in line with international standards, have *significantly expanded* the potential for indicting people who exercise fundamental human rights.

It was a damning letter, throwing down the gauntlet to the Chinese leadership. In effect, it warned President Jiang that, after years of concentrating on individual cases in a fluid situation that seemed overall to be moving in the right direction, Amnesty was back to criticizing the whole system, one that appeared to be going in reverse. 'Even the rhetoric has gone backwards,' said Amnesty in a letter to European Union governments. And in February 2000 Amnesty again went on the attack, responding to a White Paper released by Beijing in defence of its human rights accord. 'The White Paper seeks to explain away shortcomings in Beijing's human rights record by arguing that China is still a developing country and is limited by impediments of natural, historical and economic development.' But 'human rights abuses will not simply fade away with economic development. Any great leap forwards', said Amnesty, echoing Mao Zedong, 'requires a leap of political will. The ongoing crackdown on peaceful dissent is alienating and potentially destabilizing for China.'

In fact, over recent years Amnesty has gone overboard to try and meet those voices in the developing world who argue that human rights are not just about habeas corpus and free expression but include the right to work, food and shelter. At the 1993 UN Conference on Human Rights, Amnesty fought hard for the final declaration to include the argument that human rights are indivisible and independent, and that economic and social rights are as important as civil and political rights. Indeed, the US delegation took a lot of persuading to go along with this phrasing. Amnesty has no doubt that the two aspects must proceed together. The progress of one reinforces the progress of the other.

Amnesty's current preoccupations in China can be broken down into seven categories – arbitrary detention, imprisonment for offences against national security, disregard for criminal procedures, the targeting of those who attempt to contact human rights monitors, torture, the death penalty and the persecution of ethnic minorities.

- Since China signed the International Convention on Civil and Political Rights at the end of 1998 Amnesty has monitored the detention of over seventy political activists and concerned citizens. At least half are still in detention. Most of the rest have been detained repeatedly, many, taking China's signature at face value, for exercising their right to freedom of association. Although the government publicly asserts that it values highly the work of non-governmental organizations, in practice it apparently fears many of them, especially if their titles seem to challenge the *status quo* – 'The Chinese Labour Monitor', 'Corrupt Behaviour Observers' and 'Chinese People's Civil Rights Organization'.
- Since January 1999 alone China has sentenced twenty-eight prisoners of conscience, members of the 'China Democratic Party' the majority prosecuted under the revised national security offences of the 1997 Criminal Law. They either received long prison terms after unfair trials or were sent, without trial, to up to three years' 're-education' in labour camps.

Three of the most prominent prisoners of conscience are Xu Wenli, Qin Yongmin and Wang Youcai, all convicted for attempting to register the Chinese Democratic Party. They received thirteen-, twelve- and eleven-year terms respectively. They were accused of 'plotting to subvert State Power'. Only Xu had a lawyer, appointed by the state. Wang's chosen lawyer was detained several times to prevent him conducting the defence. Qin's family tried to hire a lawyer, but those in their home city of Wuham were warned not to defend him.

Tens of thousands of Falun Gong practitioners have also been arbitrarily detained by police. Many of them are reported to have been tortured or ill-treated. The government has also cracked down on other 'heretical organizations', such as a number of Qi Gong organizations which promote meditation and breathing exercises.

Talking to members of the foreign press has again become a

treasonable offence, leading to heavy prison terms for 'divulging state secrets'. One labour activist, Zhang Shanguang, was given ten years in December 1998 for giving an interview to Radio Free Asia about farmers' protests. Li Yi and Wu Ruojie, respectively a business-man and a rock singer, were similarly accused for talking to foreign journalists about the arrest of Wu's brother and three other poets, who had been planning to launch an independent literary magazine. In January 1999 Lin Hai was sentenced to two years' imprisonment for 'inciting the subversion of state power': passing on e-mail addresses to an overseas Chinese e-mail news network. Foreign jour-nalists, including those from Reuters, the Associated Press and the *New York Times*, have been detained and questioned and obliged to sign a 'confession of wrongdoing'.

• In several of the high profile prosecutions of prisoners of conscience in 1998 the authorities blatantly disregarded provisions of the much-trumpeted 1996 revised Criminal Procedure Law, which theoretically provides for greater access to legal representation, notification of relatives and public trials. In April 1998, just to take one example, Turgan Tay, a 28-year-old businessman from Gulja, Xinjiang, was sentenced to ten years' imprisonment for 'illegal' religious activities. The trial was held in secret. No lawyer, nor even a relative, was allowed to be present.

Even when the likes of Mary Robinson, the UN High Commissioner for Human Rights, visits China, the authorities, obsequious to her material comfort, totally disregard the actual purpose of her visit, to the point of parody. This happened when Chu Hailan, the wife of a dissident, tried to meet Mrs Robinson on one of her visits in 1998. Mrs Chu was detained and, what is more, beaten up. Similarly, two Tibetan monks, Kyonmed and Sandrual, who tried to present her with a letter during her visit to Tibet, were detained and have been imprisoned ever since. Prisoners have also faced severe reprisals for protests timed to coincide with visits by international delegations. One instance was when the UN Working Group on Arbitrary Detention visited Drapchi prison in Lhasa, Tibet in October 1997. Another was around the time of the visit of the European Union troika to the same prison some months later.

- Torture is inflicted on political and common criminal prisoners alike. 'Crime' is not a prerequisite for torture. Merely arguing with a policeman or other official can lead to a savage beating. Yan Zhengxue, 50 years old, earned his living as a painter. Moreover, he was certainly not a 'nobody'; he was a deputy in the Zjejiang provinces People's Congress. He was detained by the police following an argument with a bus conductor in Beijing. What happened then would be extraordinary if it were a lone case, but Amnesty have hundreds of such examples. This is what he told a local newspaper:

When we arrived at the police station, the tall thin one boxed my ears five or six times, then hit me with his electric truncheon, forcing me to the floor. Then they put handcuffs on me ... After several blows to my head and face I saw stars and fell to the floor. They pulled me to my feet by my hair and continued the beating. I reckon he hit me with about thirty blows. Another fat policeman kicked my legs, an older man stood by, watching. By now, I was nauseous and wanting to vomit ... At last I collapsed on the floor and could not struggle. Then another policeman came over and kicked me in the groin ... They went on kicking my stomach and groin. My groin was unbearably painful and I tried to protect it with my hands. They pulled me by the hair and forced me to squat. By now my hands had lost almost all feeling ...

An Amnesty report prepared in April 2000 as a comment on China's Third Periodic Report to the UN Committee Against Torture observed:

In recent years, victims of torture have included many people who simply became involved in disputes with officials, questioning their authority or attempting to uphold their rights. Officials have resorted to torture in the collection of legitimate fines and taxes. Torture as part of blackmail and extortion by corrupt officials is also frequently reported. Migrant workers, particularly young women far from the protection of family and community, are easy prey and frequent victims.

The authorities do acknowledge that torture occurs. But the numbers are played down and although it is difficult for Amnesty to come up with precise quantitative measurement there is enough evidence, it believes, to show that it is widespread and systemic.

During the early 1970s there were well-documented reports of severe torture in Guanzhou's No. 1 Detention Centre. Both men and women were shackled on a 'tiger bed'. The device consists of a wooden door laid flat on short legs with handcuffs at the four corners. A hole in the centre allows the passage of urine and excrement. Prisoners could be shackled to the 'tiger bed' for weeks on end. Other more common forms of torture include incarceration in tiny or dark cells without heat, ventilation or sanitation; handcuffing for prolonged periods; exposure to intense heat or cold; deprivation of food or sleep; and being made to sit or stand without moving for long periods. Often prisoners are beaten, whipped and kicked. Electric batons are used to give the victim powerful shocks. Prisoners are often suspended by the arms and then beaten. In many cases torture leads to death. The press does report on many such cases. Yet Amnesty is convinced they are only a fraction of the total. Moreover, the press limits itself in reporting torture cases to those that occur just after arrest. It shies away from reporting deaths in penal institutions, or those of political prisoners.

In Tibet children have been tortured. A teenager told Amnesty that he and five other youths, including some aged only 13, were kicked and beaten with belts by police officers for singing nationalist songs while out walking in Lhasa. Later, at the police station, most of their clothes were removed and they were beaten with a whip made of wires.

Although China is a signatory to the Convention Against Torture and makes regular voluntary reports to the Committee Against Torture, which monitors the Convention, its domestic legislation is inadequate in failing to criminalize all forms of torture. China's criminal law provides sanctions for two specific offences – 'torture to coerce a statement' and 'corporal punishment and abuse'. In addition, illegal and ill-treatment of illegally detained people is also an offence. However, the law does not extend to the criminalization of those who use torture to punish, intimidate or coerce. Further-more, the law only prohibits ill-treatment in a number of limited circumstances and only provides for light punishment. Relative to the high incidence of the known cases of torture, the number of judicial investigations remains on the low side.

Amnesty argues that there are at least four reasons for this. First, the procuracies have limited power to initiate criminal investigations into torture allegations. Second, the police themselves often interfere in the investigation of torture allegations. Third, there is a lack of public scrutiny of the procedures followed during an investigation. Nor are there known procedures stipulated by law on how investigations should be carried out. Not least, the fear of reprisals and distrust of the complaints system inhibit many prisoners and their relatives from making formal complaints. Yet the Convention Against Torture explicitly states that member countries should protect complainants against such intimidation.

- In China the death penalty is applied extensively, sometimes for non-violent crimes, too often for political reasons and, in many cases, simply arbitrarily. The death penalty is used more than in any other country in the world. Indeed, more people are executed in China than in all the other countries of the world combined. The actual figures are a 'state secret'. But Amnesty reckons there are over three thousand executions each year.

The death penalty has been applied for such offences as the poisoning of livestock, killing a tiger, seriously disrupting public order, embezzlement, reselling value-added tax receipts, dealing in cultural relics and pornography. The only significant positive change in the revised Criminal Law is the abolition of its use for offenders who were under the age of 18 years at the time the crime was committed.

'A young man is forced to his knees. His hands and feet are tied, his head is bowed. A soldier orders him to be quiet. A shot rings out and the man crumples to the ground. A moment later there is another shot. Another crumpled body. Again and again until dozens of lives have ended in cold blood.' The scene is a mass execution. They are not uncommon in China. Some happen in public. Most take place at discreet execution grounds after the condemned prisoners have been paraded at mass rallies or driven through the streets on the back of lorries. 'The Chinese authorities', says Amnesty, 'use the death penalty to create fear. The fear is supposed to stop crime. It does not. In many cases the death penalty is applied arbitrarily and with no safeguards against miscarriages of justice.'

Spates of executions often precede major festivals or international events. They usually accompany official announcements of anti-crime campaigns. Summary trials are particularly common during 'law and order' campaigns. The death penalty has been widely applied during crackdowns on opposition. Dozens of people were summarily executed in Beijing following the 1989 pro-democracy protests. Muslim nationalists have been executed in Xinjiang for alleged involvement in underground opposition groups or bombings.

A growing number of people are being executed each year for quite minor offences. In 1994, for instance, two peasants were put to death in Henan province for stealing thirty-six cows and $9,000 worth of agricultural machinery. Defendants can be tried without the help of a lawyer and without knowing the accusations until they reach the court. Verdicts are frequently decided before a trial as a result of political interference. Some people are condemned solely on the basis of their confession, which may have been extracted under torture. Executions can take place within a few days of sentencing. Appeals are a mere formality and rarely succeed. Examples of innocent people who were executed have occasionally been mentioned in the Chinese press. In 1995 Li Xiuwu was declared innocent seven years after he was executed on conviction of murdering a farmer and stealing.

- 'In China's many diverse regions, members of ethnic groups live under the shadow of repressive laws and regulations which deny them the right to express peacefully their natural religious or cultural aspirations. Official policies also allow those in authority to exercise their power arbitrarily and flagrantly abuse human rights.' Thus Amnesty leads off a critical report on China's rule in the Tibet Autonomous Region, the Xinjiang Uighur Autonomous Region and Inner Mongolia.

Although Amnesty itself has taken no position on the much-debated question of the political status of Tibet – is it an independent nation or not? – it has waged a strong campaign on behalf of the right of the Tibetan people to argue for independence and free speech. Since September 1987 and a resurgence of demonstrations in favour of Tibetan independence thousands have been arbitrarily detained, dozens of demonstrators shot dead and many tortured. In recent years, repression has intensified in the rural areas following a growth in unrest.

In the last few years the authorities have regularly introduced intense 'patriotic education campaigns'. Their purpose is to force Tibetans, especially monks and nuns, to denounce the Dalai Lama, the Tibetan religious leader long in exile in India, and admit that Tibet has always been part of China. As a result of the campaign, claim the authorities, 76 per cent of Tibetan monasteries and nunneries have been 'rectified'. Monks and nuns who refuse to be 'educated' face expulsion. Of some six hundred Tibetan political prisoners, 80 per cent are monks or nuns. It still remains unclear whether Gendun Choekyi Nyima, the 9-year-old boy recognized by the Dalai Lama in 1995 as the reincarnation of the Panchen Lama, is still under house arrest. The Chinese authorities have repeatedly denied requests, including that of the UN High Commissioner for Human Rights, for access to the boy.

In Xinjiang, the Muslim region of China, separatist activity has grown in vigour in recent years. Dissident organizations claim that many ethnic Uighurs suspected of supporting the separatist cause have been detained, and some executed. Occasionally, violent clashes erupt with Uighurs in gun battles with the police – as happened in 1990 and again in 1999. There are also – if rarely – incidents of bombing by dissidents. Thousands of people have been arbitrarily detained and arrests continue. Thousands of political prisoners arrested during the 1990s are still detained, some having been sentenced to long prison terms after unfair trials. Scores of Uighurs, many of them political prisoners, have been sentenced to death and executed in the last few years. Extra-judicial executions are not uncommon.

At present, in both Tibet and Xinjiang, the lid is firmly on; protest and dissidence is even less tolerated than it is in the rest of China. Only in Hong Kong, which reverted from Britain to China in 1997, are the basic freedoms of speech, protest and religious expression respected, albeit within a rather rigid political structure. The Chinese Beijing-appointed governor holds most of the power and the legislature has severe limits placed both on its powers and on its means of election. There is widespread popular support for a full democracy in Hong Kong; pro-democracy candidates won more than 60 per cent of the directly elected seats in the first elections under Chinese sovereignty, held in May 1999. Nevertheless, there is a creeping influence from Beijing in the legal area. In particular, local courts ruled that the Chinese National People's Congress had the right to override the Basic Law, the document agreed by China and Britain as Hong Kong's constitution.

The hopes that were raised during the so-called 'Beijing Spring' of 1997–8 have now withered in a premature autumn. For a brief moment intellectuals had greater freedom to debate political and economic reform. Books that before would have been banned were published. Community-based organizations continued to emerge, the government signed a major human rights treaty and some notable prisoners were released, including student leader Wang Dan. By March 1999 it seemed that, with the appointment of a liberal economic reformer, Zhu Rongji, as prime minister and the apparently successful consolidation of power by President Jiang Zemin, the spring might even turn into an early summer. In fact, the reverse has happened. 'Crackdown' is the word Human Rights Watch now uses, pointing to:

- An intensified attack on all organizations that the Chinese Communist Party perceives are a threat to its rule.
- A series of regulations that constrain free association and assembly and religious expression.
- The ongoing arrest of Tibetan 'splittists' and tightened secular control of Tibetan Buddhism.

- The stepped-up pace of arrests and executions in Xinjiang.
- A rigorous attempt to interfere with the free flow of information at home and abroad, including academic research. The Ministry of State Security is now able to track individual e-mail accounts through monitoring devices. (An estimated nine million Chinese have access to the Internet.) In the course of 1999 twenty-seven newspapers were punished for offences such as 'political errors'.

When will the outside world begin to put China into some sort of perspective? Despite its immense size, a fifth of the world's population, and the longevity of its great civilization, its possession of nuclear weapons and its permanent seat on the Security Council of the United Nations, it is not a budding superpower.

In the 1970s it was Brazil that was going to be the superstar of the decade – and perhaps for evermore. In the 1980s the talk was of Japan. In the 1990s China, Brazil and Japan came unstuck in different ways – Brazil, after decades of being the century's fastest growing economy (along with Taiwan), because it overspent and, in its massive state and social sectors, chronically underperformed; Japan because its quasi-feudal company and ministerial structures protected too well the dross as well as the gold in a system that could never bring itself to embrace capitalist meritocracy in all its parts. Now, as unemployment, inequality and crime rise, the indications are increasing that China might be looked back on as the third big falling star of the latter half of the twentieth century. China perhaps, after all, is not 'a miracle about to be performed'. In China the veneer of end-of-the-century technology and know-how is eggshell thin.

China, since the days in 1793 of the mission of Earl Macartney, emissary of King George III, has kept its distance from the West, preferring to be as 'self-contained as a billiard ball', to quote the great historian Alain Peyrefitte. It was Peyrefitte who argued in *The Collision of Civilisations* that Macartney's decision not to kowtow to the emperor gave the Chinese the impression that their civilization was denied. They withdrew into their bunker and have remained for the last two hundred years prickly, ultra-sensitive, quick to take offence and too ready to assume the worst of the West's motives.

Thus, among Sinologists, there has developed a strong school of thought that there is only one way of dealing with China – a sort of delayed, reversed, kowtow, always leaning over backwards neither to provoke nor to annoy China, even allowing China to rewrite whatever language it is negotiating in. This is combined with the propensity of many in the West, both in politics and business, to project the economic growth rates of the Deng Xiaoping era into the distant future, while taking little note of its paucity of legal and institutional framework (unlike its rival, India) to contain such endeavour. Reasoning of this kind, assuming China will soon mature into a superstate, seems to blight good sense. 'It encourages China', as the last British governor of Hong Kong, Chris Patten, has written in his provocative book *East and West*, 'to think it can become part of the modern world entirely on its own terms. Were that to happen it would make the world a more dangerous and less prosperous place. China remains a classic case of hope over experience, reminiscent of de Gaulle's famous comment about Brazil: "It has great potential and always will."'

Since the communist revolution in 1949, Western governments in their China policy 'have offered us, with rare exceptions, a choice of extremes – flab or flint, engagement or constraint'. Lurching from one to another has made little sense. President Clinton, who criticized George Bush for pampering Beijing's dictators, in mid-presidency came perilously close to doing exactly that himself.

Patten has it right: 'I'm not scared witless of the People's Republic of China, nor mesmerized by China's might and majesty. I am on balance more scared of things wrong in China – the splintering of China, the breakdown of governance. China is at the end of an era. Marxism and Maoism are dead. What does the communist party have to offer other than cynicism and decadence?' Sometimes, as Patten concludes, one has to pinch oneself to remember who needs whom most. Perhaps, to begin with, we should never forget the simple but important fact that China represents only 1.7 per cent of all Western exports added together.

It is quite pathetic, it is laughable, but above all distasteful that Western countries regularly betray each other, and, in so doing, the human rights activists inside China, in an effort to better position themselves in this quite modest market-place. If, as Patten argues, Western governments could stand shoulder to shoulder and say once and mean it, 'Stop using economic and trade threats: you are in no position to do so, it is unacceptable behaviour,' Beijing would get the message.

Only lately have cracks appeared in the unseemly union between the old time leftist/liberal fantasists who have supported 'revolution-ary' China through thick and thin and the rightist *realpolitik* habitués of the White House and European capitals who first came to Beijing to balance Moscow and who stayed on, enthralled by its vast 'potential' market.

In February 2000 the State Department in its annual human rights report noted that China's human rights record had worsened over the past year. For the first time the Department's reporting was as vigorous as that of Amnesty International and Human Rights Watch. Two months later the USA cast its vote against China at the annual meeting of the UN Human Rights Commission. At last the human rights lobby had broken through the left–right consensus that had protected China for too long.

In a major report on China, 'No One is Safe', Amnesty concluded: 'Any country that prevents domestic as well as international scrutiny of its human rights record gives the impression that it has much to hide.' In the case of China, secrecy has not prevented reports of gross human rights violations from reaching the outside world, although it does suggest that the scale of human rights violations may be far worse than can be documented. 'The secrecy also suggests that the Chinese authorities still believe they can do what they like to people and are not accountable for their actions, either internally or externally.'

Years of pressure by outside human rights bodies such as Amnesty International and Human Rights Watch seem to have brought meagre results. Government-to-government pressure has done little better. On occasion, mainly in response to American pressure, China has released a prominent political prisoner in order to ease an important negotiation or to clear the air before a visit by a head of state.

But beyond that, the impression left is less of a country genuinely attempting to improve the protection of human rights and more of a country that puts immense energy into deflecting criticism and avoiding accountability.

China joined the international consensus of states which adopted the Vienna Declaration and Programme of Action at the important 1993 UN World Conference on Human Rights. It said that 'the universal nature of these rights and freedoms [in the UN Charter] is beyond question.' In voting for this resolution, China in effect discarded its old argument that human rights was a Western cultural concept. Moreover, it also voted for a resolution which proclaimed that 'the promotion and protection of all human rights is a legitimate concern of the international community,' and, further, 'a lack of development may not be invoked to justify the abridgement of internationally recognized human rights.'

Yet at home, in successive government White Papers and in public declarations by high political figures, it continues to justify the reality that its own private concept of human rights is profoundly different from the one it voted for at the UN. China argues that human rights fall, by and large, within the domestic jurisdiction or 'sovereignty' of each country and that a country's human rights situation 'should not be judged in isolation from its historical, social, economic and cultural conditions', or 'according to a preconceived model'. The White Paper of November 1991 even claimed that political prisoners do not exist in China because 'ideas alone, in the absence of action which violates the Criminal Law, do not constitute a crime'.

However, it must be said again that the West today is undoubtedly holding China to a higher standard that it used to. That is why one must be careful in any evaluation of Amnesty reports to allow for the fact that a critique today has pocketed and taken for granted the improvements made over the last twenty years. Most Chinese go about their daily lives without significant interference by the government. They have greater room for individual choice, more diversity in cultural life, looser economic controls and increased access to outside sources of information.

There is more press freedom in China than before. Scholars can publish somewhat more freely. There is more, if not full, uncontrolled access to the outside world by means of fax and e-mails. There have been admissions by the highest authorities that all is not well in the judicial system and that reforms are necessary. There is the effect of the Trojan Horse of Hong Kong. The toing and froing between the mainland and the ex-British colony, not least by Chinese tourists and school parties, must be having some effect in persuading the Chinese that Chinese people can live contentedly and loyally under another kind of political system.

This begs the question, how can China be successfully influenced to further progress, to open up, to release its political prisoners and move towards democracy? There is little evidence that holding back on criticism of human rights practices, concentrating on trading and commercial links, and waiting for economic growth to ameliorate the political condition, will produce results. After all, Hitler, Mussolini, Franco, not to mention a host of Latin American dictators, held the highest office at a stage of economic development much further along the road than China today. On the other hand, while there is little evidence that a Western country actually loses trade opportunities by being critical on human rights issues – the Chinese do need Western markets more than vice versa – the evidence is patchy that pressure from trading sanctions gets results. The best that can be hoped for is that the drip-drip of outside opinion by the likes of both Amnesty and outside governments will slowly, almost imperceptibly, seep into the pores of Chinese society. There are, it must be said, more pores to seep into than ten or twenty years ago.

Amnesty is right to continue its pressure. What is more, it is right to lobby Western governments to come off their perch and be more outspoken. In the spring of 2000 it seemed to help to produce an important dual shift in US policy. President Clinton finally decided that the USA would criticize China in the UN Human Rights Commission (without, however, the support of the major European countries). At the same time Clinton balanced this by finally deciding that the time had come to support China's entry into the World Trade Organisation and by successfully persuading Congress to give China permanent most-favoured-nation trade status.

This is probably the right mix: the continuous drumming and tattoo of human rights lobbying, at the same time as trading, commercial and educational links are being strengthened. Over time it might work.

9

The USA – Land of the Free?

When in April 2000 the American ultra-right-wing evangelist and broadcaster Pat Robertson called for a nationwide moratorium on capital punishment, it seemed to many in Amnesty that the Rubicon itself had been crossed. Mr Robertson, who had been called an 'agent of intolerance' during the American presidential primaries by one of the Republican contenders, John McCain, has a long and rather successful record of pressuring the Republican party to support the policies of the so-called 'Christian right'. These have been characterized by opponents as viciously anti-communist, anti-abortion under whatever terms, pro-death penalty, pro the right to bear arms with minimal controls, and hostile to any advance in the welfare state, such as expanding government health coverage to the poor.

Mr Robertson's reason for his about-turn was, he said, because capital punishment is administered in a way that discriminates against minorities and poor people who cannot afford high-priced lawyers. 'We must temper justice with mercy,' he concluded.

It was yet one more voice from the right of America's political spectrum that in the late months of 1999 and during the year 2000 began publicly to somersault on their previously consistent support for the draconian use of the death penalty. Most important, perhaps, had been the decision, on 31 January 1999, of the Republican governor of Illinois to halt further executions until a study has been completed on the fairness of capital punishment. His decision, he explained, had been profoundly influenced by a group of students who had been set the task of re-examining a string of capital convictions by a professor of journalism at Northwestern University in

Figure 7. US death sentences, 1960–99

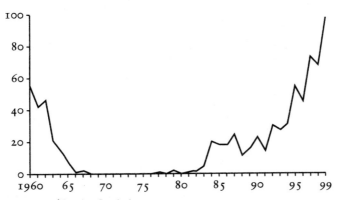

Source: Bureau of Justice Statistics

Evanston. Their investigations have so far led to the exoneration of three convicts on death row and the freeing of five others serving long jail terms.

America, after a decade of intensive re-use of the death penalty – it was suspended during the years 1972 to 1977 – is finally being pushed into a rethink. The credit is widely spread, for the USA has many groups who are active campaigners against capital punishment. Moreover, when Pope Paul II visited St Louis, Missouri, in January 1999 he not only called 'for a consensus to end the death penalty, which is both cruel and unnecessary', he personally – and successfully – appealed to the governor for a reprieve of one death-row inmate. But, undoubtedly, the systematic, thoroughly well-organized 'Rights for All' campaign launched by Amnesty at the end of 1998 to change American practice not only on the death penalty but on a host of other human rights issues has had a telling and lasting impact (see Figure 7).

'The USA was founded in the name of democracy, political and legal equality, and individual freedom. However, despite its claims to international leadership in the field of human rights, and its many institutions to protect individual civil liberties, it is failing to deliver the fundamental promise of rights for all.' Thus began Amnesty's principal campaign document. Amnesty's research over many years had convinced it that 'there is a persistent and widespread pattern of human rights violations in the USA'. Some of these arise from individual misconduct, encouraged by an institutionalized failure to hold officials accountable. Others result from inadequate systems of control or, simply, an outright refusal to recognize international standards for human rights protection. In some cases, economic policies and political trends are creating conditions in which these violations are becoming both more widespread and increasingly severe.

The picture painted by Amnesty is a grim, even sadistic one, especially for a country which prides itself on its attachment to liberty and whose foreign policy is predicated on the expansion of freedom and democracy to the far corners of the planet. The USA, with only 5 per cent of the world's population, holds 25 per cent of the world's prisoners – some two million people, three times the number in 1980, and an often unnoticed factor in keeping the US unemployment rate remarkably low.

Systematic brutality by police has been uncovered in some of the country's largest urban police departments. Across America people have been beaten, kicked, punched, choked and shot by police officers, even when they posed no threat. Behind the walls of prisons and jails, largely hidden from examination, there is more violence. Some prisoners are abused by other inmates, and guards fail to protect them. Others are assaulted by the guards themselves. As if they were criminals, many asylum-seekers are placed behind bars when they arrive in America; some are held in shackles. More than 650 people have been executed since 1977, over 500 in the past decade alone. Blacks and whites are the victims of murder in almost equal numbers, yet 82 per cent of prisoners executed since 1977 were convicted of the murder of a white person. Since 1990 the USA has executed fifteen juvenile offenders and has expressly reserved the right to use the death penalty against juveniles, even though it has ratified the International Covenant on Civil and Political Rights, which forbids the execution of those whose crime was committed while they were still children. More than thirty military personnel were imprisoned in 1991 and 1992 for conscientious objection to the war against Iraq, and were adopted by Amnesty as prisoners of conscience.

Thus it was that on 6 October 1998 Pierre Sané publicly launched Amnesty's USA campaign in Washington, DC. It was a speech of great passion. Few holds were barred:

Amnesty International has been knocking on the doors of the US Congress for the past thirty-seven years. We have been telling the US authorities that cruelty does not just happen elsewhere. Serious human rights violations are not just a foreign affair. They are happening in the US today and – worst of all – some are on the increase.

And where is the public outcry? Where are the zealous defenders of morality when a mentally ill inmate is shacked to a four-point metal restraint board for twelve weeks? When a pregnant woman is shackled during her seven hours of labour?

In UN meetings and international conferences the US leads the charge to persuade others to sign up or to point out the ways in which other signatories fall short of their solemn obligations.

On 10 December 1998 President Clinton issued an executive order affirming the US commitment to honour its obligations under the international human rights treaties to which it is a party. In doing so, Clinton raised expectations that the USA would begin to embrace international human rights standards at home, ending the country's longstanding failure to acknowledge human rights law as US law.

It was this potent mixture of hubris, ignorance and disregard that Amnesty set out to challenge. There were positive results, such as the 'conversion' of Pat Robertson on the death penalty issue, yet at the end of the campaign, as Amnesty's friendly rival, Human Rights Watch, observed in a report issued at the end of 1999, the situation remained much as it was.

At the onset of its campaign, Amnesty singled out six major cases of concern – police brutality, violations in prison, the ill-treatment of asylum-seekers, the death penalty, the use of arms, in particular disabling stun belts and guns, and America's attitude to human rights treaties.

'In the past eight years', began the Amnesty report, 'independent inquiries have uncovered systematic abuses in some of the country's largest police departments. In each case the authorities had ignored longstanding and routine police brutality in high crime districts . . . The emphasis on "the war on crime" in recent years has reportedly contributed to more aggressive policing in many areas.'

In New York, the Mollen Commission of Inquiry of 1994 reported that 'police brutality seemed to occur . . . whenever we uncovered corruption.' The commission found that the most serious abuses were concentrated in several inner-city precincts, with patrol officers protecting or assisting drug dealers, and being involved in robberies, beatings, perjury and falsification of records. It also found that the New York Police Department had failed to monitor or discipline officers accused of brutality and that a 'code of silence' among police officers had hampered internal investigations.

In 1996 Amnesty made its own investigation and found that, although steps had been taken to tackle corruption, police brutality remained a serious problem. Local community and civil rights groups told Amnesty that aggressive 'zero tolerance' policing had been accompanied by unacceptable levels of brutality. After the alleged torture of a Haitian immigrant, Abner Louima, when police officers beat him and rammed the handle of a toilet plunger into his rectum, the mayor of New York, Rudolph Giuliani, set up a task force to review community relations. The report and its recommendations were completed in May 1998. The mayor largely rejected them. However, in December 1999 a police officer was sentenced to thirty years' imprisonment for the torture of Abner Louima.

In Los Angeles, two official inquiries found that there was a serious problem with the use of excessive force, including beatings and unjustified shootings. However, a special counsel appointed to monitor reforms commended the police department for reducing excessive force between 1972 and 1997. Nevertheless, he noted a rise in brutality complaints against police officers from two inner-city police stations. At the end of 1999 a special board of inquiry was set up to investigate allegations, made by a fellow police officer, that at one police station officers beat up unarmed suspects, planted evidence and lied to cover up their actions.

In Philadelphia, in the mid-1990s, drug squad officers operating mainly in the 39th District (a poor, black neighbourhood) were accused of systematically beating and robbing suspects, planting drugs and falsifying reports. Some officers, who had operated with impunity for years, were eventually jailed. Several other major cities have been plagued by police brutality and corruption. One of the most notorious police departments was New Orleans. In the mid-1990s it underwent a major overhaul, after more than thirty officers were arrested for crimes including extortion, murder and brutality.

Despite the investigative work of various commissions of inquiry in some of America's largest cities, Amnesty's own investigation convinced it that they often lacked the thoroughness necessary to fully expose the fault-lines inside police forces. 'Officers were given the benefit of the doubt even if there was corroborative evidence of misconduct,' Amnesty concluded.

One of the main barriers to both disciplinary and criminal action is the police's 'code of silence'. There are often no independent witnesses, and officers frequently fail to report misconduct, and file false or incomplete reports to cover up abuses. Police officers cover up brutality by charging the victim or even potential witnesses with offences such as resisting arrest, interfering with arrest, or assault. The 1991 Commission of Inquiry, led by Warren Christopher, into the behaviour of the Los Angeles police noted that there was a serious problem of a failure by officers to report misconduct. In 1997 the inspector-general for the Los Angeles Police Department reported that there was still a problem. Out of nearly a hundred New York police officers interviewed during a federal investigation into the torture of Abner Louima, only two provided investigators with information. The New York task force on police–community relations reported in 1998 that the police had either taken no action, or imposed only minimal discipline, in a large proportion of complaints found to be substantiated by the independent civilian complaint review board.

Police confidence in the complaints and disciplinary process is further undermined by the secrecy of internal investigations. Police departments frequently refuse to provide information to victims, their families and their lawyers. Amnesty itself has often requested information on individual cases, only to be rebuffed. Information only becomes public in the too rare instances when there is a trial. Although there are now far more independent oversight boards than there were a decade ago, many remain underfunded and lack the power to order witnesses to appear. Some do little to publicize their operations. Many police departments fail to keep track of civil lawsuits against the police, even when one results in the payment of heavy damages, and often the outcome is not recorded in officers' files.

In the end, keeping the police on their toes is often down to the determined and tireless work of civil rights campaigners, civil rights lawyers and relatives of the victims. Without them, the situation, bad as it is, would be far worse.

In 1995 a federal court described the treatment of prisoners in Pelican Bay State Prison in California as 'a pattern of needless and officially sanctioned brutality'. The abuses included severe beatings, the cruel use of shackles and the unwarranted use of firearms. The judge found that the guards were rarely disciplined for using excessive force and that they covered up their abuses with false or inadequate reports.

Amnesty found that right across the USA in many jails and prisons such behaviour is endemic.

In some cases guards fail to stop inmates assaulting each other. In others, the guards themselves are the abusers, subjecting their victims to beatings and sexual abuse. Prisons and jails use mechanical, chemical and electrical shock methods of restraint that are cruel, degrading and sometimes life-threatening . . . Thousands of prisoners are isolated in solitary confinement for long periods. Many prisoners do not receive adequate care for serious physical and mental health problems.

Many of these practices not only violate international human rights standards, they break US law as well. But the means to prevent or redress abuse are limited and inadequate. In the face of a massive crime wave, public opinion has become more callous in recent years. There is less interest in public scrutiny and there is a climate of permissiveness that tolerates serious violations inside the penal system.

Over 60 per cent of prisoners are from racial and ethnic minorities. Half are blacks, even though they make up only 13 per cent of the US population. One reason is the disproportionate impact of drug-sentencing policies on blacks. Most of the new black prisoners are jailed for non-violent offences involving the use of drugs. Similarly, the sudden and massive rise in the number of women prisoners is because of the impact of drug laws.

Even though huge sums have been spent on prison building, the expansion has not kept pace with the rise in the prison population. Prisons are overcrowded, understaffed and often dangerous. The Justice Department has documented the conditions: overflowing toilets and pipes, toxic and insanitary environments, prisoners forced to sleep on filthy floors without mattresses, cells infested with vermin and lacking ventilation and, above all, too often, a pervasive threat of violence.

Some of the jails investigated by the Justice Department were found not to have any policies or even procedures on the use of force. There is little extra space to protect vulnerable inmates from predatory ones. In 1997 in the Yavapai County jail system in Arizona, Amnesty discovered that beatings by inmates were allegedly a daily occurrence. In Nebraska State prison, prisoners were confined together irrespective of crime or background. Rape was widespread. Contrary to international standards, some jails do not separate the convicted from the unconvicted. Those accused of minor offences may rub shoulders with those convicted of serious crimes. In Los Angeles County jail, the Justice Department has reported that inmates have preyed upon the mentally ill, stealing their food and possessions and attacking them.

The harsher atmosphere now prevalent in America has led to a toughening of the prison regime. Despite evidence that education can reduce re-offending rates, educational programmes have been cut. In many facilities exercise equipment has been removed. There has been an alarming growth in supermaximum security units in which prisoners are almost totally isolated. Mechanical means of controlling prisoners, such as electro-shock devices, have been increasingly introduced in response to overcrowded and poorly equipped prisons. In Amnesty's opinion the shift towards private management of jails has often led to unnecessary cost-cutting and even worse conditions.

In such a regime it comes as no surprise that Amnesty has been able to document severe abuse in a wide range of prisons:

- In Georgia, in June 1996, the head of the corrections department allegedly supervised the beatings of scores of handcuffed prisoners by a riot squad.
- In California, at Corcoran State prison, guards staged 'gladiator' fights between prisoners.
- In Pennsylvania, at the SCI-Greene supermaximum prison, black prisoners were regularly beaten by guards.
- At Arizona prison, following a disturbance in 1995, 600 prisoners were forced to remain handcuffed outdoors in intense heat for ninety-six hours. They were left to urinate and defecate in their own clothes.
- In 1998 the Federal Bureau of Prisons agreed to pay three women $500,000 to settle a lawsuit in which the women successfully claimed that they had been beaten, raped and sold by guards for sex with male inmates at a prison in California. The Justice Department, following an investigation of prisons in Michigan, stated: 'Many sexual relationships appear to be unreported due to the presently widespread fear of retaliation and vulnerability felt by these women.'

The cruel use of restraints, resulting in unnecessary pain, injury or even death, is widespread in the American penal system. Mentally disturbed prisoners have been bound, spread-eagled, on boards for prolonged periods. In Utah State prison, in 1995, one inmate with a history of self-mutilation was shackled to such a board for four weeks. He was left to urinate and defecate on the board, and removed only four times a week to shower.

While the USA has a voluntary code of behaviour for the use of such checks in correctional institutions, they are not mandatory. There are no nationally binding minimum standards, and international standards barring the use of chains and leg-irons are ignored. Non-violent white-collar crime offenders can get the same treatment as arsonists, rapists and murderers. Even pregnant women, about to give birth, have been shackled.

Sprays and electro-shock devices, supposedly used to subdue violent prisoners, have often been used indiscriminately. A Justice Department report into a Kentucky jail in April 1998 found that 'staff misuse and abuse weapons such as pepper spray, stun shields, and stun guns, resorting to them early and often, for both management and punishment'. The report cites a case in which a guard used a stun gun to rouse an inmate who had 'passed out'. Not surprisingly, stun weapons have been banned for use in most European countries, Canada and a number of US states.

Since the late 1980s both the federal government and individual states have built so-called supermaximum security facilities. Amnesty says it has no quarrel with the need to segregate certain prisoners for the safety of others or their own protection. But it does believe that some of the centres constitute cruel, inhuman or degrading treatment. In 1995 the UN Human Rights Commission stated that conditions in a number of such prisons were 'incompatible' with international standards. The UN Special Rapporteur on torture has criticized the treatment in H-Unit, Oklahoma, and Pelican Bay Security Housing Unit, in California.

Prisoners in supermax prisons typically spend 22–24 hours a day in small solitary cells. In some there are no windows or fresh air. There are no work, training, educational or vocational programmes. The walls and doors are solid, allowing no noise or visual contact. Often no television, radios or even books and newspapers are allowed. Contact with the outside world is kept to a minimum. In the Correctional Adjustment Centre in Baltimore, Maryland, only after the Justice Department threatened a lawsuit were prisoners allowed out for exercise, four or five hours a week.

Although states claim that their purpose is to incarcerate inmates who are violent and predatory, there is evidence, says Amnesty, that many prisoners do not warrant such a restrictive regime. A number of states incarcerate in 'supermax' units all their death-row prisoners, regardless of behaviour. Some are kept in one for relatively minor disciplinary infractions, such as insolence towards staff, or because they complained about prison conditions or even because of their political affiliations. Prison specialists say that mentally ill prisoners often end up in 'supermax' units because of behavioural difficulties, often without appropriate evaluation or treatment.

When the USA ratified the International Covenant on Civil and Political Rights it reserved the right to treat juveniles as adults 'in exceptional circumstances'. One of the Covenant's articles states that incarcerated children should be kept separated from adults. Yet the number of children held in adult facilities in the USA has increased, as states have legislated to broaden the circumstances in which children may be prosecuted. Amnesty considers the welfare of these children (well over 3,000) to be of 'grave concern, because of the extreme vulnerability to physical and sexual abuse by adults'.

Sexual abuse appears to be widespread against female prisoners too. US correctional facilities employ both men and women to supervise prisoners of the opposite sex. Indeed, US courts have ruled that anti-discrimination laws mean that prisons cannot refuse to employ men in female facilities. The UN Human Rights Committee has expressed concern at the practice, 'which had led to serious allegations of sexual abuse of women and the invasion of their privacy'. In some prisons male warders are allowed to carry out body searches of women prisoners.

'Everyone has the right to seek and to enjoy asylum if they are forced to flee their country to escape persecution,' says Amnesty in one of its reports on America. 'The USA accepts this principle and has agreed to be bound by the 1951 UN Refugee Convention. Yet US authorities frequently violate the fundamental rights of asylum-seekers by detaining them for simply seeking asylum.'

It is not just a brief detention in a holding centre while their stories and claims are cross-checked, it is a full-blooded incarceration, alongside high-risk criminals. The would-be refugees are often stripped and searched, shackled and chained, often abused, and denied access to families, lawyers and non-governmental organizations who wish to help them. Children can be separated from their families. The process of deciding whether they will be admitted to the USA or returned to where they came from can take months, even years. In recent years, the number of asylum-seekers and hence the number of detainees has soared. In 1998, the Immigration and Naturalization Service proposed new detention standards. However, these do not apply to jails, where about half of all detainees are held.

Inevitably, many asylum-seekers with a poor command of English find it near to impossible to make contact with those who might wish to help them. Some detention facilities refuse to allow lawyers access, others permit it only reluctantly, making lawyers and detainees wait for hours before a meeting.

The US prison system has been criticized by many human rights organizations over the years and by UN committees. Yet, if anything, the situation overall has severely worsened. While in some states, such as Illinois, certain non-governmental organizations have the right to inspect facilities, in fourteen states there are no jail inspection programmes of any kind. Even the Justice Department, which does have the right to investigate if it receives information that prisoners are being systematically deprived of their constitutional or federal rights, has noted 'an increased unwillingness by states to correct deficiencies voluntarily, necessitating litigation'.

Many of the people on death row in America have been responsible for brutal crimes. Families have been torn asunder and the loved ones of the victims may never recover either their emotional balance or their self-esteem. Altogether 17,000 people a year are murdered in America. Justice and punishment are necessary. Yet the evidence is overwhelming, argues Amnesty in a report on the death penalty, that in the USA a defendant who cannot afford a competent lawyer is more likely to be sentenced to death than someone with more money. Whether or not the death sentence is pronounced may be influenced more by the fact that a prosecutor or judge is due for re-election and wants to appear 'tough on crime' than by the gravity of the offence. Moreover, as the authorities attempt to speed up the time between sentence and execution, the risk of killing the innocent is increasing. Only China, Congo, Saudi Arabia and Iran execute more prisoners (they account for 85 per cent of the world's executions), and only Japan and India among the large democracies continue to use capital punishment. In recent years the world has moved increasingly in an abolitionist direction, with more than a hundred countries having now abolished the death penalty. The USA is almost isolated among the democratic nations which publicly and loudly subscribe to the Universal Declaration on Human Rights, which proclaims the right of every human being to life and freedom from cruel, inhuman or degrading treatment or punishment.

In 1972 the US Supreme Court struck down the country's death penalty laws on the grounds that they were being administered in an 'arbitrary and capricious manner', violating the US Constitution. Subsequently, several states passed new laws which, in 1976, the Supreme Court ruled were constitutional as they allowed the death penalty to be applied with 'guided discretion'.

In reality, the death penalty is administered today in much the same way as it was in 1972. Amnesty has consistently found that it is applied in a way that is 'racist, arbitrary and unfair'. Since 1977 Amnesty has published more than twenty-five reports investigating the misuse and horror of capital punishment, the American way. In 1994 it called for a presidential commission to examine and report on the use of capital punishment, to allow informed discussion outside the lightning-charged political and emotional climate which characterizes the death penalty debate. During the year 2000 not one presidential candidate, even the most liberal, questioned this American consensus. And when Bill Clinton was running for president as governor of Arkansas he broke off from his campaign to return home to confirm the execution of a convicted murderer, Ricky Ray Rector, who had been certified as mentally retarded. Ricky Rector's comprehension of his imminent execution was so limited that he left the dessert of his final meal as he wanted to 'save it for later'. Amnesty is convinced that 'the death penalty carries the official message that killing is an appropriate and effective response to killing. It is neither. It contributes to desensitizing the public to violence, and to increasing public tolerance for other human rights violations.'

When executions were resumed in 1977 a common argument was that it would help deter murder. But the evidence is overwhelming that it has no more deterrent effect than other punishments. In Canada, between the abolition of the death penalty in 1976 and the end of 1995, the murder rate dropped by 34 per cent. In 1997 the attorney-general of Massachusetts, a state that has abjured the death penalty, said: 'There is not a shred of credible evidence that the death penalty lowers the murder rate. In fact, without the death penalty the murder rate in Massachusetts is about half the national average. Maybe other states should be learning something from us.'

Indeed, the lengthy judicial proceedings in capital cases – many years between sentencing and execution – may well serve to prolong the suffering of victims' families. Without the death penalty, alternative punishments could be handed down more quickly and then the healing process could begin sooner. Yet today, with relatives of the victims actually encouraged to witness the executions, the raw emotions are re-engaged years later, re-creating the trauma and the horror of the earlier tragedy.

In many influential ways the tide continues to flow towards the executioner. A prospective Democratic candidate for governor in California launched his candidacy in late 1997 with a promise that, if elected, he would extend the use of the death penalty to serial rapists and repeat child molesters. The incumbent Republican governor of California has previously advocated the execution of children as young as 14.

Yet there are counter-currents. The moratorium on the death penalty declared by the governor of Illinois is an important indication of the unease felt by many of those responsible for its implementation. And polls show that although the death penalty remains overwhelmingly popular – some 66 per cent are in favour – that support is far less solid when follow-up questions are asked. When pollsters suggest alternatives, such as imprisonment without parole, then the 'pro' vote drops dramatically.

By now, says Amnesty, there can be little rational argument for believing that death by electrocution, hanging, gas, firing squad, or even the supposedly more humane injection, is anything but cruel. When Pedro Medina was executed in Florida's electric chair in 1997, flames shot out of the facemask, causing officials to shut down the 2,000-volt charge. Afterwards, Florida's attorney-general commented: 'People who wish to commit murder, they better not do it in the State of Florida because we may have a problem with our electric chair.' Florida's Senate majority leader observed: 'A painless death is not punishment.'

When Timmie Smith was executed in Indiana in 1996, the executioner searched for sixteen minutes for a vein in his arm. A doctor was called for, who tried unsuccessfully to insert the needle in his neck. After thirty-six minutes they eventually found a suitable vein in his foot. In 1996 Luis Mata was strapped down for execution, where he remained for the next seventy minutes, with the needle inserted, while the Arizona Supreme Court reviewed his case. He lost and the execution proceeded. His head jerked back while his face convulsed. Minutes later his chest and stomach began a series of sharp spasms.

It was Justice Blackman who told his colleagues on the US Supreme Court as recently as 1994 that 'even under the most sophisticated death penalty statutes, race continues to play a major role in determining who shall live and who shall die'. In Virginia, one of America's three leading execution states between 1908 and 1962, all those executed for rape were black. Yet only 55 per cent of those imprisoned for rape were black.

The race of the murder victim appears to be a major factor in determining who is sentenced to death. As stated previously, blacks and whites are the victims of murder almost in equal numbers, yet 82 per cent of those executed since 1977 were convicted for the murder of white persons. In Kentucky, for example, every death sentence up to March 1996 was for the murder of a white victim, despite over 1,000 victims in the state being black. Being black means that a prisoner is four times more likely to receive the death penalty than if he were white. That is the evidence of a major study carried out in 1998 by Professor David Baldus in Philadelphia. Nationwide, blacks make up 12 per cent of the country's population, but are 42 per cent of the nation's condemned prisoners.

In the late 1980s, following a request by the US Congress, the government's General Accounting Office reviewed twenty-eight studies on race and the death penalty. It found that 82 per cent of them revealed that 'those who murdered whites [were] more likely to be sentenced to death than those who murdered blacks'. An earlier move in Congress to introduce a Racial Justice Act, which would have allowed defendants to challenge their death sentence by producing statistical evidence of racial discrimination in the judicial process, was voted down and has met the same fate on subsequent occasions.

In June 2000 the first comprehensive study of all the 5,760 capital cases heard in America from 1973 to 1995 was made public.[1] Of the 4,578 cases that were appealed the authors found that there were serious flaws in more than two-thirds. The commonest causes of error were 'egregiously incompetent defence lawyers who demonstrably missed important evidence, and police and prosecutors who did discover that kind of evidence but suppressed it'. The report makes clear that at least 7 per cent of death row inmates are plainly innocent. Nevertheless, they are spending, on average, seven years on death row, while the real killers remain at large.

Only Iran, Pakistan, Saudi Arabia, Yemen, Congo, the Nigeria of the deposed tyrant Abacha and the USA have executed juvenile offenders in the last decade. (The USA has executed fifteen.) 'It is clear contravention of international law', says Pierre Sané, 'to execute those who were under 18 at the time of their crime.' The USA presumes that it is avoiding the prohibition of international law by waiting to carry out the execution until the prisoner reaches the age of 18.

At the age of only 16 Shareef Cousin became America's youngest death row inmate when in 1996 he was sentenced to death in Louisiana. Fortunately, on appeal in early 1998, he won the right to a new

---

[1] *A Broken System: Error Rates in Capital Cases, 1973–1995*, by James S. Liebman, Jeffrey Fagan and Valerie West, published online.

trial. It was only after the initial trial that his lawyers had managed to see a copy of the police statement by the principal prosecution witness, who had visually identified Cousin as the culprit. 'It was dark,' she was reported to have said, 'and I didn't have my contact lenses nor my glasses.' She said she could see only 'outlines and shapes and things'. Cousin was released in January 1999.

On 22 April 1998 Joseph John Cannon, who was 17 when he committed murder, was led to the lethal injection chamber after twenty-one years on death row in Texas. The first attempt to kill him, reported Amnesty, failed when the needle 'blew out of his arm' as the lethal solution began to flow. The court had made no allowance for the fact that his short life had been one of brutality and abuse. Despite being diagnosed as brain-damaged and schizophrenic, he had received no treatment for his mental disorders. The Pope had sent a letter to Governor Bush asking for a reprieve; so had Archbishop Desmond Tutu.

Sean Sellers was executed in Oklahoma on 4 February 1997 after spending over twelve years on death row. He was convicted and sentenced for three murders committed as a teenager.

In October 1999 the government urged the Supreme Court *not* to examine US obligations under international law, not to execute those who committed their crime under the age of 18.

In 1986 the Supreme Court ruled that executing the 'insane' is unconstitutional. However, the ruling failed to specify procedures for determining whether a prisoner is insane, and offered little protection to those suffering severe mental health problems. The Court also ruled three years later that it was not unconstitutional for the death penalty to be used against mentally retarded defendants. However, the Court did say it would reconsider the issue if there were evidence of a social consensus against the execution of the mentally retarded. Now, a significant number of states are passing laws banning such executions. Yet the practice continues.

The Supreme Court has been less forthcoming on the issue of legal mistakes. In 1984 it ruled that errors by lawyers would not merit the reversal of the sentence unless the defendant could prove that such errors had prejudiced the outcome of the case, a standard of proof that is very difficult to meet. 'The government is not responsible for, and hence not able to prevent attorney errors,' concluded the court.

The result is that many – it is impossible to say how many – prisoners have been executed because of mistakes by their lawyers. Many attorneys assigned by the court to represent capital defendants are inexperienced and lack the necessary skills. Roger Coleman, reports Amnesty, was represented at a trial by lawyers who had never handled a murder case before. They neither prepared the case properly nor investigated the evidence, including his alibi. They argued no mitigation. On appeal, he was represented by volunteer lawyers unfamiliar with Virginia's court system. Inadvertently, they filed notice of appeal to the State Supreme Court one day late; the court dismissed the appeal without a hearing. He was executed in 1992, despite serious doubts about his guilt. Similarly, in 1998 a Texas court dismissed the appeal of LaRoyce Lathair Smith because his lawyer had filed it too late. One of the dissenting judges said that the decision 'bordered on barbarism'.

Calvin Burdine, an open homosexual, was sentenced to death in a case where he was defended by a lawyer, Joe Cannon, who at an earlier court hearing referred to homosexuals as 'fairies' and 'queers'. Nor did he object to a statement by the prosecutor that 'sending a homosexual to the penitentiary certainly isn't a very bad punishment for a homosexual'. Cannon also failed to exercise his right to remove three prospective jurors during jury selection who admitted to being prejudiced against homosexuals. Cannon, who did not interview a single witness while preparing the defence, was repeatedly seen to fall asleep during the trial. Burdine, who has twice come within hours of execution, remained on death row until early in 2000, when an appeals court ruled that he be given a new trial. The state has appealed the ruling.

Texas has become notorious as the American state with the most executions. Since 1982 the state has executed 214 inmates. The next highest total is Virginia with 76. When running for president, Governor George W. Bush boasted that he left all decisions on pardons to the Texas Board of Pardons and Paroles. Yet since Texas resumed executions in 1982 the Board, to Amnesty's knowledge, has met only once to consider the commutation of a death sentence.

That only happened after a group of former and current Texas attorneys-general stated that it was highly improbable that the accused had committed the crime. In June 2000 Mr Bush announced his first stay of execution, pending DNA tests on Ricky McGinn, only twenty minutes before he was due to be strapped to a gurney and injected with chemicals that would have killed him.

Leonel Herrera was executed in Texas after the US Supreme Court denied his appeal, despite newly discovered evidence that appeared to show he was innocent. A former judge submitted an affidavit that another man had confessed to the crime. The Court ruled that there was no constitutional right to federal intervention because of new evidence when the original trial had been free of procedural error. However, in a strongly worded dissent, three justices argued that the Constitution's protection against cruel and unusual punishments did not end once a defendant has been sentenced to death. 'The execution of a person who can show that he is innocent comes perilously close to simple murder,' they said.

Last year Governor Bush vetoed a bill that its supporters said would have improved the quality of legal representation for poor defendants. He has defended the prerogative of elected judges to appoint lawyers for indigent capital defenders, despite evidence that some appointments have been tainted by patronage. In 1995 he signed a law hastening the death penalty appeals process.

The record of the Clinton administration on the death penalty cannot be said to be much better than Governor Bush's. The government has withdrawn much of its funding from so-called Post-Conviction Defender Organizations, which were responsible for most of the earlier successful appeals and releases. Most of those resource centres have been forced to close.

Amnesty has written many times to the highest reaches of the US government. The federal authorities have refused to answer its arguments in any detail. And, despite the plethora of newspaper articles and television programmes on the abuse of the death penalty right through the presidential campaign, the Democratic candidate, Al Gore, refused to make it an issue. George Bush was allowed to end his campaign without once being seriously challenged. No wonder commentators criticized Mr Gore for losing the election by refusing to bring the hard issues of capital punishment, police behaviour and gun control to the fore. It might have provided him with an extra measure of zeal among his supporters, not to mention the avoidance of a significant loss of votes to the third party candidate, Ralph Nader.

The death penalty, says Amnesty, throws into relief the essential contradiction at the heart of US human rights policy: the double standard.

The USA arguably played the most important role both in the establishment of the UN and in the drafting of the Universal Declaration of Human Rights. Both within the UN and in regional bodies, the USA has repeatedly stressed the importance of the principles of international law on human rights. Yet often the USA continues to use international law when it works in its favour and to discredit it when it does not.

For example, in 1979 the USA filed suit against Iran before the International Court of Justice (the World Court) for taking US diplomats as hostages. Yet, only four years later, when Nicaragua took the USA to the World Court for mining the harbour of its principal port, the USA refused to accept the court's jurisdiction. In 1998 the World Court ordered that the execution of a Paraguayan citizen in the USA be suspended. It argued that under the Vienna Convention on Consular Relations, to which the USA is a party, the accused had the right to seek assistance from Paraguayan consular officials, which he had been denied. Five days later, ignoring the Court, the state authorities in Virginia proceeded with the execution.

A similar case was the execution of a Mexican in Texas in 1997. He was not only denied consular access, he had signed a confession in English, a language he did not understand. While the actual killer received only a prison sentence, he was sentenced to death as an accessory to murder. After his execution, Governor Bush stated that since Texas had not signed the Vienna Convention on Consular Relations it was not bound by it!

In March 2000, the day before a German national, Walter La Grand, was due to be executed in Arizona, the German government filed a request for 'provisional measures' at the International Court of Justice. The court issued an order for the execution to be halted. The execution nevertheless proceeded and Germany announced that it was pursuing a legal claim against the USA before the court.

In his 1998 report, the UN Special Rapporteur on extra-judicial, summary or arbitrary executions said: 'The Federal Government cannot claim to represent the states at the international level and at the same time fail to take steps to implement international obligations accepted on their behalf.' The USA has the worst record of any Western country, not only in observing international human rights treaties, but in ratifying them. And often ratification when it finally passes through Congress is saddled with reservations. The Convention on the Prevention and Punishment of the Crime of Genocide (later used by the USA to justify its campaign against the 'ethnic cleansing' policies of Slobodan Milosevic of Yugoslavia) was ratified by the USA only in 1988, forty years after it signed it. The USA took twenty-eight years to ratify the International Convention on the Elimination of All Forms of Racial Discrimination after 133 other states had already ratified it. Similarly, seventy-one other states ratified the Convention Against Torture before the USA decided to do so. It was twenty-six years – and, again, after 109 other states – before the USA ratified the International Convention on Civil Rights, an instrument which it waged a long campaign to persuade China to sign up to, and which it now uses to upbraid China's human rights abuses. The USA has still not ratified the other principal treaty enshrined in the Universal Declaration of Human Rights, the International Covenant on Economic, Social and Cultural Rights. This omission allows many countries, including China, to accuse the USA of having double standards on human rights. The USA, it is said, supports human rights such as democracy or habeas corpus but doesn't support the right to have a job, education or adequate health care.

Closer to home, the USA has not ratified the American Convention on Human Rights adopted by the Organization of American States in 1969. Moreover, it has not even signed the Inter-American Convention to Prevent and Punish Torture, the Inter-American Convention on Forced Disappearance of Persons, and the Inter-American Convention to Prevent, Punish and Eradicate Violence Against

Women. Many of the Conventions would subject the USA to the rulings of the Inter-American Court, which the USA wishes to avoid, even though this attitude makes nonsense of much of its human rights propaganda in Latin America.

The USA has been adept at watering down the commitments it has made. For example, it has declared it will apply the International Covenant on Civil and Political Rights and the Convention Against Torture only to the extent that domestic law allows. It has also made informal reservations to the International Covenant on Civil and Political Rights, even though some of them are contrary to the object and aims of the treaty. Article 6.5 of the Covenant prohibits passing a death sentence on anyone under the age of 18 at the time of their crime. Yet the USA has entered a reservation. The Human Rights Committee, the UN's body of experts that monitors states' compliance with the Covenant, has said that several of the USA's reservations are incompatible with international law. In 1995, it recommended that the USA consider withdrawing them, in particular those relating to the death penalty and to the right not to be tortured.

Over the years the USA has made something of a habit of avoiding scrutiny by human rights bodies. Although it has become somewhat more open recently, it took five years to present its initial report to the Committee Against Torture, due in 1995. Two reports on its implementation of the International Convention on the Elimination of All Forms of Racial Discrimination are also overdue by five years. The USA has not recognized the jurisdiction of the Human Rights Commission and the Committee Against Torture to hear individuals' complaints that their rights have been violated under the International Covenant on Civil and Political Rights and the Convention Against Torture.

Only two countries in the world have not ratified the Convention on the Rights of the Child – the other is the collapsed state of Somalia. Yet the convention stands for the very essence of basic civilized behaviour and its principal conceptualizer and protagonist was a fine American, the late James Grant, who for years was the director-general of UNICEF.

*

Two years on, despite Amnesty's vigorous one-year campaign, the basic landscape of American law and order is essentially unchanged. Just months into the campaign Amnesty reported how, in November 1998, a 13-year-old black child, Timothy Wilson, driving a friend's pick-up truck, was shot dead after a brief chase. Six officers had pursued the truck for several miles after seeing Timothy driving erratically. All six surrounded the truck when it came to a halt in mud. Four white officers opened fire, they said, after he tried to reverse and then drove towards them. The officers were cleared of criminal wrongdoing by a local grand jury. In May 1999 a Los Angeles officer shot dead a frail, mentally ill, homeless woman, when she lunged at an officer with a screwdriver. The officer was questioning her about a shopping-cart she was pushing. In June 1999 La Tanya Haggerty, a 19-year-old passenger in a car pulled over by the Chicago police after a short chase, was shot dead when officers mistook the mobile phone in her hand for a gun.

None of these shootings, nor indeed numerous others reported by Amnesty, made many waves outside the local area, although there was in each case a huge fuss made locally. However, a few months after the Amnesty campaign got off the ground, the shooting in February 1999 of West African Amadou Diallo by New York police made headlines both at home and abroad. An unarmed Diallo was shot at forty-one times and struck by nineteen bullets. The killing triggered widespread outrage, led to an investigation by the US Justice Department and prompted the attorney-general, Janet Reno, to give her first detailed statement on police brutality, six years into her term. She recommended that complainants be allowed to file complaints without intimidation; that police and sheriffs' departments institute a vigorous system for investigating allegations thoroughly and fairly; that swift discipline be imposed when complaints are sustained; that early warning systems to identify 'repeat offenders' on forces be created; that senior officers send a signal that abuses will not be tolerated; and that the rank and file make it unacceptable to remain silent about other officers' misconduct.

The attorney-general's recommendations were not more than that

– merely suggestions for police departments to accept or ignore. The Justice Department is not prepared to consider making the millions of dollars in grants to police departments conditional on their taking steps towards curtailing abuse in their ranks. However, it did step up the number of its investigations into whether a police department exhibited a 'pattern or practice' of unchecked abuse. Meanwhile, in New York, a jury acquitted the police officers of the murder of Amadou Diallo.

What Amnesty perhaps failed to take into account was the plausible case being made for police 'toughness' by the New York Police Department. In 1993, 1,952 people were murdered in New York; in 1999 the total was 667. Overall crime has fallen by 55 per cent. (However, in both 1999 and 2000 the homicide rate began to climb upwards again.) It cannot be gainsaid that under Mayor Rudolph Giuliani and two successive police chiefs, William Bratton and Howard Safir, New York has been transformed from a very scary city into one of the safest big cities in America. Moreover, the claim that the New York Police Department has become trigger-happy does not stand up to examination. In 1990 the number killed by the police was forty-one; in 1997 it was down to eleven.

Critics argue that this fall in crime can be attributed to lower unemployment and to demographics – there are fewer criminal youths around. The police, for their part, say that in the past crime waves did not correlate with such factors, so why should they now? The police chief argues that it is a system of vigorous policing that has turned the tide.

Before Mr Giuliani became mayor, police officers had been discouraged from making arrests for drugs crimes. Now even littering or writing graffiti can lead to arrest. By dealing firmly with minor infringements of the law the police have sent a message that crime of any kind will not be tolerated. That, together with better organization, it is said, has produced the astonishing turnaround in criminal behaviour. Since 97 per cent of murder victims are black or Hispanic it is ethnic minorities who have benefited most.

Yet it is not only Amnesty that criticizes the New York police. Popular opinion at large has been alienated by police behaviour. Mr

Safir admits that the police department is now so unpopular it is 'hard to maintain morale' and recruit new personnel.

The truth seems to lie somewhere between the poles of opinion. The police have brought down the crime rate, and at the same time have killed fewer people themselves. But, day-to-day, their behaviour too often verges on the thuggish. There is too much run-of-the-mill brutality disguised as tough law enforcement. It should be possible to be both tough on crime and tough on the wayward tactics of errant officers. Amnesty may be criticized for not explaining itself better, but undoubtedly it has been right to follow its mandate and highlight police abuse that is now verging on the commonplace.

Campaigning in a climate where police 'toughness' was often excused, however excessive, was uphill work for Amnesty. The overall picture is still, as Pierre Sané observed, 'totally unacceptable'. Human rights violations in the USA are persistent and widespread. Yet along the way Amnesty did chalk up some not insignificant successes:

- Only days after Amnesty condemned the use of stun belts on unruly inmates during an American televised news programme, the New York Corrections Department cancelled its order for the devices.
- In a letter to Amnesty, the Illinois Department of Corrections stated that it has changed its policy so that no 'restraint' will be used on pregnant women in transit or at the hospital.
- The Los Angeles district attorney agreed to re-open a police programme to investigate police shootings.
- The state of Oklahoma was planning to ask for the execution of Derrick Lester, who was 15 at the time of his alleged crime. Amnesty organized constant petitioning and by the end the prosecutor had to change his fax number in an attempt to halt the deluge. Finally, the first assistant district attorney wrote to Amnesty to say the state would not seek the death penalty.
- The State Legislature of Pennsylvania passed a resolution criminalizing sexual contact between prison guards and inmates.
- The legislature of the state of Washington passed a bill criminalizing sexual contact between male guards and female prisoners. (In 1999 six more states followed suit.)

- Following an Amnesty letter-writing campaign, Shareef Cousin, the 16-year-old on death row who was mentioned on page 267, had his murder charge dropped due to lack of evidence.
- After a meeting with Amnesty, Detroit City Council called for an end of human rights abuses in Michigan's prisons.
- In Texas, Amnesty targeted Governor George W. Bush over the one hundredth execution of his governorship. It issued a report on the imminent execution of Larry Robinson, a mentally ill man. The case generated widespread media attention in Texas and elsewhere and won him an unexpected last-minute reprieve. Later in the year, the US District Court in southern Texas vacated Calvin Burdine's death sentence and ordered a new trial, accepting that his lawyer slept through substantial portions of his trial.
- Members of the Massachusetts House of Representatives voted not to reinstate the death penalty, following some powerful lobbying of prominent Irish Americans by Amnesty groups in Ireland.

The Amnesty campaign, using its international network as is always the case, spread its tentacles wide. In February 1998 it helped persuade the European Union to issue a statement regretting the execution of Sean Sellers in Oklahoma, who was 16 at the time of his crime. This was the first time the European Union had commented on an individual execution in the USA. In the spring of 2000, on the opening day of the UN's annual meeting of its Human Rights Commission, the German foreign minister, Joshka Fischer, announced that the European Union would for the first time submit an anti-death penalty resolution. The *New York Times* reported: 'The US which regards itself as a bastion of human rights found itself under attack from friend and foe alike during the first week of the United Nations' annual meetings on global democratic rights.'

For a year Amnesty activists around the world were busy trying to energize the political leadership in their own countries to put more diplomatic pressure on the USA. In Belgium, a big syringe, filled with cards written by school children with messages about juvenile justice and against the death penalty, was presented to the American embassy. In Bangladesh, the local Amnesty group sent more than a thousand letters to President Clinton and Janet Reno, appealing for a halt to the repression of women prisoners. In Nepal, more than 40,000 signatures were written on a 110-metre-long banner urging human rights protection, and presented to the US embassy in Kathmandu. In Croatia, the local group launched the USA campaign with a press conference that was widely publicized and covered on the main national television news. In the Côte d'Ivoire the campaign was launched with a press conference, attended by many ambassadors, and was widely reported. In the Netherlands 254 local Amnesty groups were working on the issues of the use of the death penalty against juveniles in the state of Virginia, police brutality in Florida and women's conditions in the prisons of Arizona.

Amnesty's far-flung campaign was perhaps more successful for the ball it started rolling – the first effort to scrutinize and publicize to a world audience the human rights record of the most powerful nation on earth – than for what it achieved. It did put US practices on the political map. Not only were some of America's penal practices discussed at the UN Human Rights Commission, they featured on the agenda of the African-American summit in Ghana and at the Organization for Security and Cooperation in Europe meeting in Warsaw.

In America, Amnesty's campaign contributed to an unprecedented debate across the country on police brutality, with President Clinton condemning the 'deeply corrosive practice of racial profiling' (a common occurence whereby police stop motorists mainly from minority groups when carrying out searches for drugs). All over the country senior officials in the judicial and prison system responded, often in a positive way, to Amnesty's lobbying. The head of the Department of Corrections in California wrote to Amnesty: 'Your organization's valuable findings and recommendations are considered when implementing new policies and procedures for female inmates . . . I was most impressed by Amnesty International's visit and report. Both were conducted in a spirit of courtesy and openness. I found all the comments constructive and valuable.' Subsequently, in California it was decided to create a new organizational structure for the state's four women's prisons.

The media coverage was nothing short of massive. Most important, it was sustained over the year, with the issues of women in prison, the death penalty, juveniles, juvenile justice and stun belts receiving the most attention. Other non-governmental organizations which have long been active on prison and police reform felt that their work had been given a push. Corey Weinstein, of California Prison Focus, wrote to Amnesty: 'It makes our work more effective to have these people scolded appropriately by the international human rights community.' Yet, for all the success, Amnesty concluded its campaign more aware than ever how incremental and arduous change is, even in an open society where criticism is allowed and the media are prepared to magnify it. Institutional inertia, and a large measure of public indifference at best, at worst hostility, are obstacles that in their own way are as difficult to surmount as the walls of a repressive dictatorship.

In April 1999 Amnesty visited Valley State Prison for Women in California. It discovered that women, some mentally ill, were held in punitive conditions, sometimes for comparatively minor infractions. In June 1999 the Justice Department held a national summit on police brutality attended by community, police and civil rights representatives. In September and October 1999 Amnesty held hearings on police brutality in Los Angeles, Chicago and Pittsburgh. In October, a state inquiry was announced into complaints of widespread sexual abuse by guards at the Fluvanna Correctional Center for Women in Virginia. On 17 April 2000 the *New York Times* carried this despatch: 'A state judge in New Orleans has removed six teenage boys from a juvenile prison after finding they had been brutalized by guards, kept in solitary confinement for months for no reason and deprived of shoes, blankets, education and medical care.'

And so it goes on. And did go on, right through the presidential campaign in 2000. It was in fact fortuitous that the governor of America's largest execution state was the Republican candidate. It acted like a lightning rod for the energies the Amnesty campaign had unleashed. The press was already alerted to the issue and thus, when a range of non-governmental organizations including Amnesty went into overdrive to highlight the inconsistencies and sheer malpractice of the Texas legal system, they found a ready audience. It became one of the most important issues of the campaign, despite Al Gore's own support for the death penalty.

Texas has accounted for one-third of all executions since 1976 and Governor Bush made no bones early on in the campaign about being proud of the fact. 'I am confident', he said, 'that every person that has been put to death in Texas on my watch has been guilty of the crime charged and has full access to the courts.' The truth is more complicated. As *The Economist* reported: 'From the moment a person is charged with a murder in Texas, he faces a system concerned less with determining whether he may actually be innocent, and more with ensuring that he ends up, neatly arranged, in the execution chamber in Huntsville.' Change will come to the USA. But only if the pressure continues.

Amnesty's rank-and-file members are good at not giving in. But they can be excused, after throwing all their combined energies at 'the bastion state of human rights', if they sometimes despair that so little progress was actually made. The USA has lived with its moral ambiguities for so long that only a great heroic shove will wake it up. One Amnesty campaign is, perhaps, but the beginning of a lifetime's work.

10

Conclusion: the World is a Better Place

Human rights – of a kind – have been around for a long time. A citizen of ancient Rome, if condemned to die, could choose to be beheaded. A non-citizen would be tortured to death, or crucified.

In more recent times, England's Bill of Rights in 1689, the American Declaration of Independence in 1776 and the French Declaration of the Rights of Man in 1789 have been seminal influences on modern institutions. Lord Acton believed that the 'Declaration of the Rights of Man made by the revolutionary movement in France had a more powerful impact on European history than all Napoleon's armies'. (Yet we must not overlook that the French Revolution's ideals were played out in the Reign of Terror to the roll of tumbrils carrying ever more victims to the guillotine.)

In post-war history two watersheds stand out in contemporary political events. The first was the United Nations' Universal Declaration of Human Rights, codified in 1948 under the influence of its presiding genius Eleanor Roosevelt. The second, perhaps more controversial, was the determination of a US president – Jimmy Carter in the late 1970s – to make the issue one of the central points of his presidency.

I have no reason to quibble with what Mr Carter told me in Vienna in 1994: 'There is no way that Amnesty International, for all its wonderful work, can play the same role as the president of the United States can play.' What was missing, however, from the end of that sentence were the words 'if he wants to'. That certainly applied to Carter himself, who was, to say the least, inconsistent in the application of his human rights norms. Even in his final speech as president before the Democratic party congress he almost exclusively lambasted the Soviet Union for its falling short, ignoring the many parts of the world where the US gave tacit support to unsavoury regimes for geopolitical reasons. But he did lay down, particularly within the Democratic party, precepts by which the actions of future presidents could be judged and which could be used by organizations like Amnesty International to hold the politicians to account.

Nothing perhaps illustrates more sharply the gap in thinking between those who try to integrate human rights into everyday geopolitical thinking and those such as Amnesty who stand apart from day-to-day political compromise and insist on an untarnished standard, than the debate over the bombing of Yugoslavia in 1999. NATO claimed it was a crusade to forestall the ethnic cleansing of the Albanian people of the province of Kosovo. But in fact the bombing turned out to be nothing less than the precipitating event in the ethnic cleansing, which, contrary to NATO propaganda, did not occur on a massive scale until after the bombs began to drop.

Amnesty, although critical of the bombing at the time, did not issue its blockbusting press release until thirteen months after the event. It had taken that long for its thorough checking processes to be completed. But once Pierre Sané had taken the final decision to go public in May 2000, it became quickly apparent this was the essence of Amnesty's long tradition: to stand apart from governments, even democratic ones, and to question means as well as ends. On 7 June the Amnesty press release went out, with a copy sent simultaneously to the US State Department, the foreign ministries of Britain, Germany and France and NATO headquarters in Brussels. The *New York Times*'s Steven Erlanger began his despatch: 'In an extensive report that has infuriated Nato leaders Amnesty International said that Nato violated international law in its bombing over Yugoslavia by hitting targets where civilians were sure to be killed. Amnesty accused Nato of war crimes, of "breaking the rules of war", said that those responsible "must be brought to justice" and asked the UN criminal tribunal on the former Yugoslavia to investigate these allegations.'

Ironically, this perhaps showed that the Pentagon generals who, three years ago, had waged a bureaucratic war against President Clinton to water down and, in the end, oppose the creation (which initially he had strongly favoured) of a permanent International Criminal Court for trying war crimes had focused their attention in the right direction. Their intuitive alarmism, which many at the time thought was overdone, turned out to be essentially correct. The human rights lobby has the wind in its sails and is going about its business in a way that is pushing its ship forward at a fast rate of knots. Over the last decade, it has won world-wide ratification of the Genocide and Torture Conventions, the creation of a UN High Commissioner for Human Rights, the establishment of *ad hoc* War Crimes Tribunals for ex-Yugoslavia, Rwanda and Sierra Leone, and not least, the arrest and detention in Britain of General Pinochet of Chile.

Standing at NATO's doorway, it will not be long before Amnesty will be on the steps of the Pentagon itself. The reasons the Pentagon gave to President Clinton for opposing an International Criminal Court[1] – that other nations would not allow the USA to write into the treaty language that would in effect give cast-iron guarantees that US troops could never be arraigned before it – now can be seen as prescient. It will be deeply ironic if the human rights cause to which an American president in the 1970s gave so much of a fillip should progress to the point where it is hoisting the USA with its own petard.

But that, indeed, is what Amnesty is up to. Case by case, the logic of its own mandate is leading it more and more into a head-on clash with the liberal democracies. Contrary to the current widespread opinion, given voice to by such diverse personalities as David Holbrooke, Clinton's ambassador to the UN, the Canadian writer, Michael Ignatieff[2] and the Oxford don, Timothy Garton Ash, the

---

[1] For a fuller and profound discussion of the growth and extension of the norms of international jurisprudence, see 'Judging War Crimes' by William Pfaff, in *Survival*, 42/1 (Spring 2000).

[2] To quote Michael Ignatieff: 'The military campaign in Kosovo depends for its legitimacy on what fifty years of human rights has done to our moral instincts, weakening the presumption of state sovereignty, strengthening the presumption in favour of intervention when massacre and deportation become state policy.'

pursuit of human rights is not particularly well served by military action. War is war, even if it is launched in a 'good' cause, and human rights is too often the loser, however stringent the control exercised by democratically elected politicians of their fighting machine. Indeed, if the preservation of human rights is really the first and paramount purpose of policy, the whole approach to the kind of political impasses that lead to war becomes very different. Simply put, one avoids the recourse to war and leaders are compelled to search for alternative ways of dealing with the situation. Naïve? Although the issue has not been exclusively human rights, one can see an example of how such an approach could work out in practice with US policy towards North Korea, an uncompromising dictatorship.

In this case Clinton had to find an alternative to war because the USA feared if it chose the military option North Korea might well retaliate against a US/South Korean ground invasion with the two or three nuclear weapons it is supposed to possess. Apart from the devastation this would cause in South Korea, it might lead to the loss of over 50,000 American troops.

There have been any number of reasons why since 1994 America could have decided to get tough with a country that gave many indications that it had serious ambitions not just to build a nuclear bomb but to develop a long-distance missile to deliver it. Even today North Korea is the arch-demon for those who advocate the necessity of building an anti-missile shield to 'protect' the USA from nuclear attack from a 'rogue' country.

Yet, contrary to many of its basic instincts, the Clinton administration used the soft glove rather than the mailed fist. Indeed, North Korea is now the main recipient of US aid in Asia. The USA supplies free much of the country's fuel oil needs and a good part of its food requirements. At the same time South Korea and Japan are building, free of charge, a state-of-the-art light-water reactor capable of supplying most of North Korea's electricity needs for years to come.

In retrospect, it seems amazing that debate in Washington in 1994 was almost dominated by those discussing the best way of bombing North Korea. US intelligence had discovered that North Korea was about to remove spent nuclear rods from a cooling pond to recover plutonium, sufficient to make four or six nuclear bombs to add to its supposed (but never proved) stockpile of two or three. Former Secretary of State Henry Kissinger, former National Security Advisor Brent Scowcroft and former CIA chief Robert Gates loudly went public with calls for battle. The saving grace was that they ended up shooting each other in the foot. Gates and Scowcroft argued that the USA should immediately bomb the North Korean reprocessing plant before the cooling rods could be transferred to it. This, they said, would minimize the risk of radioactive fallout. Kissinger advocated immediate tough sanctions and unspecified 'military action'. But his timetable miraculously allowed time – a short three months while the rods cooled – both for a conference of the nuclear-haves and for sanctions to work. Military action should occur, he said, only if North Korea refuelled its reactor or started to reprocess its plutonium from the cooling rods. However, this seemed to ignore Scowcroft's and Gates's point about the dangers of an aerial bombardment on reprocessing facilities. Nor did any of them appear to worry that North Korea might use the two or three nuclear bombs they said the country already had to repulse an American attack.

In fact, the three of them talked themselves into the ground and made it easier for ex-president Jimmy Carter to journey to Pyongyang on a peace mission and pave the way for a deal with Kim Il Sung to accept a nuclear freeze. In return, the USA would be committed to working with South Korea and Japan to build two conventional power-producing nuclear reactors.

Since then there have been all manner of ups and downs in the USA–North Korean relationship. Congress nearly sabotaged the agreement fashioned in the wake of Carter's visit by reneging on White House commitments to begin liberalizing the USA's trade and investment and ending sanctions. Kim Il Sung died, to be succeeded by his son, Kim Jong Il, who took the best part of five years to show he was firmly in the saddle. In 1998, when North Korea test-fired a long-range rocket over Japan, it seemed that Pyongyang was determined to play out its role as the world's number one agent provocateur. Later in 1998, US intelligence spotted a massive hole being dug suitable for exploding secret triggers for a nuclear weapon. In the end, for a payment, the USA was allowed to inspect the hole and found that a hole was all it was.

Not without a great deal of political contortion, the USA over the years has managed in the end to convince Pyongyang of its good faith. North Korea, for its part, has reciprocated by drawing in its horns, albeit often at the last moment. Most important, it has honoured the freeze.

Meanwhile, South Korean president Kim Dae Jung – an ex-Amnesty prisoner of conscience – has pursued his so-called 'sunshine policy' with the North. Despite immense opposition from the old guard, he has succeeded in sustaining it to where the temperature of the Cold War between North and South began to rise so the waters were unfrozen enough for a highly successful summit to take place in June 2000. At the end of 2000 Secretary of State Madeleine Albright broke more of the ice with her visit to Pyongyang.

The North Korean peace is one of President Clinton's rare positive foreign policy achievements. The Pentagon's influence for once was stymied by North Korea's supposed possession of nuclear weapons, and, this time, willy-nilly, other less confrontational means had to be tried. Six years of carrot rather than stick has not produced the end of narrow-minded, dictatorial communism in North Korea, but it has averted war and the immense human suffering and dislocation that is its inevitable corollary. It may have persuaded the regime to begin to loosen up on the human rights front, although it will be perhaps another six years before there is confirmation of that in a society that has made almost a religion out of moribund political and economic activity.

The North Korean example, for all its inadequacies, is a parable of our times. It demonstrates that progress can now often be made by engagement in moving nations out of their entrenched positions. Endless confrontation can be endlessly counterproductive. There is no conclusive evidence that isolating or cornering a nation succeeds in moderating its behaviour. Carl Bildt, the former prime minister of Sweden, made this point more effectively than most in an icily ironic essay on Yugoslavia and the Kosovo war penned for *Prospect*. (Bildt, at present the UN Secretary-General's special envoy for the Balkans, is a man of political leanings, if elections are anything to go by, too far to the right for most of his countrymen.)

'The Baby Bombers', as the editor headlined the piece, was a wake-up call for the baby-boomers, now in the higher reaches of Western political power, 'who have never learnt about war and power the hard way' and who, with their 'smart wars – high rhetoric, high altitude and high technology; smart bombs for smart politicians', believe there is a 'third way in war'. Bildt wrote of meeting Gerd Schmueckle, a retired German general who was wounded six times on the Russian front during the Second World War, but then served in the highest positions inside NATO. Perhaps, said the general, it is a question of generations. While the war veterans are losing their hair and teeth, the new generation suddenly has a different attitude towards war. For Schmueckle, war was associated with horror beyond imagination, leaving deep psychological scars on individuals and nations. Bombs, he said, 'do not create peace: instead they breed hatred for years, perhaps for generations'.

Two years on we can see the truth of this in Yugoslavia. The bombing did not forestall ethnic cleansing, it appeared to precipitate it. And it has bequeathed a cauldron of mutual hatred and a political potage that no amount of NATO and UN policing and Western economic aid can clear up, even if it were forthcoming in something like the quantities promised – another example of the war-time rhetoric that misled the public. Reading the public statements of Bernard Koucher, the UN man responsible for the reconstruction of Kosovo, and General Klaus Reinhardt, the local NATO commander, is to sense that they are often close to despair.

Aficionados of Carl Bildt had the chance to pursue his thinking, one year after the bombing, in *Survival*, the quarterly journal of the International Institute for Strategic Studies. This is a much more lengthy discourse on the limits of force, and looks not just at Kosovo but at Bosnia before the conflict. Its essence is to challenge what has now achieved the status of conventional wisdom – the idea of the supremacy of air power.

Bildt argues that the Dayton agreement that brought an end to the fighting in Bosnia was 'far more a victory for diplomacy than for force'. He certainly doesn't deny that the NATO air operation, initiated on 30 September 1995, 'had a significant psychological impact during its first few days', but the political momentum that led to the accord came about primarily because of a new diplomatic approach. 'The essential diplomatic innovation was the willingness of the US to accept some of the core demands of the Bosnian Serbs; demands that the US previously had refused even to contemplate. In particular the Bosnian Serbs had consistently demanded a separate Republika Srpska inside a weak Bosnian framework.'

After Dayton, there was an unforgivable lull in Western diplomatic activity. Neither the European Union nor the USA were willing to launch any serious diplomatic initiatives to head off the brewing crisis in Kosovo. Albanian opinion inside Kosovo, once more fluid and open to diplomatic options, was allowed to harden, leading to the birth of an armed insurrection and driving the population into the embrace of the Kosovo Liberation Army. The West, misreading the lesson of Bosnia, tried to head off Serbian repression with the threat of air power. Thus when diplomacy failed – and the Rambouillet agreement demanded much more from Slobodan Milosevic than the 'peace agreement' which ended the war – the West had little choice but to make good its threats.

The air operation, however, could not prevent a major humanitarian disaster. Whether it triggered it, Bildt, more cautious than I, just says 'will remain a subject of debate'. But he adds scathingly that 'despite all the talk about a revolution in military affairs, Kosovo brutally demonstrated that the axe remains the superior short-range precision-guided weapon when it comes to one man killing another; there is very little that increasingly long-range and high-tech weaponry can do about it.'

Two years on, we have to live with the now seemingly insoluble Kosovo problem handed over to the UN, to the world. (Poor old rest of the world. That was its reward for kicking up a fuss about the UN Charter being abused by the West's unilateral decision to bomb.) The UN is supposed to find the peace that Western bombs could not deliver, even though, in Bildt's view, 'there is no agreed framework for either the internal or external order of Kosovo'.

Perhaps we can suggest the direction of an alternative way with a question: what would it have taken to draw Milosevic's sting in the early days of the crisis in Yugoslavia – a move to offer Yugoslavia, as has recently been offered to Turkey, a chance of entering the European Union if the peace were kept? Or perhaps it would have been sufficient to offer post-communist Yugoslavia massive amounts of aid to effect a transition to modern capitalism, as long as human rights were respected. (Sums which now, in retrospect, would seem modest compared with what the West has subsequently had to spend via the UN, NATO and the humanitarian relief agencies.)

Or what would it have taken to persuade the Hutu-run government of Rwanda to shelve its contingency plans for massacring the minority Tutsis? Even if every member of the Hutu élite had to be bribed with ten Mercedes each it would have been peanuts compared with what was spent in feeding the fleeing refugees both inside and outside the country. More seriously, a programme instituted even as belatedly as the early 1990s (there had been many earlier smaller-scale pogroms from 1959 on to give warning aplenty of what was to come) to deal with the underlying issues of land-shortage and lack of agricultural development together with the ill-training of the institutions of government, in particular local administration, the courts, the police and the army, would have cost a significant amount, but then again nothing compared with later sweat, guilt and even expenditure.[1]

As a foreword to Amnesty's yearbook for 2000 Pierre Sané penned an essay with the provocative title, 'Soldiers in the Name of Human Rights'. It was an intellectual's demolition job on the modern-day crusader school of thought. 'Are invasion and bombardment by foreign forces justifiable in the name of human rights? And have external military interventions succeeded in winning respect for human rights?' he asked. His reply in five lines is this: 'Amnesty International has long refused to take a position on whether or not

---

[1] A fuller perspective of this tragic land would also take into account two points: (1) while tens of thousands of Hutu participated in the genocide of 1994, millions did not; (2) with a thirty-five-year exception, between 1959 and 1994, the Tutsis have been oppressors of the Hutu majority for centuries.

armed forces should be deployed in human rights crises. Instead, we argue that human rights crises can, and should, be prevented. They are never inevitable. If government decisions to intervene are motivated by the quest for *justice*, why do they allow situations to deteriorate to such unspeakable injustice?'

Inevitably, given Amnesty's current preoccupations, Sané points to Yugoslavia. The NATO governments which bombed Belgrade are the same governments that were willing to deal with Slobodan Milosevic's government during the break-up of the original Yugoslavia and were unwilling to address repeated warnings about the growing human rights crisis in Kosovo. As long ago as 1993 Amnesty was arguing in public: 'If action is not taken soon to break the cycle of unchecked abuses and escalating tensions in Kosovo, the world may again find itself staring impotently at a new conflagration.'

A similar argument, continues Sané, can be made for the West's other great preoccupation during the 1990s – the dictatorial regime of Saddam Hussein, defeated and driven back after an attempted invasion of neighbouring Kuwait. It was Amnesty which called for international pressure on Iraq in the mid-1980s, especially after the 1988 chemical weapons attack by Saddam Hussein's troops on the town of Halabja which killed an estimated 5,000 unarmed Kurdish civilians. Amnesty also drew attention at this time to Saddam's notorious conduct towards his political enemies, incarcerating and torturing their children. Yet Western governments were then four-square behind Iraq as it fought a First World War-type conflict of attrition with its neighbour Iran, whom the USA could not forgive either for its fundamentalist stridency or for taking hostage the diplomats of the US embassy a few years earlier. The West simply turned a blind eye to Saddam's human rights violations, while it sold him increasingly sophisticated weapons of war.

Sané is also right to question the rhetoric of Western governments. When they do intervene they say they are motivated by *'universal values'*. 'But why', asks Sané, 'is the international community so selective in its actions?' The imposition of UN sanctions on Libya or present-day Iraq stands in marked contrast to the non-imposition of sanctions on Israel for refusing to comply with UN Security Council resolutions. The actions over Kosovo and East Timor beg the question of why little or nothing was done in Rwanda, Chechnya or Turkey.

In Turkey, over 3,000 Turkish villages have been destroyed, three million people internally displaced and thousands of Turkish civilians killed by the Turkish security forces during its running war with the guerrillas of the Kurdish Workers' Party. Western arms supplies have continued unabated, and Turkey has recently been accepted as a candidate for European Union membership with little sign that she is committed to giving the Kurds more political space.

This begs another question, argues Sané. If the motivation of governments is 'peace', as they often claim, why do they fuel conflicts by supplying arms or allowing their nationals to trade in arms? Despite the recent rapid increase in wars in Africa, arms exports to the region doubled last year, mainly small arms such as assault rifles and sub-machine guns that have been virtually ignored by those who seek controls on nuclear, chemical and biological weapons, yet which appear to be the weapons that cause most of the damage in most of the wars. In the case of East Timor, two of the major powers who argued for international intervention – the USA and the UK – were also the major suppliers of arms to the Indonesian government, whose security forces were responsible for widespread and systematic violations of human rights in East Timor.

(Sané, it should be added, also applies his jaundiced eye to those governments who do commit the human rights abuses that prompt the international community on occasion to belated action. National sovereignty is not the sovereign right to kill dissenters, or those of another ethnic group. 'National sovereignty was won', says Sané, who grew up in Senegal, then a French colony, 'by people that did not make their sacrifices only to succumb to oppression and violence at the hands of their own leaders.')

The history of the last few years has demonstrated vividly that those who seek to do good by military intervention find, more often than not, that it is a double-edged sword. Failure is more likely than success.

In Kosovo, Amnesty has shown, months after the NATO air

strikes, 'violence is being committed on a daily basis against Serbia, the gypsies and moderate Albanians'. During 2000 the level of murder, abductions, violent attacks, intimidation and house burning was almost as high as in June 1999 when NATO peacekeeping troops were first deployed.

In Somalia, seven years after a UN military intervention – in which, in fact, the US army acted as an autonomous agent – there is no functioning government and no judiciary. Continued fighting, especially in the south, imperils hundreds of thousands of people already suffering famine. The UN forces themselves committed serious human rights abuses. And the unsuccessful attempts of the US Rangers to arrest one of the guerrilla leaders diverted them from the ostensible purpose of their mission. They killed and arbitrarily detained hundreds of Somali civilians, including children.

Sané does not try to argue against intervention in every situation. He observes how disastrous it was in Rwanda when the UN pulled out its forces as the mass killings began, and up to a million people died in the ensuing genocide. Yet, Sané argues, if we have our wits about us and not just our reactive impulses, we will observe that none of the human rights tragedies of recent years were unpredictable or unavoidable. A year before the genocide in Rwanda, the UN Special Rapporteur on Extrajudicial, Summary or Arbitrary Executions warned of what was to come. Amnesty, for its part, repeatedly exposed the Indonesian government's gross violations of human rights, not just in East Timor, but also in Aceh, Irian Jaya and the rest of Indonesia. Sané concludes his argument: 'We fear now that our pleas for action on other countries are similarly being downplayed. When some human rights catastrophe explodes, will we again be expected to see only military intervention as the option?'

All of which brings Sané back to his main point: prevention. 'Prevention work may be less newsworthy and more difficult to justify to the public than intervention in times of crisis. It requires the sustained investment of significant resources without the emotive media images of hardship and suffering.' It's the hard day-to-day slog of human rights vigilance – using diplomatic measures to persuade governments to ratify human rights treaties and implement them at home. It means ensuring there is no impunity and that every time someone's rights are violated, the incident is investigated and those responsible brought to justice. Not least, it means speeding up the establishment of the International Criminal Court.

It also means that governments must be prepared to condemn violations of human rights by their allies as well as their foes. It demands a halt to the sale of arms to human rights violators. It means ensuring that economic sanctions do not hurt the wrong people – as in Iraq, where it is estimated that 40,000 children a year die because of the tight sanctions on essential foods, medicines and hospital equipment.

Sané is careful to acknowledge that some forms of UN peace-keeping may be necessary (he cites UN Secretary-General Kofi Annan's criteria[1] for action as taking the debate in the right direction). He is equally careful to make clear that Amnesty as an organization has to stand apart 'from the clamour for armed action' even in 'the face of immediate suffering'. Amnesty is preoccupied, he says, by the danger that 'human rights' might be usurped to justify the military ambitions of powerful states. And, he asks, why should Amnesty be forced to choose between intervention and inaction?

Why should we be forced to choose between two types of failure when the successful course of action is known? The best we can do is to ensure that whatever route is chosen, we do what we can to contain the suffering and let the powerful know our anger. Prevention of human rights crises is the correct course. The problem is not lack of early warning, but lack of early action. Only by protecting human rights everywhere, every day, will we render the debate over humanitarian action obsolete.

Amnesty International is at a major turning-point. It has questioned the orthodoxies – even the liberal ones – of our age with a

---

[1] • The scale and nature of the breaches of human rights.
 • The incapacity of local authorities to uphold order and their complicity in the violations.
 • The exhaustion of peaceful means to address the situation.
 • The ability of the Security Council to monitor the operation.
 • The limited and proportionate use of force.

daring that could not have been even contemplated forty years ago. In challenging NATO's engagement in what, in the West, was a fairly popular war with Yugoslavia and in arguing that most of the efforts of the international community led by the West to use force to uphold human rights are often counterproductive, it has staked out what has been described as an extreme position.

Extreme today? The conventional wisdom tomorrow? Amnesty, in fact, is testing the waters. The Danish philosopher Kierkegaard wrote that 'we have to live life forwards but we can only understand it backwards'. Indeed, it is impossible to decide if Amnesty's judgement is definitely correct and its timing right by peering into the future. Yet a look backwards, at least to the end of the Cold War in the late 1980s and, better still, further back, gives a clear picture that there is enormous momentum in the human rights cause. Moreover, many things related to it, from the number of military conflicts to the health of young children, have improved sharply for the better. We live in a world which, on balance, despite all its many wars, poverty, refugees, weapons development, arms sales and human rights abuses, are actually changing for the better at a rate quite unprecedented in human history. Amnesty has been both part-instigator and part-beneficiary of this tide. What is needed at this time is men and women with the necessary insight to seize the moment: to take the rising tide and push the boats even further out to sea; to be demanding of our institutions, systems and traditions; above all, to challenge our orthodoxies.

The signs are mostly, though not in every case, propitious, which ever way one looks at it, political, military, economic or social. Is such a conclusion naïve? Won't historians be able a hundred years hence to look at the end of the twentieth century much as we now look at the end of the nineteenth and say, 'Unfortunately the peace and prosperity of that moment was but an interlude before the bloodiest century in mankind's history'? Will they conclude, as Aldous Huxley did, that 'Every road towards a better state of society is blocked, sooner or later, by war, by threats of war, preparations for war. That is the truth, the odious and unacceptable truth'?

The pessimists of our day have grist for their mill – in 1999

President Clinton announced he wanted the largest rise in the military budget since the end of the Cold War build-up under Ronald Reagan; the conundrum of how best to contain and restrain Iraq and North Korea remains imperfectly answered; civil wars that target civilians more than soldiers are being fought all over the place; nuclear weapons are proliferating in states that don't have the secure command and control systems of the old nuclear powers; and the American plan to build a national missile defence, even if it means abrogating unilaterally the Anti-Ballistic Missile Treaty, could mean destabilizing relations with not only Russia but with China and India too.

Yet despite these ominous developments the big picture *is* good, arguably far better and more inherently stable than it was in 1899. Major war, involving the most powerful industrialized states, those capable of massive destruction far and wide, is much less likely than it has ever been. Unlike in previous ages neither economic, religious nor ideological forces point us or push us in the direction of war. War, *pace* Lenin, in the age of nuclear and high-tech weapons, is a loss-making enterprise. Virulent religious strife, once the cause of so much bloodshed in Europe, is now limited to former Yugoslavia – and even there, with the fall of Milosevic, an end to it may be in sight. Communism in Europe is practically dead and the credo of the West, democracy, does not lend itself to wars of conversion. War, moreover, has lost most of its glamour. Honour and heroism, the old virtues for every war from the time of the *Iliad* to General Douglas MacArthur, got lost in the jungles of Vietnam. President Clinton, a draft-dodger, came to power by defeating two Second World War heroes. Despite the occasional recourse to cruise missiles, he can hardly be regarded as a martial figure.

The state is no longer made by war for the purpose of making war. The modern industrial state is, *par excellence*, an economic institution. Democracy, not so long ago an uncertain, precarious achievement, is today deeply embedded in all the most advanced economies. And democracies do not seem to go to war with each other either. Elections, increasing political and economic transparency, the separation of powers, the media constantly on the watch, the urge of young men to make money not war and, in Europe, not least, the formation of the single currency, make serious all-out war a remote possibility. (Let us put on one side the aberration of Margaret Thatcher's mini-war with the Argentine generals as 'two bald men fighting over a comb', and such off-the-wall analyses as Martin Feldstein writing in *Foreign Affairs*, who argues that a future collapse of the single currency could lead to a new European war.)

But this sense of common security is, of course, confined to Europe, North America and Japan – and, it should be added, South America, which, for all its historic tendencies towards bravado, is, over the last two centuries, the continent that has gone to war least.

In the Middle East, all the old-time ingredients of war-making are present – financial greed over a scarce resource and religious fervour, combined with the new-time ingredients of modern weapons. Still, combative though many of the countries in the region tend to be, they lack the capacity to wage major war in the World War sense. Outside the Western world only China and Russia could do that. And it is these two states that hold in their hands the peace of the twenty-first century, to make it or break it.

Russia, potentially dangerous, claims a sphere of influence in the territory of the former Soviet Union; China in the South China Sea. Yet neither are in any real sense preparing for major war. Both are essentially inwardly preoccupied and neither are committed, as were their orthodox communist predecessors, to the violent overthrow of present-day political, military and economic arrangements.

'The practice of war, once the prerogative of the strong, instead is increasingly the tactic of the weak,' argues Michael Mandelbaum in the quarterly journal, *Survival*. His argument, eloquently developed at length, is that 'the great chess game of international politics is finished, or at least suspended. A pawn is now just a pawn, not a sentry standing guard against an attack on a king.' We'll still have our Kashmirs, Iraqs and Rwandas but, over time, they are becoming less numerous and the stakes for the rest of the world are lower. That doesn't mean that this new century won't have some bad wars. Doubtless, there will still be plenty of those. But major war, involving a clash of the best-armed gladiators, with convulsions on a scale that twice consumed the young men and the innocents of the twentieth century, could be in abeyance.

Nevertheless, even if the point about large-scale inter-state war is accepted, many would argue – I have even heard Pierre Sané make this point – that the number of ethnic wars is on the increase. The media certainly work on the assumption that tribal and nationalist fighting is rising on a frightening scale. But they are wrong. The modern era of ethnic warfare peaked in the early 1990s.

Every year for the past decade, the authoritative Stockholm International Peace Research Institute (SIPRI) has monitored the course of world conflicts and every year since the end of the Cold War the number has fallen, from thirty-five down to twenty-five. Gone into the history books, in all likelihood, are such conflicts as the Chittagong Hill Tracts dispute in Bangladesh, a long-running local sore, and Somalia, that managed in its momentary severity to sabotage a new era of UN peacekeeping. If it wasn't that the number of wars is rising in Africa, the world-wide fall in conflicts would be even more dramatic.

Confirmation for the analysis made by SIPRI comes from a major new study carried out by the Minority at Risk Project at the University of Maryland. Professor Ted Gurr, the project leader, wrote in *Foreign Affairs* in early 2000: 'The brutality of the conflict in Kosovo, East Timor and Rwanda obscures the larger shift from confrontation towards accommodation. But the trends are there, a sharp decline in new ethnic wars, the settlement of many old ones, and a pro-active effort by states and the international organizations to recognize group rights and to channel ethnic disputes into conventional politics.'

It was only a few years ago that US Secretary of State Warren Christopher, commenting on the outbreak of ethnic strife in countries such as Somalia, Zaire and ex-Yugoslavia, asked, 'Where will it end? Will it end with 5,000 countries?' It was a gross misjudgement. Two-thirds of all new campaigns of ethnic protest and rebellion in the last fifteen years began between 1989 and 1993. Since 1993 the number of wars of self-determination has been halved. During the 1990s sixteen separatist wars were settled by peace agreements and ten others were checked by cease-fires and negotiation.

Governments and media have been culpable in cultivating a weary cynicism about the inexorable growth in ethnic conflict. They have misled us. Concerted efforts by a great many people and organizations, from UN agencies to Amnesty International, from Médecins Sans Frontières to religious groups, from Sweden's small, private Transnational Foundation for Peace and Future Research to the large intergovernmental Organization for Security and Cooperation in Europe, have helped bring about a sea-change.

The list of countries where the problems of ethnic conflict looked until quite recently potentially ominous but which are now vastly improved is a long one. Baltic nationalists have moderated their treatment of Russians. Hungarians in Slovakia and Romania are no longer under threat. Croatia's new moderate government is respecting minorities. Likewise, conflicts between the central government and India's Mizo people, the Gaguaz minority in Moldova and the Chakma tribal group in Bangladesh's Chittagong Hills have all diminished. Nationalists willing to continue fighting for total independence, such as the rebel leaders in Chechnya and East Timor, are, increasingly, few and far between. Central governments, for their part, appear to be becoming more flexible and sensible about devolving power. One of democratic Russia's most important but least-noted achievements has been its peacefully-arrived-at power-sharing agreements with Tatarstan, Bashkiria and forty other regions. It is important to know that the large majority of these conflicts were brought to successful conclusion without outside military intervention.

A list almost as long can still be made for ethnic disputes unsolved. But what we have learnt in the last few years is that the pool of ethnic conflicts is not infinite; that the ultra-pessimism of just a few years ago was misplaced; and that human beings can settle for less, as long as the dominant party recognizes the underdog's integrity and gives it enough room for manoeuvre.

Side by side with these developments over war and conflict has been the remarkable spread of democracy in recent years. Every December the New York-based Freedom House publishes its annual survey of democratic trends. In 2000 it concluded that 'There were major gains in liberty in 1999 and 2000 and there now exists the largest number of politically free countries in the history of mankind.' Contrary to popular Western belief, there are more people in the Third World living under democratic governance than there are in the West. What is more, thanks to transformation in Nigeria and Indonesia, the majority of the world's Muslims are now living in countries that practise democracy. This end-of-century survey finds that only 36 per cent of the peoples of the world live in countries that are not free – and the overwhelming proportion of those are in China. Two-thirds of the world's countries, 120 of them, have achieved democratic rule.

Yet still the argument continues: is the glass half-full or half-empty? That, in fact, it's nearly full seems to be ignored by most of our active political class, who seem to believe they thrive personally if they can paint the world blacker than it is, with only the prowess of their own country able to sort it out.

The Russian parliamentary election should be a salutary reminder of how the democratic pulse works: overturning the debilitating practices that accrete to any working body politic and breathing new life into those hackneyed words, 'a new mandate'. Maybe, after all, insiders, once given the vote, have a better feel of how to correct the course of their country than the *realpolitik* politicos in foreign parts. The atmosphere *has* changed for the better. Democracy has been throughout the century a slow, uncertain but, in the end, steady cumulative process and now it is a hard thing for anyone to block, at least for any length of time. While one can worry, and sometimes despair, about the homogenized uniformity brought about by many aspects of globalization, one can only rejoice in this phenomenon.

At the beginning of the twentieth century there were only 55 sovereign polities. (There are now 192.) Not one enjoyed fully competitive multiparty politics with universal suffrage. A mere 12.5 per cent of mankind lived under a form of government that could be described as somewhat democratic, although suffrage was generally limited to males. Even as recently as mid-century there were only 22 functioning democracies and a further 21 restricted democracies. They accounted for a mere 12 per cent of the globe's population.

Meanwhile, totalitarian communism had spread to govern one-third of the world's people.

But the last quarter of a century in particular has seen a tremendous acceleration in democracy's spread. One doesn't have to be too gullible an optimist to imagine that the first decade of this century could well see the dawn of a near-totally democratic world. To say democracy and its handmaiden liberty are now only Western constructs is as foolish as saying that rice is only an Asian food. Any long view of history, with rather more time-span than the life of McDonalds, will realize that the cultures of the world have been cross-fertilizing each other for thousands of years.

Of course, democracy has had some high moments before, but then regressed; as in pre-war Europe with the rise of fascism and subsequently the spread of communism. In Iran, in the early twentieth century, democracy was the constitutional order but then the monarchy reasserted itself and since then Iran has never known, until the last couple of years, real democracy. Even today, an elected parliament and president are circumscribed by the independent, and constitutionally superior, power of the chief religious leader. In Egypt in 1923 there was universal suffrage and a parliament with considerable power. But it didn't last long and, as was made abundantly clear in the country's recent controlled elections, Egypt shows little sign of being able to shed the military's totalitarian grip.

There is a powerful, if pessimistic, school of thought that argues that democracy will never take real root in the Muslim world. Yet we can see a significant and widespread pro-democracy ferment in much of the Muslim world and important steps towards democratic reform under way in many Islamic countries. Six out of 42 predominantly Muslim states now have democratically elected governments: Albania, Bangladesh, Indonesia, Kyrgyzstan, Mali and Turkey. In fact, if one takes into account these six Muslim democracies, add in Nigeria, where half the population is Muslim, and the Muslims who live in Europe, the Americas and India, a majority of the world's 1.15 billion Muslims live under democratically elected governments.

In several Arab states, the passing away of old monarchs has led to reform. In Morocco, under the new king, there is a much greater tolerance of opposition parties. In Jordan, under its new king, press laws have been relaxed and there have been competitive elections at the municipal level. In Lebanon, although still under Syrian domination, there have been relatively pluralistic local elections. In Kuwait the national legislature (albeit elected by exclusively male suffrage) has wide legislative authority and the emir's decrees are subject to its approval.

Qatar, an oil-rich state on the Persian Gulf, may itself have progressed only to the point at which it allows open elections at the municipal level. But it is the home of the Al-Jazira television station, which has become a major source for the spread of the idea of openness and democratic practice. It includes regular debates on theology, democracy and human rights and allows wide-ranging interviews with dissidents and political exiles from throughout the Arab world.

In 1984 Iran's representative at the UN said that the Universal Declaration of Human Rights 'represented a secular understanding of the Judaeo-Christian tradition'. Saudi Arabia abstained in the vote on it in 1948.[1] The Saudi delegate to the UN said that the provision for religious liberty in the Declaration violated Islamic law. But he was answered by the delegate from Pakistan, who argued that Islam supported freedom of conscience. And today the delegate of Iran to the UN can be heard speaking of the desirability of democracy for his country and the full observance of human rights.

Islam, as Christianity before it, is evolving at a rapid pace. Many Muslims today, including a number of its most informed religious leaders, argue that many so-called 'traditional' Islamic practices, the forms of punishment and the attitude to women and non-Muslim minorities, are not Islamic at all, or at least not mandated in all circumstances. Most Muslims indeed understand their religion's essentials as a message of tolerance, compassion and social justice.

It came as no surprise that at the UN Conference on Human Rights

---

[1] For a fuller discussion see 'International Law, Universal Rights, the Global Dilemma', by Richard Reoch in Jonathan Power (ed.), *Vision of Hope – 50 Years of the United Nations* (Regency Press, 1995).

in 1993, meant to review and renew the commitments made in 1948, the Islamic world was split. In the end, however, there was an overwhelming endorsement of resolutions that reaffirmed the validity of the original Declaration,[1] and indeed extended its scope. Even China and Saudi Arabia felt compelled to cast their vote in favour of the consensus. The African and Latin American countries in particular had fought hard for such a meeting of minds. The universality of human rights was reaffirmed. The final declaration states that 'The universal nature of these rights is beyond question. All human rights are universal, indivisible, interdependent and interrelated.' Thus, the entire spectrum of human rights was endorsed without division, an amazing, if under-reported, step forward for mankind.

The Vienna Declaration also stated that 'the human person is the central subject of development'. Human rights were reaffirmed as including not just civil and political rights, but the broader range of economic, social and cultural rights, together with the right to development. The first set of human rights was seen as guaranteeing freedom from fear; the second set dealt with freedom from want. In retrospect, it is surprising that the two sets should have been seen as somehow contradictory. Even up to the middle of the Vienna Conference, the USA was arguing that social and economic rights were not so important.

Yet the progress we have witnessed in the last fifty years in civil and political rights has come about, in part, because of advances in economic, social and cultural rights. The two have a symbiotic relationship. The swift advance of political rights is so much easier where the standard of living is rapidly rising. The rise of authoritarianism is more likely where there are either great disparities in incomes or a general, widespread economic malaise. Contrariwise, democracy is more likely to provide the climate for economic advance and steps towards a more benign distribution of income.

Proponents of so-called 'Asian values' – the Chinese, prime minister Mahathir bin Muhammad of Malaysia or ex-prime minister Lee

---

[1] A number of Third World countries including India, Chile, Cuba, Lebanon and Panama played an active and influential role in the drafting of the Declaration.

Kuan Yew of Singapore – dispute this. They attribute growth in south-east Asia to the Confucian virtues of obedience, order and respect for authority. 'The exuberance of democracy leads to indiscipline and disorderly conduct which are inimical to development,' says Mr Lee. (Yet it was only a generation ago that observers of the Confucian ethic blamed it for much of Asia's economic backwardness.) They claim that the suspension or limiting of human rights is a sacrifice of the few for the benefit of the many.

Yet anyone who has visited Japan will know it's perfectly possible for Asian societies to embrace modernity without discarding the virtues of respect, order and obedience. Besides, if one looks at the Western world with a broader view than focusing on, say, San Francisco, there are a lot of so-called Confucian values at work in the West. Family values are certainly enormously strong in Italy and Spain. Collective obligations are taken more seriously than possibly anywhere else in the world in Scandinavia. (And you can see how both strands in European culture have been transported to parts of America.)

Democracies, in fact, tend to make economic reform more feasible. Political checks and balances, together with open debate on the costs and benefits of government policy, give the public both a sense of involvement and a stake in reform. One reason India has never been overwhelmed by unexpected famine as China and Ethiopia have is the free press. In India the press has always alerted the central government to what was going on in the distant countryside long before the cautious bureaucrats got round to filing their grey reports. (And when India under Indira Gandhi introduced a state of emergency suspending parliament, the electorate, mainly uneducated peasants, took the first opportunity to throw her out.) India now seems poised to become the greatest economic success among the larger Asian developing countries, overtaking China.

All countries in the end come up against the reality that nearly all the world's richest countries are free, and nearly all the poorest are not. If dictatorship made countries rich, then Africa and Latin America would, by now, be economic heavyweights. (The fact that countries such as China and South Korea progressed rapidly on the economic front under dictatorship probably owed itself to the

Confucian work ethic rather than the dictatorship. But even that seems to work better – as in Hong Kong and modern-day South Korea – if there is room for democracy.) A study made by Surjit Bhalla,[1] formerly of the World Bank, examined ninety countries over the period 1973–90. It found that civil and political freedoms do promote growth. Other things being equal – in particular economic freedom – an improvement of one point in civil and political freedom raises annual growth by approximately a full percentage point.

More recently, after extensive research, Freedom House concluded in a study published in 2001 that 'there is a high and statistically significant correlation between the level of political freedom as measured by Freedom House and economic freedom as measured by the Wall Street Journal/Heritage Foundation survey.' This study effectively answered the old conundrum of whether the large number of prosperous countries are free as a consequence of their prosperity and development or whether prosperity is a consequence of basic political and civic freedoms. Economic growth is certainly possible in an unfree political culture, but political freedom accelerates it. Repressive countries with high and sustained growth rates, such as China, are the exception rather than the rule.

In the long run even the most apolitical capitalist learns to appreciate a political structure that will protect his property, both material and intellectual. A dictatorship, however benign, is always more vulnerable than a democracy. It can be more easily overthrown and its policy simply reversed. Democracy and the freedoms that usually go with it – an independent judiciary, freedom of expression, the enforcement of contracts and the inbuilt pressures of free trade – give the businessman what he wants for the long run, while offering the educated classes an outlet for their opinions and the workers a safety valve for their grievances.

The economic and social advance of the so-called Third World, in the main, has been spectacular, according to the UN's annual Human

[1] 'Free Societies, Free Markets and Social Welfare', unpublished paper presented at Nobel Symposium on Democracy, University of Uppsala, Sweden, 1994.

Development Report. The poorer countries have covered as much distance in human development during the past thirty years as the industrialized world did in over a century. A child born today in a developing country can expect to live sixteen years longer than one born thirty-five years ago. The mortality rate of children under 5 has been halved. Between 1980 and 1999 the proportion of underweight children in developing countries fell from 37 per cent to 27 per cent, and that of stunted children from 47 per cent to 33 per cent. The proportion enrolled in primary school has risen from less than a half to nearly three-quarters. The percentage of rural families with access to safe water has risen from less than 13 per cent in 1970 to more than 71 per cent in 1999. The proportion of couples using modern contraceptives has risen from almost nothing to more than 50 per cent. Average family size is falling in almost every country. Although the South's average per capita income is only 6 per cent of the North's, its social progress has been so effective that its average life expectancy is now a remarkable 80 per cent of that of the rich industrialized world, and its average literacy rate a significant 66 per cent.

It is noteworthy that such progress has been made despite inadequate resources, an often inhospitable international economic climate and, in many countries, not always the wisest or most responsive of governments. If this kind of momentum can be achieved in less than perfect conditions, then it is not hard to imagine the further steps that can be made in a more democratic, socially aware and responsibly managed world.

The unmet needs are vast: 800 million people go to bed hungry every night; a billion people eke out the barest existence in perpetual poverty; more than a billion people are without safe water; and 1.5 billion people have no access to primary health care. Contrary to some the claims of the 'globalization' school, the progress that has been made is not because of world-wide economic growth, it is because of the hard, humdrum work of introducing better health services and the rapid growth of primary schools – and the often derided work of the aid agencies. Out of 124 Third World countries for which there are adequate statistics, only 21 had a per capita growth rate of 3 per cent or more each year between 1995 and 1998. No fewer than 100 countries – in the Third World and Eastern Europe – have experienced serious economic decline over the past three decades.

It is true, however, that the remarkable US-led boom of the 1990s – threatened for only a brief period by the Asian economic crisis of 1998 – has enabled positive growth to spread. It is also true that it is the countries most open for freer trade that have the best record for economic growth. The challenge is to combine high levels of human development, low unemployment and rapid economic growth, creating a 'virtuous circle' in which worker productivity rises and triggers an increase in real wages, which in turn attracts more investment in human capital, in education and in access to social services.

The pace-setters in this kind of development are the east and south-east Asian nations, led by Japan. Not only have they grown fastest; they also have been the most fair in their distribution of income and assets such as land and credits. Not least, they have built on growth by investing in health and education for all, however poor. South Korea has surged in a single generation from rags to riches. In 1945 only 13 per cent of adults had any formal schooling. By 1990 the average time spent in school was 9.9 years, higher than in the industrialized countries.

Still, great areas of economic backwardness remain, especially in parts of Africa and South America. At the same time, right through the Third World there is more drug and alcohol abuse, more deaths on the road and more pollution. Homicide rates around the world (the most reliable measure of individual violence) have increased very fast, particularly in Africa, Latin America and China (however, Asia and the Pacific have declining rates). Globalization may be necessary for further progress but there can be no question that it is sharpening disparities of income, even as the proportion of people living in extreme poverty is falling.[1]

[1] However, over the last century, the world as a whole has become more equal. Today's mainly Anglo-Saxon and Third World phenomenon of increased inequality may well be a temporary aberration. For further discussion see 'Inequality – the Long View', by Paul Ormerod, in *Prospect*, August 2000.

There is an answer to the dilemma. There is no country on earth that cannot afford to do more for their poor. What is needed is better targeting and use of the money set aside to relieve poverty. Simply to ensure that young girls get educated would make the world of difference not just to the rate of poverty and population increase, but to the future growth of violence.

Which brings us back to the need for more human rights – so that the voice of the downtrodden can be heard more easily and can carry more political weight. Kofi Annan, the UN Secretary-General, in a speech made in Tehran University in 1997, argued against those who see authoritarian leadership as the one that can best serve the poor. 'When have you heard a free voice demand an end to freedom?' he asked. 'When you have heard a slave argue for slavery? When have you heard a victim of torture endorse the ways of the torturer? Where have you heard the tolerant cry out for intolerance?'

On balance, most of the world's people do live in the best of economic times. This has had a marked impact on the progress made in extending the range and practice of human rights. Equally, the advance of human rights in a political and personal sense has produced a resonance that has spilt over into its economic and social arena, pushing the leaders of developing societies to be more responsive to the needs of the poor. Ironically, one can see this process at work even in societies such as Pinochet's Chile, Suharto's Indonesia or Lee's Singapore. It was part of their justification for spurning 'Western human rights' that they could point to how much progress there had been made in helping the poor. (But for every 'benign' dictator who cared about the poor there have been a dozen who cared not a whit, and the poor had no chance to vote them out. Only a handful of the authoritarian governments out of the hundreds that have existed have been economically enlightened.)

If we do live in 'the best of times', the inevitable question is what next? In terms of treaties and declarations the human rights lobby now has a tremendous range of tools at its beck and call. Since the Universal Declaration of Human Rights we now have a total of sixty-seven human rights instruments, embracing 'The Right of

Self-Determination', 'Prevention of Discrimination', 'War Crimes and Crimes Against Humanity, including Genocide, Slavery, Servitude and Forced Labour', 'Torture and Detention', 'Nationality, Statelessness, Asylum and Refugees', 'Freedom of Association', 'Employment Policy', 'Political Rights of Women', 'Rights of the Family, Children and Youth', and 'Social Welfare, Progress and Development'.

This is the tremendous hard-won legacy of the post-war generation. The question now is what will the post-Cold War generation do with it? One important, perhaps the most important, avenue to explore is to continue to extend the frontiers of international law. International law offers the world the best choice of avoiding war. If law were observed, military might – and even the enforcement procedures of the Security Council – would become increasingly redundant. Yet if there is no law, all the enforcement in the world will not achieve its objective. Many of the norms of international law, particularly on human rights, are already respected by domestic courts. Many regional institutions already operate by international law, such as the European Court of Justice. The World Bank and the World Trade Organization have their own legal tribunals for arbitrating investment and trade disputes. How far are we prepared to subordinate national loyalties before a law that transcends individual cultures and societies but is just and avoids conflicts?

A number of 'good global citizen states' need to take the lead if we are to build a world of 'laws not of men' in which the powerful or the cruel do not necessarily get their way and the vulnerable, the outspoken and the preyed-upon have the chance to show that nobody and no nation is above the law. The UN Charter made a bold beginning. It established the International Court of Justice, the World Court. This 'cathedral of law' may be the most imaginative of all the constructs of the UN's founding fathers. However, it is limited to hearing cases only between states. Moreover, it has jurisdiction only when disputing states agree to abide by its decisions. Too few countries give this consent automatically.

Nevertheless, with its active jurisdictional responsibility for over 400 international treaties, it has made steady if slow progress. It has ruled on such issues as the question of rights over the continental shelf affecting Tunisia and Libya, a frontier dispute between Burkino Faso and Mali, and Nicaragua's action against the USA for mining the waters of its main port. Although the number of cases is relatively small, the court's influence is far greater. A judgement can fix precedents and shape the future interpretation of principles and treaties in the whole field of international law.

So great, in fact, is the implicit power of the court that a decision by one nation to refer a case to it can greatly exercise the mind of any other government that might be affected by the decision. For example, in 1974 Australia and New Zealand asked the court to rule on the extremely sensitive matter of responsibility for trans-boundary radioactive pollution, citing France as the government responsible. Before the case could be heard the president of France publicly declared his government would cease atmospheric nuclear testing.

It was not, however, until February 1993[1] that the UN created a court to deal with questions of individual criminal behaviour. A Bosnian Serb, Duscan Tadic, arrested in Germany, was accused of killing, raping, beating and torturing Croats and Muslims during the 'ethnic cleansing' in north-western Bosnia, and his arrest was initiated by the then recently created ad hoc war crimes tribunal on ex-Yugoslavia. Not long after, the Security Council established a parallel tribunal for Rwanda. (In August 2000 it also created a third tribunal, for Sierra Leone.) Then in Rome in June 1998 came the formal vote to establish by treaty an International Criminal Court to try war crimes *wherever* they occurred. Now the task is to get this up and running, to win ratification from the maximum number of states. Sixty ratifications are needed for the court to begin to function. However, it is clear that the USA will not be one of them. Although

---

[1] When in early 1992 I wrote a prominently displayed column in the influential *Los Angeles Times* arguing for an International Criminal Court I received but one letter – from a University of California law professor who said he had had the same idea and written about it in an academic journal, but that no one in government was responsive and debate on the subject was dead in the water. Then the war in ex-Yugoslavia shook up everyone's complacency. It is a mark of how things can change once the human rights activists seize a cause.

Up To $5 Million Reward

Wanted

For crimes against humanity

Slobodan Milosevic
President of the Federal
Republic of Yugoslavia

For genocide and crimes against humanity

Radovan Karadzic **Ratko Mladic**

Milosevic, Karadzic, and Mladic have been indicted by the United Nations International Criminal Tribunal for the Former Yugoslavia for crimes against humanity, including murders and rapes of thousands of innocent civilians, torture, hostage-taking of peacekeepers, wanton destruction of private property, and the destruction of sacred places. Mladic and Karadzic also have been indicted for genocide.

To bring Milosevic, Karadzic, and Mladic to justice, the United States Government is offering a reward of up to $5 million for information leading to the transfer to, or conviction by, the International Criminal Tribunal for the Former Yugoslavia of any of these individuals or any other person indicted by the International Tribunal.

If you believe you have information, please contact the nearest U.S. embassy or consulate, or write the U.S. Department of State, Diplomatic Security Service at:

REWARDS FOR JUSTICE
Post Office Box 96781 • Washington, D.C. 20090-6781 U.S.A.
email: mail@dssrewards.net • www.dssrewards.net
1-800-437-6371 (U.S.A. Only)

Figure 8. Wanted poster put up by the United States across Bosnia to advertise rewards for the capture of three Serbian leaders (*Associated Press/State Department*)

at the end of 2000 President Clinton surprised everyone with his announcement that the USA was signing (but not ratifying) the statute creating the court, the USA remains determined to protect its soldiers and officials from falling under the court's jurisdiction.

William Lace, convenor of the Coalition for an International Court, an umbrella group for more than 1,000 human rights groups, including Amnesty International, has argued that exempting citizens of countries that have not ratified the treaty would be counterproductive. 'It would drastically undermine the effectiveness of the Court and would provide an opening not only for the US to protect its officials and soldiers but also for the so-called rogue countries the court should have as its primary focus.'

Amnesty's legal experts are puzzled at the strength of US opposition, as the treaty gives countries whose citizens are charged with international crimes the right to try them in their own courts, as the USA had frequently done in the past when US soldiers were involved in criminal activity overseas. The court can in fact only prosecute when governments are acting to shield individuals from their national courts.

Of course, the unspoken problem is what would happen if the court should attempt a prosecution of a case that the US authorities don't consider a war crime. The bombing of ex-Yugoslavia is indeed a perfect example of what could happen. Is it enough to say the court will be wise and cautious enough not to seek a major confrontation with the world's superpower? Or perhaps on occasion, it should do so. There the matter rests and Amnesty and its allies will have their work cut out to bring American public opinion around. Probably the best way to do that is to wait for the court to show its mettle. If it can deal with some future Pinochets, Saddam Husseins and Milosevics – or be seen to be deterring such kind of behaviour on the world stage – then the vigour of US opposition may begin to wither.

The second task for the new generation is to build on the recent work of Amnesty in bringing the notions and principles of human rights to the board-tables of the business community. In the first thirty years of its existence Amnesty practically ignored the role that companies play in the social arena, particularly when they invest in a developing country. But in 1991 Amnesty International's British branch set up a Business Group under the chairmanship of a former senior executive of Shell Oil, Sir Geoffrey Chandler, to encourage companies to be aware of the human rights impact of all aspects of their operations; to use their legitimate influence in support of human rights in all countries in which they operate; to give effect to the Universal Declaration of Human Rights; to implement Amnesty International's Human Rights Guidelines for Companies; to include a specific commitment to human rights in their statements of business principles and codes of conduct; and to make their human rights policies explicit, ensuring that these are integrated across all functions, monitored and audited. 'There is no hiding place,' says Chandler. 'To go without a policy in human rights is to go naked into a dangerous world.'

A report published by Amnesty together with the Prince of Wales Business Leaders Forum in April 2000 signalled the beginning of a campaign by activists to hold corporate behaviour to standards that many multinational corporations had once sought to dismiss. The report cites as one example the experience of the Royal Dutch/Shell Group in Nigeria's Niger Delta in the mid-1990s, when the oil company's activities were caught between a repressive military regime and increasingly vocal protesters, in particular Amnesty members, demanding that a greater share of Shell's production be channelled into the local community. The conflict led to the execution of nine activists in 1995 and, afterwards, demands for a boycott of Shell products. The result, the report notes, was that Shell revised its business principles to commit itself to upholding human rights. It led also to a revision of Shell's rules of engagement with the State security forces to accommodate the UN Basic Principles on the Use of Force and Firearms and the UN Code of Conduct for Law Enforcement Officials. All Shell security personnel now receive training in operating procedures that are consistent with these.

In recent years Shell has become more active in its efforts to protect human rights in the Delta. After the arrest of activist Baton Mittee and others during the January 1998 Ogoni Day celebrations, Shell appealed for the highest standards of human rights to be upheld.

Shell lobbied the government for the withdrawal of the Mobile Police from Ogoni land and for the release of Baton Mittee. On both counts Shell were successful. Robin Aram, Shell's vice-president for External Relations and Policy Development, observes: 'There is an emerging consensus that for peace and stability to be restored to the Niger Delta, the communities must view themselves as net beneficiaries from oil production. Achieving that shift in perspective is no easy task, given the legacy of past failures by governments, persecution by security forces, inter-ethnic values and the sense that oil companies have put profit before principles.'

A survey by the Ashridge Centre for Business in Society, published in April 2000, found that human rights issues had caused 36 per cent of the biggest 500 companies to abandon a proposed investment project and 19 per cent to disinvest from a country. Oil, gas and mining companies have set the pace, with European companies in the lead. Among the retailers Levi Strauss, the Body Shop and the Co-op Bank have long built human rights into their decision-making criteria, but they remain a tiny minority on the world stage.

During the late 1990s the role of companies and human rights made its way up to the level of governments. The triggering issue was the belated discovery that diamond mines, particularly in Angola and Sierra Leone, were being exploited by warlords to fund their lethal, no-holds-barred insurgencies. In June 1998 the UN imposed a world-wide ban on importing diamonds from Angolan mines that were not under government control.

A special study commissioned by the United Nations Security Council accused diamond-cutting centres in Antwerp, Bombay and Tel Aviv of processing diamonds without regard to origin. Likewise, it was critical of the De Beers Group, the giant of the world's rough diamond trade, which controls 70 per cent of the trade in uncut stones. This prompted De Beers to announce in March 2000 that it would begin issuing written guarantees that its stones did not originate with African rebels. And in June the British government, which was heavily involved in peacekeeping in the Sierra Leone civil war, called for a world-wide boycott of stones emanating from rebel-held areas in the country and from its neighbour Liberia. In July 2000 the

UN Security Council, voting on a British resolution, announced a ban on the trade in so-called 'conflict diamonds'. Now there are serious moves afoot to respond to a call from Amnesty for the diamond industry to monitor and self-police the traffic in what are also called 'blood diamonds'.

The old issues – political prisoners, disappearances, torture and executions – will continue, as always, to take most of the time of Amnesty's staff and membership. But making the courts and the business community more effective bastions of human rights is a short cut to an improved recognition of the essential value of human rights for the inner workings of societies everywhere.

Morality is not the only reason for putting human rights high on the foreign policy and business agendas. Self-interest plays its part. Political freedom goes hand in hand with economic freedom. That in turn is good for trade, prosperity and a fairer distribution of income. Moreover, those governments that treat their own people with a sense of tolerance and respect tend to treat their neighbours in the same way. Dictatorships were responsible for the last century's two world wars, indeed, for most wars before and since. Democracies that practise the importance of human rights do not take up arms against each other. The human rights that Amnesty International battles for involve contesting the human wrongs of not just the false imprisonment of non-violent political activists, as Peter Benenson first thought, but the human wrongs of dictatorship, war and economic disadvantage.

Index

PUBLISHED IN PENGUIN

Values for a Godless Age   Francesca Klug

The Story of the United Kingdom's New Bill of Rights

When the Human Rights Act (HRA) came into force in October 2000, the United Kingdom at last acquired its own Bill of Rights. In this clear and accessible guide, one of its architects spells out its huge significance for us all. Francesca Klug, joint winner of the 1998 *Times*/JUSTICE award for an outstanding contribution to civil justice, tells the story of how the idea of rights has evolved from the late eighteenth century to the present day. The HRA marks a historic turning-point and has an immense potential to transform our lives. This powerful book will help us seize the opportunity.

'The most useful and informative book I have read on the Human Rights Act' Kirsty Walk, *Newsnight*, BBC 2

Crimes Against Humanity   Geoffrey Robertson QC

First used at Nuremberg to condemn the Nazi rulers, the concept of 'crimes against humanity' gave universal recognition to the need to hold political leaders accountable for the wars, genocide and torture which disfigure our world. In his powerful and timely book, Geoffrey Robertson QC is cautiously optimistic about bringing tyrants and torturers to heal, but unsparingly critical of the corruption, hypocrisy and political bias of international diplomacy. Nevertheless, as we go into the twenty-first century, we are, he explains, on the brink of a new era of human rights – the age of enforcement.

'A fine work, scholarly and impassioned' Anthony Julius, *Mail on Sunday*